# Political Aid and Arab Activism

What does it mean to promote "transitions to democracy" in the Middle East? How have North American, European, and multilateral projects advanced human rights, authoritarian retrenchment, or Western domination?

*Political Aid and Arab Activism* examines transnational programs in Egypt, Jordan, Morocco, Yemen, Lebanon, Tunisia, Algeria, the exceptional cases of Palestine and Iraq, and the Arab region at large during two tumultuous decades. To understand the controversial and contradictory effects of political aid, Sheila Carapico analyzes discursive and professional practices in four key subfields: the rule of law, electoral design and monitoring, women's political empowerment, and civil society. From the institutional arrangements for extraordinary undertakings such as Saddam Hussein's trial or Palestinian elections to routine templates for national women's machineries or NGO networks, her research explores the paradoxes and jurisdictional disputes confronted by Arab activists for justice, representation, and "nongovernmental" agency.

Sheila Carapico is Professor of Political Science and International Studies at the University of Richmond and Visiting Professor of Political Science at the American University in Cairo. The author of *Civil Society in Yemen: The Political Economy of Activism in Modern Arabia* (Cambridge University Press, 1998), she has also researched and written about Yemeni, Egyptian, and Arab political activism; American foreign policy in the Middle East; and the politics of international political aid.

D0916101

## Cambridge Middle East Studies

**Cambridge Middle East Studies** has been established to publish books on the nineteenth- to twenty-first-century Middle East and North Africa. The series offers new and original interpretations of aspects of Middle Eastern societies and their histories. To achieve disciplinary diversity, books are solicited from authors writing in a wide range of fields including history, sociology, anthropology, political science, and political economy. The emphasis is on producing books affording an original approach along theoretical and empirical lines. The series is intended for students and academics, but the more accessible and wide-ranging studies will also appeal to the interested general reader.

*A list of books in the series can be found after the index.*

# Political Aid and Arab Activism

*Democracy Promotion, Justice,*
*and Representation*

SHEILA CARAPICO

*University of Richmond*

CAMBRIDGE
UNIVERSITY PRESS

# CAMBRIDGE
## UNIVERSITY PRESS

32 Avenue of the Americas, New York, NY 10013-2473, USA

Cambridge University Press is part of the University of Cambridge.

It furthers the University's mission by disseminating knowledge in the pursuit of education, learning, and research at the highest international levels of excellence.

www.cambridge.org
Information on this title: www.cambridge.org/9780521136914

© Sheila Carapico 2014

First published 2014

*A catalog record for this publication is available from the British Library.*

*Library of Congress Cataloging in Publication Data*
Carapico, Sheila.
Political aid and Arab activism : democracy promotion, justice, and representation / Sheila Carapico, University of Richmond.
    pages   cm
Includes bibliographical references and index.
ISBN 978-0-521-19991-9 (hardback) – ISBN 978-0-521-13691-4 (pbk.)
 1. Democratization – Government policy – United States.   2. United States – Foreign relations – Middle East.   3. Middle East – Foreign relations – United States.   I. Title.
JZ1480.A55C37   2013
327.1–dc23      2013003969

ISBN 978-0-521-19991-9 Hardback
ISBN 978-0-521-13691-4 Paperback

# Contents

# Tables and Figures

# Dedication and Acknowledgments

This work is dedicated to my parents, whose own parents named them Gino Enrico Ciarapica and Catherine Christina Maloney, respectively, but who later became the loving couple Gene and Katie Carapico.

Among the joys of an academic career is membership in communities of scholars who share knowledge, ideas, and experiences. I have had the privilege of association with groups and networks whose collective wisdom is respected in this book. Yemen scholars, including researchers at Sana'a University, the Yemen Center for Research and Studies, the French Center in Sana'a, and the American Institute for Yemeni Studies, among others, taught me whatever I know about cross-cultural research. The collective known as MERIP, especially the editors and members of the editorial board of its flagship publication *Middle East Report*, were role models of intellectual imagination and politically conscious scholarship. The University of Richmond has been generously supportive. I benefited from short-term associations with Human Rights Watch, the Middle East Institute, the Institute for the Study of Islam and Modernity in the Netherlands, the Fulbright program in Yemen, and the American Research Center in Egypt. Colleagues at the American University in Cairo shared deep insights into Egyptian, Arab, and Middle Eastern politics during some amazing times. I cannot list the round-tables and workshops where a community of Middle East specialists shared and questioned findings and analyses and enjoyed good dinners; but I want to thank the conveners and my co-panelists in the United States, Europe, and the region.

I am thankful to many individuals who helped shape this book. Several colleagues offered valuable comments on early drafts of the chapters that follow or conference presentations based on them. I appreciate candid criticism and kind encouragement from Diane Singerman, Benoît Challand, Lisa Hajjar, Rabab El-Mahdi, Lila Abu Lughod, Lori A. Allen, Ellen Lust, Iris Glosemeyer, Imco Brouwer, Abla Amawi, Jeannie Sowers, and anonymous Cambridge University Press readers. At different stages of its evolution, Louis Tremaine and Lisa Wedeen read and suggested revisions to drafts of the entire manuscript; I am especially grateful to them. In addition, Marsha Pripstein Posusney, Samer Soliman, Eva Bellin, Amat al-Alim al-Soswa, Holger Albrecht, Joel Beinin, Manal Jamal, Anna Würth, Vickie Langohr, Joe Stork, Chris Toensing, Nubar Hovsepian, Zachary Lockman, Gary Shapiro, Laleh Khalili, Ellis Goldberg, Muhammad Abd-al-Malik al-Mutawakkil, Reem Saad, Ted Swedenburg, Marilyn Booth, Khaled Fahmy, Oliver Schlumberger, Doug Wood, Jamila Raja, Hamud al-Salahi, Ezzedine Choukri Fishere, Bahgat Korani, Waleed Hazbun, Arang Keshavarzian, Shelagh Weir, Sari Hanafi, Asef Bayat, Kevin Cherry, Greg Gause, Roger Owen, Kristina Touzenis, and Zohra Merabet each, in their own ways, offered inspiration and/or intellectual support for this project. As the beneficiary of so much feedback, support, and foundational research, I have only myself to blame for any remaining analytical or empirical lapses.

On a more nuts-and-bolts level, graduate research assistants at AUC Karim Hamdy and Adam Mattatal helped me track down details. Michelle Woodward guided me through the selection and procurement of visual images. Beth Ann Howard gave production assistance and Gehan Wissa provided logistical backup. This book would not have come to fruition without the professional care of Marigold Acland and Sarika Narula of Cambridge University Press. Ronald Cohen was the manuscript editor and Diana Witt prepared the index.

# Introduction

## *Political Aid in Theory and Practice*

Jackbooted security forces raided the offices of foreign and Egyptian political think tanks on December 29, 2011, confiscating computers, records, cell phones, maps, documents, and cash. Five of the organizations targeted were overseas branches of the federally funded quasi-non-governmental National Democratic Institute (NDI), International Republican Institute (IRI), the International Center for Journalists, Freedom House, and Germany's Konrad Adenauer Foundation. The others were locally headquartered professional advocacy organizations, including the Egyptian Organization for Human Rights and the Arab Center for the Independence of Judges and Lawyers. The Minister of International Cooperation, Fayza Aboulnaga, often nicknamed "the iron lady," and a "Mubarak holdover," had asked prosecutors to investigate what foreign democracy brokers were up to, how Egyptian organizations received foreign aid, and whether they all had official authorization.

This news event was spun in various directions. That evening, Dawlat Soulam, a bilingual Egyptian-American, gave a scathing in-depth interview on a Channel 2 TV program called *The Truth (al-Haqiqah)* about why she and six colleagues had already resigned their jobs at IRI. She complained of blatant anti-Islamist bias in party training, CIA officers posing as democracy experts, grant-making according to ulterior motives, deliberate provocation of sectarian tensions, and anti-Egyptian prejudices expressed by drunken consultants at after-hours expatriate social gatherings. Soulam's accusations fed tales in Cairo's state-run media and unofficial rumor-mills about colonial agents undermining Egyptian sovereignty and fomenting instability.

Across town the following day, spokespersons for more than two dozen independent Egyptian civic organizations including the Egyptian Initiative for Personal Rights and the Cairo Institute for Human Rights Studies held a press conference. They expressed outrage at the inordinately forceful crackdown on independent agencies that had been monitoring parliamentary elections or documenting human rights abuses before, during, and after the popular revolt that forced President Husni Mubarak from power. These organizations, their attorneys, and international rights advocates braced for another round in a long series of litigations. Several of them had already faced court charges mostly related to unauthorized receipt of foreign funds for political activities, but also including treason or other trumped-up accusations. One friend of this group wrote at the time that "while many Egyptians seem to have bought the official line that this was a long-overdue move aimed at subjecting foreign NGOs to local legislation and thus correcting a momentarily injured Egyptian sovereignty, pro-democracy activists suspect that the true purpose of the trial is nothing less than intimidating human rights organizations, and some even fear that the ultimate goal is to close down not only foreign but all human rights organizations working in Egypt."[1]

There was an outcry from Washington. Former Republican presidential nominee John McCain and former Secretary of State Madeline Albright, chairs of the boards of IRI and NDI, respectively, denounced the heavy-handed harassment of American-funded 'non-governmental' pro-democracy workers. President Barack Obama and Secretary of State Hillary Clinton chimed in. Congress suspended payment on $1.3 billion of military aid to Egypt (for fighter jets, army tanks, riot control gear, and intelligence consultations) before deciding to maintain this pivotal security arrangement. In the event, once bail was paid to allow most of the foreign defendants to evacuate around March 1, only Egyptians and permanent residents of Egypt employed by four foreign organizations actually stood trial. As this cased stretched into 2013, the new Egyptian government proposed legislation further restricting associational freedoms and access to resources from abroad.

How can we sort through such conflicting claims and testimonials about justice, imperialism, and pushback? European, Canadian, and American experts in 'political transitions' had been working in Arab countries for a couple of decades. After the end of the Cold War, more intently after 9/11/2001, and in another spurt after the 'youth' uprisings in 2011, professional democracy brokers (and some amateurs) flocked to the region with projects to upgrade legal systems, institutionalize competitive

[1] Khaled Fahmy, "The Truth About Fayza," *Egypt Independent*, February 26, 2012.

elections, encourage female participation, and organize liberal civic networks. Drawing on dollars, pounds sterling, and euros, often cooperating with United Nations programs, they were employed inside Egypt, Jordan, sometimes Lebanon, the Maghreb countries, Yemen, and the two exceptional ill-fated cases of Palestine and Iraq. They offered technical advice, collected data, wrote assessments, conducted seminars, ran public information campaigns, and made grants to national or regional public advocacy think tanks for projects on human rights, political reform, civil society, and related topics. Involvement varied over time and space. In some countries, foreign experts offered boilerplates for commercial legislation; in Iraq, Americans created new courts. To different degrees, foreigners participated in electoral events as technical consultants or volunteer monitors. Many donors worked directly with public sector or parastatal institutions such as parliamentary libraries or national councils for women. Other projects provided grants and training to civil society organizations defined as NGOs or CSOs. More broadly, democracy brokers sponsored or co-sponsored virtual networks and transnational conferences on topics such as how to run electoral campaigns, lobby for reforms to family law, or battle press censorship.

This book investigates how such projects work, their proximate outputs, and the experiences of practitioners.

## QUESTIONS AND PRELIMINARY ANSWERS

My task is to describe and analyze the dynamics of Western or multilateral organizations' programs 'promoting' Arab transitions from authoritarianism in the context of national, regional, and international politics in the Middle East during two tumultuous decades. The main research question is not *whether* political aid 'worked,' but rather *how* it worked, in actual practice. What work gets done, how, by whom, to what effect? Who gets what, when, where, and how? What were the actual channels, mechanisms, and institutional practices – inter-governmental, for instance, or non-governmental? Where are the sites of interaction inside or beyond national boundaries? Who are the agents, intermediaries, and audiences? How were goals relating to justice, representation, women's rights, or civil society framed, routinized, or contested? How did theories about political transitions mesh or clash with pre-existing legal jurisdictions, political institutions, and public civic spheres? When, why and how did client governments embrace or reject overtures? How did initiatives jibe with the aspirations, inspirations, and counter-hegemonic claims of civic activists? What did professionals and close-hand observers see as the proximate benefits or risks? How relevant is applied transitology to indigenous struggles for fair and decent governance? Does political aid advance social justice, representative political institutions, and popular empowerment; or authoritarian retrenchment; or imperial domination – or what?

In response to the basic question of how democracy promotion works in practice, I venture a simple answer, a basic argument, a composite theoretical structure, and a bottom-line political point. The simple answer is that political-development assistance consists of projects that are carried out by specialized professional agencies working through cross-national institutional channels. The specificities warrant further investigation. The straightforward argument is that institutional arrangements and professional practices across and inside national domains are contextual, complex, and often contested. Regardless of nationality, professionals know that transnational engagements in matters of law, elections, gender, and what is 'non-governmental' intersect with international and domestic power arrangements in complicated, sometimes counter-intuitive ways. The paradoxes encompass but go beyond what a famous historian called the collocation of "megalomania and messianism" in macro-level American foreign policy.[2] Agents and participant observers reflect ruefully on the mixed motives, messages, and blessings of political aid; ironic convergences of empowerment and power; ethical and practical dilemmas; differently scaled legal-political jurisdictions; grandiose plans gone awry; confluences and disruptures between domestic and international regimes; banal competition over symbolic capital, institutional access, and monetary advantage; and the rarified experience of conferences in fancy off-shore locations.

Amidst these complexities, I suggest that it helps to break political aid into its component parts, goals, and fields of specialization. The formal organizing thesis around which this book is structured is that practitioners and researchers in four key sectors – the rule of law sector, projects dealing with formal electoral politics, gender programming, and funding for civil society – each identify distinctive terminologies, establishments, and contradictions. Legal scholar-practitioners explore layered articulations, harmonizations, and rifts between and among legal regimes. In Iraq, the disruptures were colossal. It is in the field of elections that Western powers earned their reputation for hypocrisy, because in the Middle East the 'high politics' of geo-strategic alliances so often contradicted professional

---

[2] Eric J. Hobsbawm, "Spreading Democracy," *Foreign Policy* (Sept/Oct 2004) 40–41.

election monitoring and/or design. Feminist intellectuals and gender specialists debated cultural and institutional ways of 'representing' women. Civil society promotion and hostile counterattacks caused scholars and activists (not that these are mutually exclusive categories) to consider what it means to be governmental or not, national or not; and to analyze ironic convergences and separations between sovereign and transnational manners of governmentality.

My colleagues cited in this book variously have analyzed the salience of enduring authoritarianism; the diffusion of international law; armed interventions; feminist internationalism; neo-liberal globalization; and paradoxical interactions between or among these trajectories. Many grappled with ironies, contradictions, and dialectics: 'the West' both does and does not 'promote' human rights, ballot-driven political transitions, the struggles of Arab women, and civic freedom; democracy promotion is – but is not simply – an imperial venture; political aid might undermine or upgrade authoritarianism. There is an overarching tone of irony. I am going to suggest that seemingly antithetical hypotheses are concomitantly valid because contradictory trajectories are in play.

Beyond a straightforward answer, a narrative argument, and a thesis structure, *Political Aid and Arab Activism* aspires to solidarity with independent human rights defenders, election monitors, feminist activists, and independent advocacy organizations. We want to understand the reasoning of government officials; but our sympathies are with colleagues accused of purveying Western agendas. Therefore the evaluation of political aid must provide enough experiential and epistemological nuances to counter either vicious smear campaigns against politically engaged activist intellectuals or the sanctimonious naiveté of the Washington establishment. We seek, in other words, to confront complexities facing the mostly bilingual agents and actors caught between these conflicting narratives. The way to do this is to read the reports and commentaries they publish about their experiences and frustrations. This is a political point, but also a research strategy.

## WHAT DOES IT MEAN, PROMOTING POLITICAL TRANSITIONS?

The "work" discourses must be investigated along two axes: (1) examining a text's or ideology's logics – the assumptions the discourse implies, its context-dependent uses, and the possibilities it forecloses; and (2) investigating the rhetoric's effects – the ways in which that discourse is mediated, reiterated, and transmitted, and how it is assessed and resignified over time through political organizations, extraordinary events, and everyday practices.[3]

We understand the first of these axes – the ideological postures of donors – better than its routines, outputs, and denouements overseas. Although later in this book I will cite books, reports, and articles generated by the political-aid industry, as well as academic studies of programs dealing with law, women, and civil society, most scholars are not familiar with praxis-level implementation. The undifferentiated notion of 'democracy promotion' is too abstract for empirical investigation. Political scientists comparing political change in authoritarian systems frequently referred nebulously to Western inspiration and influence but often paid little attention to the exact roles of foreign experts or the precise pathways of donor involvement. Instead 'transitologists' offered mostly descriptive policy studies of the 'supply side' of donor motivations, strategies, and intentions, on the one hand, or studies of the purely endogenous, domestic conditions favorable to democratic transitions, on the other.[4] The most prominent works specifically about democracy promotion combine open advocacy for government funding with policy advice for donor agencies.[5]

The transnational democracy complex is so well-funded, professionalized, and prolific that in-house publications virtually flood the market with a steady stream of books and articles. The applied transitology genre is written for policy-makers, in an omniscient, imperative voice: experts tell donors, governments, and activists what they 'should' or 'must' do – or perhaps failed to do – to 'get things right.' I will draw upon the accumulated expert knowledge generated by full-time researchers, much of which is insightful and smart. Still, let us distinguish theoretically inspired academic inquiry from the professional policy genre that generates action recommendations. How-to policy manuals certainly make negative assessments of inconsistencies and wrong-headed policies, and many specialists

---

[3] Lisa Wedeen, *Peripheral Visions: Publics, Power, and Performance in Yemen* (London: University of Chicago Press, 2008) 217.

[4] Amichai Magen, *Evaluating External Influence on Democratic Development: Transition*, Center on Democracy, Development, and The Rule of Law, Freeman Spogli Institute for International Studies, Stanford University, CDDRL Working Paper 111, March 2009, Palo Alto, California: 18–20.

[5] See, for instance, Larry Diamond, *The Spirit of Democracy: The Struggle to Build Free Societies throughout the World* (New York: Times Books/Henry Holt, 2008); the classic piece by Thomas Carothers, "The End of the Transitions Paradigm," *Journal of Democracy*, 13:1(2002) 5–21; Tamara Coffman Wittes, *Freedom's Unsteady March: America's Role in Building Arab Democratization* (Washington: Brookings Institution Press, 2008).

acknowledge that in the Middle East American democracy promotion in particular has a bad name. Trade publications do not, however, entertain alternative hypotheses, cite critical explanations, or pay much attention to commentary from purported beneficiaries. Democracy promotion is described in very general terms as providing practical, advisory, technical and financial support to 'democratic agents' overseas, usually working with foreign governments but sometimes provoking authoritarian back-lash.[6] Specialists distinguish technical advice for government institutions from support for civil society groups, noting that either way, almost all political aid consists of information services via consultancies, conferences, or grants for research and/or outreach projects.[7] Tools for critically analyzing the effects of advice and information are few and rather rudimentary, however, and the appraisal effort is largely driven by agency-financed research on how donors meet mission-statement goals.[8] My purpose in this book is to analyze policy and professional practice; it is not to give policy advice.

Since the majority of policy papers and books on the topic are written from Washington's point of view, some readers will instinctively think of democracy promotion as Uncle Sam's soliloquy, for better or for worse. The autobiographical account is often told as the saga of a lone super-power in the Middle Eastern theater introspectively trying to reconcile ideals and insecurities. Given massive deployments, forceful interventions, arms exports, world-conquering military expenditures, and the preponderant American role in Iraq, perhaps Egypt, and the Israel/Palestine conundrum, this realist focus on the intentions driving American unilateralism makes sense. Even the juxtaposition of sentimental idealism with the calculations of a self-interested rational actor can be a useful heuristic for understanding contradictory official transcripts issued by professional

---

[6] These points have been made by Peter Burnell, "From Evaluating Democracy Assistance to Appraising Democracy Promotion," *Political Studies* 56 (2008) 414–434; Amichai Magen, "The Rule of Law and Its Promotion Abroad: Three Problems of Scope," *Stanford Journal of International Law* 51 (2009) 51–115; Michele Acuto, "Wilson Victorious? Understanding Democracy Promotion in the Midst of a 'Backlash,'" *Alternatives* 33 (2008) 461–480.

[7] Tamara Cofman Wittes and Andrew Masloski, "Democracy Promotion under Obama: Lessons from the Middle East Partnership Initiative," Saban Center for Middle East Policy Paper 13, Brookings Institution, Washington, May 2009.

[8] See the statistically sophisticated multivariate cross-national analysis of correlations between USAID democratic governance funding and measures of democratization in Steven E. Finkel, Anibal Pérez-Liñán, and Mitchell A. Seligson, "The Effects of U.S. Foreign Assistance on Democracy Building, 1990–2003," *World Politics* 59 (2007) 404–439: 438.

democracy brokers, the State Department, the Pentagon, and/or political leaders. Moreover, many Middle East specialists advance the counter-narrative of a superpower determined to dominate the region using tools including political aid. Nonetheless, this book is not only about American intentions, Americans abroad, or anti-Americanism.

To the contrary, singular focus on the U.S. juggernaut tends to obfuscate analysis in two ways. First, and for our overall purposes, foremost, it over-determines rather than investigates outcomes. The path-dependent projection of superpower discourages serious exploration of what happens next – how various actors 'over there,' on 'the receiving end,' interpret transcripts and reproduce institutional practices. Preliminarily, then, we might pause to con-sider how people in different countries might view the cover photograph for this book showing Marines mounting the statue of Saddam, or what the act of casting ballots signified for Iraqis in 2005, or what a voter with purple ink on her finger was communicating when she flashed a V-sign to a photographer?[9] Later we will try to understand how various actors react to, act upon, or re-purpose the symbolic and institutional default modes of political aid in specific contexts. This includes (but is not limited to) authoritarian pushback.

The second reason to eschew a narrow focus on American policies is that it can artificially and misleadingly separate them from the work of UN, European, Canadian, and other agencies. Narcissistic monologues belie the cosmopolitan intellectual roots and transnational networks of democratic internationalism. Lofty ideals, capitalist expansion, and geo-strategic superstructures fuse in a 'democratic peace' or 'pacific union' theory of enlightened multilateralism that is grounded in universal, not uniquely American, values.[10] Most contemporary innovations in interna-tional law, expertise in elections, and gender rights originate outside the United States, as we will see. The conference circuit is very multicultural. A Washington industry insider described a "democracy bureaucracy" loosely centered in the dense institutional complex in the District of Columbia but dispersed worldwide and lacking a "command and control center."[11] Going further, a conservative Republican decried a "post

---

[9] On the importance of signification, see Lisa Wedeen, "Conceptualizing Culture: Possibilities for Political Science," *The American Political Science Review* 96:4 (2002) 713–728.
[10] The interplay of idealism, realism, and economic reasoning in enlarging the pacific union was analyzed by Michael W. Doyle, *Ways of War and Peace* (New York: W. W. Norton, 1997).
[11] Thomas O. Melia, "The Democracy Bureaucracy: The Infrastructure of American Democracy Promotion," Discussion Paper for the Princeton Project on National Security Working Group on Global Institutions and Foreign Policy Infrastructure, Washington, September, 2005: 1–2.

democratic" "global governance regime" ... "promoted and run by complementary and interlocking networks" of leftist "Sixty-Eighters."[12] All in all, as we will see, Uncle Sam may steal the limelight, but other roles are pivotal to plot development. Ergo, this is not a book about American foreign policy as told from Washington's perspective, nor a study of Arab reactions to American initiatives. International law, multinational initiatives, and cosmopolitan codes of behavior transcend American foreign policy objectives and hegemonic aspirations.

If American might is just one arc that requires scrutiny, how can we conceptualize the political development enterprise? Very broadly, social scientists offer two main sets of hypotheses about the global governance regime. The more sanguine view, if you will, accentuates the catalytic power of ideas institutionalized in signatory conventions that gradually gain compliance from increasing numbers of states. This 'constructivist' paradigm holds that transnational networks gradually universalize norms, rules, institutions, and procedures governing sovereign and even non-state behavior in particular issue areas.[13] International regimes share distinctive catchphrases, templates, and standards via conferences, training, documentation, web-links, and institution-building activities. They constitute "epistemic communities" of knowledgeable specialists to generate and disseminate the "reasons, habits, expectations, and compelling arguments" for cosmopolitan processes and policies.[14] Now, one realist argument is that the superpower delegates implementation of

[12] John Fonte, "Democracy's Trojan Horse," *The National Interest* (Summer 2004) 117–118. Referring to leftist protests in the United States, France, and other Western countries in 1968, Fonte warns that national sovereignty "is increasingly circumscribed by the growing strength of the global institutions, laws, rules, and ideological norms."

[13] Robert Keohane, *After Hegemony: Cooperation and Disorder in World Political Economy* (Princeton: Princeton University Press, 1984), argued that the United States was the prime mover in some, but not all, international regimes. Initially a theory of inter-governmental institutions, the concept of regimes was later applied to the grey area of non- and quasi-non-governmental organizations, according to James Bohman, "International Regimes and Democratic Governance: Political Equality and Influence in Global Institutions, *International Affairs* 75 (1999) 499–513.

[14] Emanuel Adler and Peter M. Haas, "Conclusion: Epistemic Communities, World Order, and the Creation of a Reflective Research Program," *International Organization* 45:1 (1992) 367–390: 372. See also Andrew P. Cortell and James W. Davis, Jr., "Understanding the Domestic Impact of International Norms: A Research Agenda," *International Studies Review*, 2:1 (2000) 65–87; Rodger A. Payne, "Persuasion, Frames, and Norm Construction," *European Journal of International Relations*, 7:1 (2001) 37–61; and Amitav Acharya, "How Ideas Spread: Whose Norms Matter? Norm Localization and Institutional Change in Asian Regionalism," *International Organization* 58 (2004) 239–275.

some high principles to allies and multilateral institutions in order "to facilitate construction of an order conducive to its interests."[15] This is certainly a hypothesis worth entertaining. Liberal internationalists reply, however, that universal norms, multilateral efforts, leadership from 'middle powers' such as the Netherlands and Canada, polyglot teams, and 'non-governmental' organizations minimize the perception of meddling in domestic politics, thereby increasing the acceptability of democracy assistance. They distinguish, in other words, inter-governmental institutions and transnational regimes from American imperialism, arguing – normatively, heuristically, and empirically – for multilateralism over unilateralism.[16] In each field of investigation in this book some thoughtful analysis shows how international regimes express universal values, influence state reforms, or bolster the efforts of activists to defend against despotism. Moreover, this perspective encourages recognition that Arab jurists, elections monitors, feminists, and civic activists are agents, and not simply recipients, of cosmopolitan norms. In the best-case scenarios, international rights conventions, techniques for exposing electoral fraud, transnational women's advocacy, and support for independent intellectual production empower a social justice vanguard to work for better governance. The resources of political aid might tip the balance in their favor.

However, other progressive scholars associate dense vertical networks radiating from Europe and North America with neo-liberal globalization's assault on states and their welfare projects. Human rights regimes, election monitoring, gender empowerment agendas, and NGO networks can all perpetuate global capitalist expansion and modes of governmentality dictated by the World Bank, the International Monetary Fund, and the World Trade Organization. From this perspective, limited political reform initiatives are meant to subjugate national sovereignty to Western

---

[15] G. John Ikenberry and Charles A. Kupchan, "Socialization and Hegemonic Power," *International Organization* 44:3 (1990) 283–315: 284.

[16] Jon C. Pevehouse, "Democracy from the Outside-In? International Organizations and Democratization," *International Organization* 56:3 (2002) 515–549: 523, suggests that international rather than purely bilateral involvement may reassure business elites and military officers. To offset criticisms of overt and covert manipulations of elections in Central America and Southeast Asia, Washington financed more multilateral efforts, according to David P. Forsythe and Barbara Ann Rieffer, "US Foreign Policy and Enlarging the Democratic Community": *Human Rights Quarterly* 22: 4 (2000) 998–1010. This argument for multilateralism was applied to Iraq by Rob Jenkins, "Collateral Benefit: Iraq and Increased Legitimacy for International Trusteeship." *Dissent* 53: 2 (2006) 72–75.

corporate hegemony.[17] "Democratic evangelism," accordingly, was about "mobilizing discourses," constructing "frameworks for thought," "creating foot soldiers," and providing "yardsticks" to measure compliance with new standards.[18] It was intended to foreclose prospects of mass mobilizations of "the Arab street" or in the form of "politics from below."[19] These were not only Arab concerns. In 'sub-Saharan' Africa as well, "the ascendancy of form over content" conveyed a "legitimization of disempowerment."[20] Washington-based "democracy makers," the think tanks in the U.S. government, World Bank offices, and the so-called NGO sector comprised of IRI, Carnegie, and others generated modes of knowledge conducive to American dominance, for instance by subsuming human rights under the more managerial notion of good governance, effectively consigning culturally sensitive field workers to 'double agent' roles. As one scholar observed, the genius of this formulation is the premise that political transitions evolve from bureaucratic-authoritarian conditions via expert consultation rather than by popular mobilization.[21] This managerial rendition obscures issues of global democracy and histories of struggles over rights and representation in the West.[22] Instead of taking

---

[17] Larbi Sadiki, "To Export or Not Export Democracy to the Arab World: The Islamist Perspective," *Arab Studies Journal* VI: 1 (1998) 60–75; Moheb Zaki, *Civil Society and Democratization in Egypt, 1981–1994*, Cairo, Dar Al Kutub for *Konrad-Adenauer-Stiftung* and The Ibn Khaldun Center, n.d.

[18] Hisham M. Nazer, *Power of a Third Kind: The Western Attempt to Colonize the Global Village* (Westport, Connecticut, and London: Praeger, 1999), xxiii, 13–15. NGOs' "simplistic narratives" and "zealous rationale," he wrote, constituted "nodal links" in a hegemonic discourse, and human rights "a fetishized commodity… and, simultaneously, a fungible political currency" 103–107.

[19] Assef Bayat, "Transforming the Arab World: *The Arab Human Development Report* and the Politics of Change," *Development and Change* 36:6 (2005) 1225–37; Lila Abu-Lughod, "Dialects of Women's Empowerment: The International Circuitry of the Arab Human Development Report 2005," *International Journal of Middle East Studies*, 41:1 (2009) 83–103. Galal Amin, *The Illusion of Progress in the Arab World: A Critique of Western Misconstructions* (Cairo: American University in Cairo Press, 2006); Mark Levine, "The UN Arab Human Development Report: A Critique," *Middle East Report Online*, July 2, 2002.

[20] Claude Ake, "The Democratisation of Disempowerment in Africa," in Hippler, ed., *The Democratisation of Disempowerment: The Problem of Democracy in the Third World* (London: Pluto Press, 1999) 70.

[21] Nicolas Guilhot, *The Democracy Makers: Human Rights and International Order* (New York: Columbia University Press, 2005).

[22] Johan Galtung, "Alternative Models for Global Democracy," ed. Barry Holden, *Global Democracy: Key Debates* (London and New York: Routledge, 2000) 142–161; Johan Galtung, "A Structural Theory of Imperialism," *Journal of Peace Research* 8:2 (1971) 81–117; Alan Gilbert, *Must Global Politics Constrain Democracy? Great-Power*

mission statements and in-house publications at face value, critical scholars invite us to consider how developmental "regimes of truth" were disseminated, professionalized, and institutionalized by conventional aid agencies.[23]

Arab rights advocates and plenty of expatriate professionals contemplated these arguments as they applied in specific post-Cold War contexts. Participants in human rights conferences and women's networks frequently discussed, debated, and disagreed about the extent to which international aid for political transitions offered intellectual, material, or mechanical assets for reform projects; provoked authoritarian backlash; and/or perpetuated Euro-American supremacy. It was clear to many that conceptually elegant analyses could be vulgarized as propaganda for dictatorship or for imperialism. The vision of an enlightened evangelical 'West' exporting legal rights, electoral practices, gender equality, and basic liberties morphed into apologetics for hubris and belligerence. On the other side, Arab police-states whipped up xenophobic sentiments against 'colonial meddling' to muzzle and scapegoat citizen rights-defenders. I want to ponder these perspectives, without giving grist to either mill, in order to investigate the anomalous interchanges between them and to appreciate the perspectives of civic activists caught in the middle.

It can already be anticipated that self-fulfilling postulates about political aid – as mode of empowerment or exercise of power – offer insights but don't really explain how it works in practice. What are the events? Who is there; who says what; what do they document about what was said? If projects harmonize procedures or parlances – how so? What's the difference between sending consultants, hiring 'locals,' and providing grants? What are the implications of working through governmental, parastatal, or non-governmental channels, respectively? To give a concrete example: what are the political-institutional ramifications of working inside judiciaries, through national human rights ministries, with independent national watch-dogs, or by fostering pan-Arab transnational 'NGO' networks – and how do they vary by circumstance? Is monitoring elections a way of catching ballot thieves red-handed, a supplement to conventional espionage, a roadmap for authoritarian upgrading, or all of these things? How,

---

*Realism, Democratic Peace, and Democratic Internationalism* (Princeton, Princeton University Press, 1999).

[23] Arturo Escobar, *Encountering Development: The Making and Unmaking of the Third World* (Princeton: Princeton University Press, 1995).

by what mechanisms, to what extent, under what circumstances, does political aid in different sectors reproduce technocratic practices – or not?

## METHOD AND SCOPE

Decades ago, a famous sociologist observed that *projects* are the "privileged particles"[24] of development. In this research, the units of analysis are projects: discrete, named, finite activities underwritten by donors and implemented by contractors or intermediaries working with indigenous partners or counterparts. If foreign aid is the sum of development projects, then, for our purposes, political aid is its projects. To understand how democracy promotion works, therefore, we would need to appreciate how iterative activities are cumulatively framed, professionalized, institutionalized, and politicized in 'real life.'

I began this research by attending events, visiting offices, talking to people, reading news articles, and learning what agencies named what kind of projects in which countries in the Middle East. Next, I searched backward to the web sites of democracy assistance agencies for their mission statements, lists of projects, partners, and partners' project lists and sponsor links. This exercise provided an overview of activities.[25] My ambition singlehandedly to code and catalogue 'all' projects turned into an unwieldy data file that imploded under the hundreds of separate initiatives by new actors in Iraq and the proliferation of transnational grant-making agencies in the twenty-first century. Nonetheless, tracking two decades' worth of projects yielded an unusually large pile of anecdotes. Thirdly, in pursuit of depth, and most revealingly, I pored over reports, evaluations, scholarly publications, and published or online commentary, mostly written in English by professionals and practitioners. I relied on their writings rather than on interviews in order to capture what they wanted to say rather than what I wanted to know, and by way of analyzing texts and transcripts. Although I did a lot of participant observation 'in the field,' therefore, published or posted first-hand, on-site accounts are the main source for the analyses that follow. Also I relied mostly on readily available English-language sources to which international experts have access.

---

[24] Albert O. Hirschman, *Development Projects Observed* (Washington, Brookings Institution, 1967) 1.
[25] I described my preliminary findings in Sheila Carapico, "Foreign Aid for Promoting Democracy in the Arab World," *The Middle East Journal* 56:3 (2002) 379–395.

The overview project catalogue yielded some basic descriptive information. First, perhaps obviously, democracy promotion differs from humanitarian aid that provides emergency relief directly to disaster victims or refugees; conventional bilateral or multilateral socio-economic development cooperation; or military assistance in the form of training and equipment for armed forces. Normally, both development aid and military aid are inter-state arrangements negotiated diplomatically and administered through official channels. Both consist mostly of loans for material goods and grants for expert services. Conventional bilateral and multilateral development aid agencies do fund political projects in good governance, decentralization and civil society as part of their overall developmental mandates, and most political aid originates in the group of about two dozen wealthy capitalist aid donors known as the Organization for Economic Cooperation and Development (OECD). However, in addition to conventional providers of what the OECD calls overseas development assistance (ODA), democracy brokers include a range of quasi-non-governmental and transnational agencies and subcontractors situated in different operational niches in and beyond 'the state.' Parastatal publicly subsidized national political foundations include the German *Stiftungen*, the National Endowment for Democracy (NED), NDI and IRI, the Netherlands Institute for Multiparty Democracy, and many others. Among the numerous new quasi-multilateral public entities were the European Union's Anna Lindh Foundation for the Dialogue between Cultures and its Network of Democracy Think Tanks, the U.S.-led Foundation for the Future, and a group based in Stockholm known as International IDEA. With the exception of a few mostly U.S.-based foundations with private endowments such as the Ford, Soros, and Carnegie foundations and the Carter Center, virtually all of them relied on public sector budgets.

Next, only some countries in the Middle East and North Africa (popularly known in English by the acronym MENA) featured prominently in project records. No non-Arab countries were candidates for concerted overt efforts. Israel, the top beneficiary of American security and financial assistance worldwide, was already classified as an advanced liberal democracy not in need of reform or guidance, so although some Israeli peace and human rights groups fund-raise in Europe, few if any judicial advisors or election monitors go to Israel. Turkey, a NATO member aspiring to join the European Union, was scarcely mentioned in project lists for the MENA region except under the broad-ranging Euro-Mediterranean network. At the opposite end of the spectrum, the hostile pariah government of the

Islamic Republic of Iran was beyond the scope of overt initiatives for democratic enlargement. Donors placed Arab League members Sudan (now North Sudan), Mauritania, and Somalia under their Africa bureaus. This left just the Arab countries, by which I mean the places where Arabic is the main official, spoken, and media language.

Not all Arab countries were targeted, however. Rather, lists of projects, office locations, and even attendees at transnational conferences mostly featured nine countries. These were *not* the wealthy oil-exporting monarchies of the Gulf, net donors of development assistance adamant about the sanctity of their dynastic traditions, whose stability was considered a vital American interest. Nor, prior to 2011, were the rogue dictatorships in Libya and Syria, or Iraq under Saddam Hussein, included (however much North Atlantic powers had hoped for regime change there and in Iran). Whether there were clandestine activities via covert institutional channels in Libya before the 2011 NATO intervention or in Syria is beyond the scope of this study.

Candidates for political aid were the Western-leaning, often-called 'moderate,' post-colonial, Third World places where most of the Arab region's roughly 360 million people live. Unlike either the tidy well-to-do Gulf Cooperation Council (GCC) states or the belligerent rogues, they were the places where OECD aid agencies, the World Bank, and the United Nations Development Programme (UNDP) already maintained an active presence: client regimes, low-to-middle income, debt-ridden and dependent to varying degrees on conventional socio-economic development loans, grants, and policy advice from Western, Gulf, and multilateral sources. They were seven sovereign countries and two exceptional cases of political development under conditions of occupation: Egypt, Jordan, Morocco, Yemen, Algeria, Tunisia, and Lebanon; and Palestine during the Oslo era and Iraq after the second Anglo-American invasion. Egypt, Palestine, and Iraq are the most prominent cases overall, in terms of activities and scholarly analysis.

The OECD's Development Assistance Committee (DAC) keeps track of official ODA transfers, and publishes data provided by its member states. By contrast, aggregate figures for political aid through various governmental, parastatal, and quasi-multilateral channels are harder to come by. Tables 1 and 2 give proxy evidence of rank orders and magnitude. Table 1 shows the Middle Eastern recipients of official bilateral American aid via the Agency for International Development (USAID)'s Democratic Governance program for a fourteen-year period ending in 2004. It does not necessarily include all USAID projects for civil society or women or

TABLE 1. *Middle Eastern Recipients of USAID Democratic Governance Assistance during 1990–2004 (by amount and number of years)*

| | | |
|---|---|---|
| Algeria | $3.7 million | 8 years |
| Bahrain | $1.3 million | 2 years |
| Egypt | $334.3 million | 14 years |
| Iraq | $523.6 million | 3 years |
| Jordan | $28.3 million | 5 years |
| Lebanon | $28.5 million | 11 years |
| Morocco | $3.6 million | 7 years |
| Oman | $0.6 million | 2 years |
| Qatar | $0.8 million | 1 year |
| Saudi Arabia | $0.4 million | 1 year |
| Tunisia | $11.2 million | 5 years |
| Turkey | $0.9 million | 4 years |
| West Bank and Gaza | $155.4 million | 11 years |
| Yemen | $6.6 million | 8 years |

*Source*: Steven E. Finkel, Anibal Pérez-Liñán and Mitchell A. Seligson, "The Effects of U.S. Foreign Assistance on Democracy Building, 1990–2003," *World Politics*, 59 (2007) 404–439: 438.

TABLE 2. *Major Donors to Top Arab Aid Recipients circa 2007/08*

| | |
|---|---|
| Algeria | France, Spain, EC, Belgium, Arabs, Germany, Italy, Japan, Canada, Korea |
| Egypt | US, EC, Germany, France, Arabs, Japan, Denmark, IDA, Spain, Austria |
| Iraq | US, Germany, Japan, France, Italy, Austria, Australia, Sweden, UK, Spain |
| Jordan | US, UNWRA, Germany, EC, Japan, Arabs, Israel, Spain, Italy, Canada |
| Lebanon | Arabs, EC, US, France, UNWRA, Italy, Germany, Spain, Turkey, Norway |
| Morocco | France, EC, Germany, Arabs, Japan, Spain, Italy, US, Belgium |
| Palestine | UNWRA, EC, US, Norway, Germany, Japan, Spain, Sweden, France, Canada |
| Tunisia | France, EC, Germany, Japan, Italy, Spain, Belgium, UK, Arabs, Canada |
| Yemen | IDA, Germany, Netherlands, US, EC, UK, Arabs, Japan, France, WFP |

*Source*: OECD data. UNWRA is the UN agency that assists Palestinian refugees; Arabs are GCC donors; IDA is the branch of the World Bank that deals with the most impoverished countries; the WFP is the World Food Program.

American projects funded under the National Endowment for Democracy, the Middle East Partnership Initiative, or other channels. It shows that Iraq, Egypt, and the West Bank and Gaza were the top recipients; Gulf countries are included but the tab is a comparative pittance. Table 2 shows the top donors to the main Arab ODA recipients circa 2007. These rankings vary from year to year. At that time, the United States was the major donor of economic development assistance to Iraq, Egypt, and Jordan, in that order. The European Union, France, and other OECD donors played larger roles in the other sovereign countries and Palestine. The two lists of recipients and donors roughly seem to correlate with the activities of democracy brokers in the Middle East and North Africa (MENA) region described in the rest of this book.

The data in these two tables show conventional assistance to nine Arab ODA recipients. However, project records for democracy promotion show additional significant spending on co-sponsored transnational conferences or networks at the Arab or Mediterranean regional level. The steady stream of workshops, summits, and declarations, sometimes coordinated by UN organizations, allow prominent Arab professionals from these countries to meet with European, North American, and international experts to exchange information and ideas. This interesting quasi-non-intergovernmental sphere of intermittent interaction in luxury conference facilities and in cyberspace goes largely unnoticed in studies that usually focus on, say, American policies, or programs inside Egypt. Yet it is very much part of the work democracy brokers do. Investigating this regional dimension is one of the original contributions of this book.

Conspicuously, democracy promotion is an informational enterprise, idealist in the sense that it aims to shape norms and values. Compared with the hardware-and-firepower of military assistance or the brick-and-mortar or syringes-and-books provisions of conventional development aid, political aid mostly delivers words, knowledge, ideas, and publicity. Project activities and outputs are studies, reports, advice, seminars, and educational materials; expenditures go toward consultant salaries, travel expenses, printing costs, and technology and software. More than conventional ODA, democracy promotion produces and reproduces codes and categories of information and disseminates professional practices.

More specifically, however, as already suggested, operational expertise is specialized. There's hardly any such thing as a 'democracy project,' per se, it turns out: professionalism means specialization. Projects, experts, detailed accounts, and scholarly inquiry are refined into several distinct subfields. These are displayed in the project typology shown in Table 3.

The justice/human rights/rule-of-law sector is perhaps the most highly specialized, and Chapter 1 cites a rich trove of academic and legal scholarship on the intermingling of transnational, Arab, and national legal regimes. The second important category of political aid has to do with

TABLE 3. *A Typology of Projects Promoting Arab Democratization*

| | Legal-Judicial Sector | Electoral Representation | Civic Sector |
|---|---|---|---|
| **Research** | Legal sector analysis | Pilot/background | Studies of civil |
| | Human rights reports | studies | society |
| | Legislative | Needs assessments | NGO directories |
| | documentation | Mapping exercises | Research grants |
| | Digital inventories | Election monitoring | Gender analysis |
| | Translation of | Public opinion surveys | Publications |
| | documents | Parliamentary records | Documentaries |
| | Constitutional | Studies of gender | · |
| | research | quotas | |
| | Criminal registries | | |
| **Pedagogy** | Expert consultations | Voter education | NGO workshops |
| | Law schools & | Party campaign | Women's |
| | programs | training | empowerment |
| | Human rights | Women candidate | Advocacy training |
| | training | programs | Web sites/ |
| | Media campaigns on | Parliamentary | handbooks |
| | rights | exchanges | Media seminars |
| | Seminars/workshops | Poll-worker training | Study tours |
| | Professional | Election publicity | Fund-raising |
| | exchanges | Local monitor | manuals |
| | Commercial | training | |
| | harmonization | | |
| **Institutional** | Courts recording | Election commissions | Think tanks |
| | Penal system | Parliamentary offices | Media centers |
| | Introducing | Local councils | Women's advocacy |
| | legislation | Automated voting | Chambers of |
| | Law libraries | Ballots, ink, boxes | commerce |
| | Bar associations | Election monitors | Universities |
| | Human rights | Parliamentary | Global NGO |
| | organizations | libraries | networks |
| | Transnational | | Labor unions |
| | institutions | | Arab regional |
| | Iraq's High Tribunal | | conferences |

voting and representation, the crux of what most people mean by democracy and democracy promotion. Here the specialized academic literature is rather thin, but the industry documentation and commentary on the American role are particularly robust. Consultants, critics, and constituents have written extensively about the third major subset of activities engaging civil society defined as advocacy NGOs. This is a well-researched and well-theorized field covered in analyses of the 'non-governmental' obsessions of neo-liberal globalization as well as studies of civil society in Egypt, Palestine and other countries. Last, but hardly least, grants officers, activists, and scholars have thought creatively about the complicated issues surrounding Arab women's empowerment via legal, electoral, and civil engagement, so there is a unique body of gender research. In each sphere, practitioners faced contradictory challenges.

This book's four main chapters consider these subfields and the relevant literatures. Each examines both a sector and a significant contradiction. They are arranged to be accessible to non-Middle East specialists and to build a cumulative analysis. Chapter 1 on Legal Jurisdictions considers historical articulations among municipal, Arab, European, and international legal regimes before investigating what specialists call 'legal harmonization.' Responding to other scholars' invitation to consider the dissonant ways political aid might erode and/or reinforce states' legal authority, the first half of the chapter investigates relationships between national and transnational legal jurisdictions historically and in the context of specific contemporary project funding for law schools, national human rights councils, non-governmental networks, or new information technologies. It looks at how practices are folded into existing municipal-legal arrangements inside the sovereign domains. The rest of the chapter delves into the exceptional American project to layer some new courts and laws atop the existing Iraqi Arab-style judicial system, mostly as told by some of the leading, ultimately disenchanted, legal consultants and experts involved.

Although a certain trope about 'Western pressure to hold free and fair elections' persists in the English-language mass media, the historical record suggests otherwise. Celebration of Kuwait's non-partisan male-only post liberation balloting, mute reactions to an Algerian military coup that blocked an Islamist victory at the polls, orchestration of voting for the Palestine Authority under the Oslo Accords, fanfare surrounding Iraq's problematic post-invasion elections, rejection of the outcome of the 2006 Palestinian vote, delicate understatements of vote-rigging in Egypt, and other examples cumulatively suggest that the United States in particular sought publicity and/or outcomes conducive to its power. The chapter on elections covers these stories, but also less-studied rubrics of an incipient transnational elections regime. This regime provides expert advice on the design and administration of electoral systems; trains poll-workers, campaign managers, and others; and/or applies an increasingly sophisticated methodology for local and foreign monitors to document what happens in polling stations and vote-tallying centers. The chapter examines specific expert and documentary activities in different Arab elections between the early 1990s and the end of 2010, as reported by track-record organizations such as the EU Elections Unit, the International Foundation for Electoral Systems, NDI, Canadian groups, the Carter Center, and specialized United Nations agencies. Foreign experts, trainers, and monitors had a complicated and sometimes controversial relationship to national authorities, as IRI was reminded when its offices were raided amidst intensive election-season monitoring and training activities. The chapter considers the ways foreign democracy brokers did or did not work in various Arab elections to harmonize internationally accepted routines, and how those activities imbricated with national and international power struggles.

The second half of the book shifts register. It eavesdrops on interpersonal encounters and confrontations over the discourses and resources earmarked for women's empowerment and civil society, respectively. Drawing on first-hand scholarly analyses, industry reports, conference presentations, and journalistic commentary, these two chapters are less about international relations and geo-strategic issues than about processes of globalization and cosmopolitanism. The third chapter, Patronizing Women, asks how 'regimes of truth' are interpreted and put into action by Arab women and other actors. I draw on women's internationalism as well as on rich feminist critiques of the 'dialects' of 'transnational feminist governmentality.' Still, again the question is: then what? How do bilingual practitioners and/or 'native' audiences react to and act upon the UN-centered gender regime? How are its generalizations institutionalized? What are the politics of this? The chapter is divided into two parts. The first part quotes extensively from transcripts of cross-cultural exchanges in an effort to reveal how women receive, resignify, or reject rather didactic messages. Some Western readers will be surprised by the sarcasm. The second part traces organizational pathways with parallels to national human rights institutions, and anticipates some of the conflicts and controversies over non-governmental funding channels. One of the paradoxes in this chapter – the enigma of institutionalized idealism – is conveyed by years' worth of images of First Lady Susanne Mubarak leading Egypt's International Women's Day celebrations applauded more by foreigners than by Egyptians.

The chapter on so-called NGOs, GONGOs, and DONGOs looks into fierce disputes over legislation, registration and funding of civil society organizations as defined by domestic and transnational regimes. This investigation takes us into the frontier zones of 'non-governmental,' sometimes extra-territorial, activities, and thus necessitates refined notions of transnational regimes; centrifugal and centripetal forces of globalization; and the dual meanings of 'denationalization.' The main plot line follows the backlash from Arab governments allied with the West, notably the contentious string of disputes, re-legislations, and court cases leading up to the 'foreign funding' trial in Egypt in late 2011. In these inordinate events, I also had to include a glimpse into outlandish feedback loops of anti-terror legislation and crackdowns in 'the West' eerily similar to long-standing restrictions on non-governmental funding imposed by Arab dictators. Like the chapter on women, this one cites leading bilingual intellectuals' sometimes incredulous reactions to both nationalist and imperial parlances.

Given the locations of the main donor agencies, political foundations, and sub-contractors, it is almost impossible to avoid characterizing them collectively as 'the West' or 'Western.' This pseudo-geographic designation carries several distinct, often contrary, connotations, however. An over-arching concept of Western Civilization features in English as the bearer of great democratic ideals from the ancient Greek philosophers, Judeo-Christian traditions, and the European Enlightenment. Equally, the term is often used as shorthand for stable liberal democracies and the values they share. 'Western' also refers to European-looking people, and in some usages seems synonymous with 'English-speaking.' Another euphemistic rendering also calls it 'the international community,' as in expatriate communities of diplomats, development experts, and democracy brokers who reside in several Arab capitals. Alternately, the North Atlantic Treaty Organization, NATO, 'the Western alliance,' is the world's dominant military force, formerly opposed by the Soviet-led 'eastern bloc.' Another use of the term describes the Group of Seven (G-7) strongest capitalist economies – the United States, Great Britain, France, Germany, Japan, Canada, and Italy – or the larger club of capitalist donor countries that make development policies for the rest of the world through their membership in the Organization for Economic Cooperation and Development, the OECD. This 'West,' the center of the world capitalist system and its financial institutions the World Bank and the International Monetary Fund, also goes by other geographic designations: 'the global North' and 'the core countries.' Similarly, yet contrarily, in the post-colonial Third World, and in Arabic usage, 'Western' is often an adjectival descriptor of imperialism signifying alien, domineering, insidious, and haughty. I will try to keep these alternative meanings distinct, while acknowledging that in everyday conversation and extraordinary events they merge and overlap in ambiguous, contradictory, and very political ways.

To those who used to imagine 'the West' and 'the Arab world' as two parallel universes, conferences and partnerships would seem like intergalactic portals. The analogy is not entirely inept because so-called 'missions' almost always entail intercontinental air travel, Arabic-English (or French) translation, and glassed-off suspension in extra-territorial space. I like the allegory of missions, projects, and meetings as inter-scalar, boundary-crossing, ephemeral portals where dual realities may co-exist or collide.

If projects, branch offices, and conference halls are portals, however, collectively they constitute a sort of denationalized-transnationalized frontier between national and transnational domains. In the late twentieth century, a vast, mostly non-profit, publicly funded industry had set up shop in Cairo, Jerusalem, Amman, Rabat, Sana'a, and other, mostly Mediterranean, locales. Downtown convention centers or offshore resorts hosted endless workshops and conferences. A whole cadre of think tanks staffed by liberal Arab or bi-national intellectuals, many of them educated in the finest Western universities, emerged as democracy brokers in their own right, so to speak, translating and reinterpreting universal norms into Arabic vernaculars and national histories. Under extraordinary circumstances, Ramallah, Jerusalem, Baghdad, Irbil, Amman, and Cairo became destinations for global experts in law, elections, and empowerment. Doha and Casablanca offered even more upscale beachfront venues. These spaces defy binary categories of Western/Arab, native/foreign, state/nongovernmental, and expert/activist.

Of course, 'the West' and 'the Arab world' never were two parallel universes. European or 'Western' history evolved in part in interactions with ancient Mesopotamia, Egypt, and the Holy Land, through Roman conquests, Mediterranean trade, Arab scholars' preservation of Greek manuscripts, and the Crusades. The Middle East has been touched by two twentieth-century European wars, post-Ottoman British and French mandates, European Zionism, OECD dependence on Arabian oil, the Israel-Palestine conundrum, two U.S.-led wars in Iraq, 9/11, and so on, not to mention Mercedes cars and McDonald's hamburgers. The first chapter explains something about the historical processes of legal layering and Arab-regional legal harmonization, before analyzing interfaces of political aid with already hybrid legal systems. It opens with the morose execution of the deposed dictator of Iraq, images of which suffice to dispel fantasies about the virtuous superiority of Western, or specifically American, justice. The chapter also sets the stage for subsequent discussions of elections, women's rights, and the campaign to reform Arab NGO laws.

# I

# Legal Jurisdictions

On December 30, 2006, Saddam Hussein al-Takriti was hanged by a noose around his neck after being convicted of ordering a massacre of Iraqi citizens in 1982 in a place called Dujail. The videotape broadcast worldwide showed witnesses jeering as his body convulsed through the gallows. The trial had been an exercise in legal pluralism, the multicultural intermingling of legal orders. It dramatized some complexities of international interventions in the rule-of-law sector. The tyrant was captured by American forces and sentenced by an Iraqi High Tribunal organized and financed by the Occupying Authority. He was not charged with genocide, war crimes, or crimes against humanity under international law. Nor was he indicted for all his administrations' atrocities. Rather, the verdict was rendered under the 1969 Iraqi Penal Code derived from an antecedent law promulgated by Great Britain under its League of Nations mandate and consistent with the Napoleonic code introduced by the Ottomans in their Mesopotamian provinces. Conducted in Arabic and Kurdish by Iraqi judges and prosecutors, the proceedings reflected Ottoman, customary, French, British, and Egyptian influences on Iraq's courts system, and some American elements, but not more recent precedents, norms, and mechanisms in international criminal prosecution.

Few other initiatives were as sensationally fraught as the one culminating in this gruesome death chamber spectacle, and very rarely are foreign interventions as determinant as the American role in the Dujail proceedings. Yet multicultural legal systems and evolving transnational norms frequently call into question what system of laws applies in what circumstances. Inevitably probing the shifting confluence of municipal and transnational jurisdictions, legal development projects in post-colonial states and the Palestinian territories often confronted ambiguities between and among layers of judicial authority. Scholars posed these contradictions between law as a bulwark against police states and law as a tool of empire.

The prosecution of Saddam Hussein embellished these issues. The hybridity of the extraordinary Dujail tribunal and sentence further illustrated why the variables West/Arab, national/foreign, and state/non-state are what scholars like to call 'false binaries': actually they are continuous rather than dichotomous variables. Democracy-assistance projects in the legal sector navigated gradations between international and domestic law. Often they operated in the Arab "*qawmi*" layer between global and national ("*watani*") ecosystems of executive bureaucracies, parliaments, courts, bar associations, parastatal national human rights institutions, criminal justice systems, and local think tanks and advocacy groups. Where exactly projects go, and for what purposes, are inherently contentious. Just as law is fundamentally political because it is constitutive of political order, so are projects dealing with the nature and practice of law. This chapter investigates these politics broadly and historically for the region as a whole, and then examines the extraordinary experiment in creating a new constitution and courts for Iraq. Overall, it is a study of quarrelsome politics of legal pluralism and legal layering as influenced by foreign funders and experts.

## JUSTICE AND DISCIPLINE

In the global arena, even before the turn of the millennium, the enigma was that human rights advocacy could be seen, as one theorist put it, "as a movement for international justice or as a cultural project for 'civilizing' and emancipating 'savage' cultures."[1] The first view, the identification of democracy brokers with a worldwide social justice movement, begins when Northern rights advocates petition their elected representatives to legislate compliance with the Universal Declaration of Human Rights and other international covenants. Advocates contend that these instruments confer ethical and signatory obligations to intrude into the judicial affairs of non-compliant countries, specifically with political aid and aid conditionality. All states have a duty to protect and promote civil, political,

---

[1] Makau Mutua, "Human Rights International NGOs: A Critical Evaluation," in Claude E. Welch, Jr., ed. *NGOs and Human Rights: Promise and Performance* (Philadelphia: University of Pennsylvania Press, 2001) 151–163:151.

economic, social, and cultural rights and freedoms. It is a matter of giving international regimes, or sets of vocabulary, practices, and institutions governing state behavior in a particular domain or issue-area, the force of law. Thus, for instance, the mission of Canada's International Centre for Human Rights and Democratic Development (known as "Rights and Democracy") was to implement the Universal Declaration. Succinctly stated, according to the director of the British foreign aid agency (DFID), external actors' "legitimate interest" in good governance derives from the Declaration as well as the public's right to hold Parliament accountable for the way its aid money is spent.[2]

Ostensibly, then, national political foundations and foreign aid programs help systematize supra-national peremptory norms. Democracy brokers work alongside independent monitoring groups (of which the best known are Amnesty International and Human Rights Watch), international federations (such as the *Union Internationale des Avocats* and the *Fédération internationale des ligues des droits de l'Homme*), and evolving global institutions (such as the International Criminal Court). The legal-constructivist premise is that through monitoring, information exchange, and enforcement, principled norm entrepreneurs and international judicial institutions raise *jus cogens* peremptory norms around which rights defenders, jurists, journalists, opinion entrepreneurs, and educators can lobby officials or ultimately bring suit against transgressors.[3] Enthusiasts trust political aid from strong democracies and democracy brokers working within legal regimes to make other states enforce overriding principles.[4]

---

[2] Andrew Goudie, "International Development: Beyond the White Paper is a Good Government Agenda Practical? An Approach to Governance," speech to the Overseas Development Institute, Department for International Development, March 25, 1998.

[3] Kathryn Sikkink, "Human Rights, Principled Issue-Networks, and Sovereignty in Latin America," *International Organization*, 47:3 (1993) 411–441. For theoretical elaboration, see Harold Koh, "How is International Human Rights Law Enforced," *Indiana Law Journal* 74 (1998) 1396–1417; and Kathryn Hochstetler, Ann Marie Clark, and Elisabeth J. Friedman, "Sovereignty in the Balance: Claims and Bargains at the UN Conferences on the Environment, Human Rights, and Women," *International Studies Quarterly* 44:4 (2000) 591–614.

[4] A widely cited classification distinguishes enforcement regimes, monitoring and review regimes, formats for international policy coordination, information-exchange regimes, and international promotion or assistance regimes. Political aid for legal development is promotional, and also geared toward policy coordination. Jack Donnelly, "International Human Rights: A Regime Analysis," *International Organization* 40:3 (1986):599–642. However, Guilhot, *The Democracy Makers*:182, points out that studies of regime-building centered on "issue networks" rarely distinguish government-funded political aid administered by policy entrepreneurs from the work of activists in the philanthropic sector.

Democracy promotion in the field of law overlaps only partly with human rights advocacy, however, because legal-development assistance addresses commercial law and policing alongside human rights protection. When the World Bank, the European Community, and USAID talk about legal reform, good governance, judicial upgrading, and the rule of law, their points of reference are corruption, commercial courts, bankruptcy procedures, financial and regulatory legislation, protections for corporate investment, and international trade rules. The main USAID-funded American Bar Association (ABA) program in continuing legal education in Egypt, for instance, partnered with the Cairo Regional Center for International Commercial Arbitration and Cairo University's Faculty of Law; and one of the main Middle East Partnership Initiative (MEPI) rule of law programs centered on strengthening commercial law. The World Bank slogan of 'transparency,' meaning that international auditors inspect national accounts, gives the notion of 'rule-of-law' a distinctly capitalist flavor. Critical scholars scrutinized the ambivalent dynamic between human rights discourses and a mercantile 'market discipline' stressing the legal protections of contracts, patents, copyrights, investment, financial transactions, and property at the expense of humanitarian values regarding life, health, community welfare, and protection from state violence.[5] They indicated that discrepancies between Europe's oft-stated fidelity to human rights and its assurances to friendly but undemocratic elites exposed the Continent's priorities to be trade advantage and control of South-North migration.[6] Thus, even as the Mediterranean aid policy explicitly invoked democratic governance, it perhaps sub-consciously aligned investment codes, fiscal systems, some regulations, public sector arrangements, and elements of civil society with European and global models while taking care not to disturb underlying patronage-based polyarchic structures too much.[7] The universalization of American law is mostly about the global reach of American corporate law firms, according to one

---

[5] Tony Evans elaborates this position in "International Human Rights Law as Power/ Knowledge," *Human Rights Quarterly* 27:3 (2005) 1046–1068, not, as he says, to reject human rights claims but rather to understand the discourses in terms of both empowerment and domination.

[6] Roderick Pace, Stelios Stavridis, and Dimtris K. Xenakis, "Parliaments and Civil Society Cooperation in the Euro-Mediterranean Partnership," *Mediterranean Quarterly* 15:1 (2004) 75–92.

[7] Patrick Holden, "Hybrids on the Rim? The European Union's Mediterranean Aid Policy," *Democratization*, 12: 4 (2005) 461–480.

analysis.[8] Overall, then, some scholars insist that the neo-liberal conception of rule of law is alienated from the human rights ethos.

A more ominous overtone of 'rule of law' connotes 'law and order.' Post-modern and post-colonial scholars point to ways political and military aid to fortify client states' capacities lawfully to patrol, investigate, apprehend, prosecute, process, and incarcerate constitute a mode of regimentation and domination. Framed this way, law is a sophisticated non-kinetic weapon in an arsenal for pacification of the badlands. Washington's Cold War establishment folded the progressive concept of human rights into instruments of good governance better understood as regulation than compliance with international law.[9] The rule of law was advanced as a discursive tool combining administrative techniques with norm internalization such that societies would learn to restrain themselves.[10] Theoretically, these techniques of social control rendered the inscrutable and disorderly Orient governable and susceptible to regulation.

The Manichean fantasy of civilization versus barbarism was both animated and caricatured after 9/11/2001. The new millennium dawned on extraordinary, unsettling antipathies around the rule of law, the nature of law, and legal domains, most notably in the Middle East. American's praetorian responses to death and destruction in New York and Washington – the War on Terror, the invasion of Iraq, and other actions – sparked controversies about the intersection of sovereign prerogative and international law, trade-offs between civil liberties and national security, and the competence of the nascent International Criminal Court. In the name of fighting terrorism, the United States now not only resorted to extra-legal renditions, torture, and extended detention without trial, but exported these contortions through new military assistance packages emphasizing synchronized policing and espionage.[11] American attitudes toward international law and human rights standards were called "inescapably schizophrenic" by the director of the Cairo Institute for Human

---

[8] R. Daniel Kelemen and Eric C. Sibbitt, "The Globalization of American Law," *International Organization*, 58:1 (2004) 103–136.

[9] Nicolas Guilhot, "Limiting Sovereignty or Producing Governmentality? Two Human Rights Regimes in U.S. Political Discourse," *Constellations* 15:4 (2008) 502–516.

[10] Giovanni Bassu, "Law Overruled: Strengthening the Rule of Law in Postconflict States," *Global Governance* 14 (2008) 21–38. 'Donors' refers to multilateral and bilateral agencies, foundations, and NGOs acting as a multiagency 'team' of foreign entities inside host states.

[11] Beth Elise Whitaker, "Exporting the Patriot Act? Democracy and the 'War on Terror' in the Third World," *Third World Quarterly* 28:5 (2007) 1017–1032: 1017.

Rights Studies.[12] Indeed, in a turnabout of monitoring, many Arab human rights defenders either took it upon themselves to publicize abuses in the Abu Ghraib and Guantanamo prisons or refused American money and advice altogether.[13] A study for the Rand Corporation, specialized in sober strategic policy advice for the U.S. military, acknowledged that "preemptive counterterrorism measures against returning jihadists provided a convenient pretext for the dragnet arrests of a broad spectrum of domestic opponents" by Arab autocrats opting for more rather than less oppression in the name of combating terrorism.[14]

Forcible regime change in Iraq posed extra, monumental conundrums of jurisdiction starting with the legality of the military operation under international, or even American, law.[15] In terms of Iraqi legal development, initially it seemed that American notions such as the constitutional separation of powers and Miranda rights would be "superimposed" rather than "indigenized," as a study of constitutional developments under foreign occupation put it, "grafted onto Iraq's existing patchwork of Sharia-, Egyptian-, and French-based code."[16] Instead of bringing American civilian law to bear, another scholar argued that "juridico-democratization" enabled American officers to construe justice in military rather than civilian terms and to focus litigation on past rather than present crimes.[17] Yet another scholar deemed Abu Ghraib prison a site of unseemly

[12] Bahey Eldin Hassan, "Democratize or Disintegrate," _al-Ahram Weekly_ No. 862, 13–19 September 2007. He continued: "In the morning they call for democratic reform in some countries and at night they use the secret prisons of those same countries to torture those whom the CIA's illegal extraordinary rendition flights deliver for the purpose of extorting confessions."

[13] Shadi Mokhtari, _"After Abu Ghraib: Exploring Human Rights in America and the Middle East"_ (Cambridge: Cambridge University Press, 2009) provides a wealth of interview-derived commentary on this reverse human rights scrutiny.

[14] Frederic Wehrey et. al., _The Iraq Effect: The Middle East after the Iraq War_, Rand Project Air Force, Santa Monica, 2010: 80–83.

[15] A succinct argument and long bibliography were offered by Ronald Kramer et al., "The Supreme International Crime: How the U.S. War in Iraq Threatens the Rule of Law," _Social Justice_ 32: 2 (2005) 52–81. Laurence Whitehead, "Losing 'the Force'? The 'Dark Side' of Democratization after Iraq," _Democratization_, 16: 2 (2009) 215–242, contends that the suspension of a substantial state's sovereignty with neither full prior international authorization nor the democratic consent of the Iraqi people raised serious doubts about the conceptual foundations of the Western pro-democracy consensus.

[16] Stanley Nider Katz, "Democratic Constitutionalism after Military Occupation: Reflections on the United States' Experience in Japan, Germany, Afghanistan, and Iraq," _Common Knowledge_ 12:2 (2006) 181–196.

[17] Samera Esmier, "The Violence of Non-Violence: Law and War in Iraq," _Journal of Law and Society_ 34 (2007) 99–115: 111.

conjunctures of U.S., Islamic, military, criminal, and international human rights law, positing that both the prison and the military trials extended the American system of punishment to contradictory spaces simultaneously foreign and under U.S. jurisdiction.[18] Condemning the fallen tyrant to death for some of his horrific crimes by a Iraqi High Tribunal established under military occupation was also a discriminating application of American, Iraqi, and ad hoc law.

## LEGAL PLURALISM

Some Western Christians and Jews, imagining Arab legal artifacts of an early Islamic heritage untouched by the positive example of European justice, heuristically juxtapose enlightened modern law and its ideal-typical antithesis, egregious "sharia." Serious academic research has shown how this misleading simplification glosses over historical realities of colonial rule, legal cross-breeding, and the forging of human rights conventions.[19] Even in the sphere often thought to exemplify discordance between European and Arab-Islamic law – personal status or family law – scholars advised against exaggerating the extent to which Islam accounts for gender discrimination and downplaying the extent of legal assimilation from Europe. Instead of placing Muslim legal practices in a parallel legal universe, comparative legal history is cognizant of dynamic inter-cultural interactions.[20]

Comprehension of forays into the judicial sector must begin, then, with recognition of past patterns of multicultural legal absorption and accommodations essential to long-distance trade. Problematizing the historical narrative about legal rationality 'spreading' outward from Europe, social scientists offer notions of cultural flux, junctures, disjunctures, and

---

[18] Michelle Brown, "Setting the Conditions for Abu Ghraib: The Prison Nation Abroad," *American Quarterly*, 57:3 (2005) 973–997.

[19] Henry F. Carey, "The Postcolonial State and the Protection of Human Rights," *Comparative Studies of South Asia, Africa, and the Middle East* 22: 1- 2 (2002) 59–75 analyzed the paradoxical ways colonial policies underlaid both contemporary human rights abuses and protections; Samuel Moyn, "Human Rights in History," *The Nation* August 30-September 6, 2010, explained that human rights conventions replaced national self-determination with international obligations to intervene to protect individual liberties.

[20] Ann Elizabeth Mayer, "Reform of Personal Status Laws in North Africa: A Problem of Islamic or Mediterranean Laws?" The *Middle East Journal* 49 (1995) 432–46 argued that the impact of the universal secular ideal of non-discrimination (as embodied in CEDAW) is often overlooked.

reconfigurations between and among legal systems.[21] Especially (if not only) under colonial administration, multiple legal orders were spliced together with multifaceted, multilayered "articulations" that left usually significant pre-existing elements intact.[22] Moreover, as global agencies and processes nowadays impinge on the hypothetical exclusivity of sovereign legal domains, Third World governments adapt with innovative national regulatory configurations, adjusting jurisdictional boundaries, negotiating reconciliations of national with international law, and importing devices conducive to their own governance projects.[23] In contemporary crisis situations where the rule of law has disintegrated, perhaps, international experts play roles more reminiscent of colonial than Westphalian standards. They build courts, train magistrates, and draft constitutions. Nonetheless even in catastrophic cases such as Rwanda this is a mitigated rather than unidirectional process.[24] Some research suggests that the localization, or indigenization, of a transnational ethos matters a lot.[25] But adjustments reflect political interests as much as normative ideals. It would be naïve to imagine that the outcome would be "justice" pure and simple.

Modern Middle Eastern legal systems were already composite tapestries in the twentieth century. Crossroads of trade and civilizations for millennia, North Africa, the eastern Mediterranean, and the Arabian Peninsula preserved legacies from Hammurabi's code, Abrahamic traditions, classical Greek philosophy, Roman law, and early and medieval Islamic jurisprudence. They also accommodated tribal, religious, and national jurisprudence with Napoleonic, Ottoman, British, Soviet-style, and international commercial, civil, and criminal law. The Ottoman *millet* system that honored local communal law, late Ottoman Tanzimat reforms derived from French penal, land, commercial, and maritime standards, practices from the British Raj in India, the League of Nations mandate system, colonial amalgams of European, native and mixed courts,

[21] Arjun Appadurai, *Modernity at Large: Cultural Dimensions of Globalization* (Minneapolis: University of Minnesota Press, 2006).
[22] Lauren Benton, *Law and Colonial Cultures: Legal Regimes in World History, 1400–1900* (Cambridge: Cambridge University Press, 2002).
[23] Saskia Sassen, *A Sociology of Globalization* (New York: W. W. Norton, 2007). Mainly focused on economic globalization, Sassen mentions international courts and human rights NGOs in the process.
[24] Barbara Oomen, "Donor-Driven Justice and its Discontents: The Case of Rwanda," *Development and Change* 36:5 (2005) 887–910: 888–889, 892.
[25] Amitav Acharya, "How Ideas Spread: Whose Norms Matter? Norm Localization and Institutional Change in Asian Regionalism," *International Organization* 58 (2004) 239–275.

statutory legislation, tribal (common law or '*urf*) methods of adjudication, and other elements all helped shape contemporary judicial sectors.

The Palestinian arrangement, for instance, was cobbled from Ottoman, British, and later Israeli military law, Jordanian rule in the West Bank, Egyptian law in Gaza, and *millet* precedents. Via India, Britain introduced common law courts and judicial education in the Crown Colony of Aden, whose institutional framework persisted in socialist South Yemen during the era of Soviet influence; in the North, by contrast, Ottoman regulations were overlaid on indigenous Zaydi and Shafa'i jurisprudence; both Yemens adopted some Egyptian laws and legal institutions: upon unification, "the rule of law" was ferociously disputed. French civil law most thoroughly permeated colonial Algeria, but also affected Moroccan, Tunisian, and Egyptian systems under occupation, influenced Lebanese and Syrian legal development in the mandate era, and reached elsewhere indirectly. Moroccan law incorporates Spanish and Jewish elements; several countries have Christian and sometimes Jewish as well as Islamic family courts. Legal education in the Egyptian capital includes not only the famous historic al-Azhar University's *Shari'a* institute, but also the Arabic, French, and English law faculties at Cairo University and Ein Shams University and specialized judicial training. Moreover, there are differences between Shi'a and Sunni legal traditions, and within each sect among different schools of law. Far from the simplistic juxtaposition between "*Shari'a*" and "law," then, there has been an amalgamation of legal legacies, heavily influenced by colonial and post-colonial codifications and long litigious battles to centralize courts under executive-run justice ministries.

The outcome of these deep, multifaceted historical influences has been rather robust and strikingly similar Arab judiciaries.[26] Calling them robust is not to glamorize modern bureaucracies plagued by Third World conditions, patrimonial concentration of power, managerial caprice, and extra-judicial excesses, but rather to recognize the relative integrity and professionalism of courts. Even in Iraq, where the oppressive national security apparatus obliterated most alternative loci of legitimacy, arriving American interlocutors were surprised to find that "a relatively decent judiciary had persisted."[27] More or less shared genealogies, common experiences with

[26] Nathan J. Brown, *The Rule of Law in the Arab World* (Cambridge: Cambridge University Press, 1997).

[27] Larry Diamond, *Squandered Victory: The American Occupation and the Bungled Effort to Bring Democracy to Iraq* (New York: Henry Holt & Co., 2005), 149, describing the findings of the Coalition Provisional Authority. Sylvia De Bertodano, "Were There More

modern imperialism, and intra-regional osmosis led to a fair degree of legal harmonization facilitated by the common language of legal Arabic.

Thus it is possible to discern a trans-Arab legal legacy that complicates a simple bifurcation between domestic and exogenous. Like that of Iraq, most systems feature centralized hierarchical court structures and civil law procedures drawn from the Napoleonic inquisitorial model but incorporating modified, codified Islamic elements, especially in matters of personal status, family law, and rules of admissible evidence. Refined in Egypt under Ottoman, French, and British tutelage, this pattern was reproduced elsewhere after independence, often on the advice of visiting Egyptian experts, and usually in the context of centralizing authority over formerly independent local (tribal and *Shari'a*) judges. More than either the spread of Western enlightenment or the imposition of imperial order, often this was an elite governance scheme.[28] North Yemen, for instance, grafted an Egyptian-style office of prosecution (borrowed from France a century earlier and modified subsequently) onto Yemeni concepts and courts.[29] Such hybridizations occurred amidst agitations over state appropriations of legal authority. It is hardly surprising that recent 'foreign' rule-of-law interventions would also be disputatious.

Given the woeful record of Arab governments regarding treatment in police custody, capital punishment, due process, gender equality, freedoms of expression and association, and resort to brute force, one might suppose perennial Arab estrangement from international negotiations on universal rights. This is also inaccurate. The post–World War II era of the early Cold War was also a period of rapid decolonization when newly independent Third World countries sought a voice in international negotiations, including the shape and language of human rights declarations. Of course, G-7 countries wanted to author international declarations and wield them for political purposes, but the actual process was far more multilateral, cosmopolitan, and also contentious than prevalent narratives in English and French indicate. Diplomats from Muslim countries were closely engaged in deliberations on the Universal Declaration and the Covenant on Civil and

Acceptable Alternatives to the Iraqi High Tribunal?" *Journal of International Criminal Justice* Minneapolis, 5:2 (2007) 294–300, noted that unlike other post-conflict societies, Iraq had a properly functioning legal system and a cadre of experienced independent jurists without strong links to the Ba'ath party.

[28] Nathan J. Brown, "Law and Imperialism: Egypt in Comparative Perspective," *Law and Society Review*, 29:1 (1995) 103–125.

[29] Brinkley Messick, "Prosecution in Yemen: The Introduction of the Niyaba," *International Journal of Middle East Studies* 15 (1983) 507–518.

Political Rights (which most closely reflects an American notion of individual rights and liberties) and the Covenant on Social, Economic, and Cultural Rights (more reflective of socialist or newly independent states' conception of social justice). Saudi, Egyptian, Yemeni, Moroccan, Iraqi, Syrian, Libyan, Sudanese, and Tunisian delegations joined debates on freedom of religion and family law, cultural issues they argued amongst themselves; and also anti-colonial concerns with self-determination, social justice, entitlements of non-state parties to petition the UN, and the rights of people in non-self-governing territories.[30]

Rights-speak was wielded within Middle Eastern states both by and against governments. The domestic and regional currency of abstract principles was manifested in official and unofficial human rights organizations established in Iraq and Egypt in the early 1970s, in their subsequent regional proliferation, and in Arab League actions from the 1960s onward: the convening of a Permanent Arab Human Rights Commission, the declaration of Arab Human Rights Day, and the saga of an Arab Charter for Human Rights issued by the League in 1994.[31] Many of these gestures were the product of inter-Arab politics, to be sure. Yet however demagogic, these postures indicated the populist appeal of human rights semantics in counter-imperialist rhetoric circulated in the Arabic-language official media.

The United Nations partition of Palestine in 1947, Israeli administration of all of Jerusalem, the West Bank, and Gaza in the wake of Israel's victory in the 1967 war, Israel's treatment of the indigenous population, and its subsequent military engagements in the Palestinian territories and Lebanon all served to galvanize Palestinian and elite interest elsewhere in the Arab world in the Geneva Conventions, rights of national self-determination, international justice, human rights, and eventually the International Criminal Court. From 1967 onward, even as Zionist concerns about Holocaust remembrance and terrorism diverted Western attention away from the unique problems of Israeli occupation, rights idioms increasingly permeated Palestinian narratives about the injustices committed against them, and wider Arabic-language discussions of rights

---

[30] Britain, France, and the United States argued that rights covenants apply only to citizens of states, and many Americans then insisted that they did not apply to African-Americans. There were women in the Iraqi, Moroccan, and Libyan delegations, incidentally. On these negotiations and debates, see Susan Waltz, "Universal Human Rights: The Contribution of Muslim States," *Human Rights Quarterly* 26.4 (2004) 799–844.

[31] Abd al-Allahi Ahmad Naim, "Human Rights in the Arab World: A Regional Perspective," *Human Rights Quarterly* 23.3 (2001) 701–732.

and justice.[32] A Palestinian human rights NGO – *al-Haq* ("the Right") – appeared in 1976, followed by many other (including the Israeli Information Center for Human Rights in the Occupied Territories, *B'tselem*) rights and cause lawyering agencies organized around land, citizenship, due process, free movement, administrative detention, and freedom of expression as well as self-determination.[33] Sovereignty, a right to anti-colonial resistance, and the rules of war acquired special semantic salience, and the perceived failures of the UN, the United States, and Europe to redress authentic grievances deepened suspicions that international and humanitarian legal norms gave cover to other Western designs.

Skepticism about Western narratives notwithstanding, universal principles of judicial integrity, fair trials, the rule of law, and justice resonated widely. In obviously non-democratic settings, virtually everyone agreed in principle to norms including judicial review, due process, constitutional interpretation by courts, and judicial restraint on presidential and legislative excesses.[34] Because such disparate entities as American-style corporate law firms, human rights lawyers, the Judges' Club, and the Muslim Brotherhood all rallied around demands for a strong, independent judiciary, wrote a prominent Egyptian scholar, "rule of law" aid projects helped empower legal practitioners as instrumental decision makers on multiple questions of public concern: thus the historical facts of legal intermingling and foreign intervention in legal education made it difficult to either embrace the rule of law as a panacea or dismiss it out of hand as a colonial ploy.[35] This is a well-recognized, wide-ranging discrepancy.

---

[32] Lori A. Allen, "Martyr Bodies in the Media: Human Rights, Aesthetics, and the Politics of Immediation in the Palestinian Intifada," *American Ethnologist* 36: 1 (2009) 161–180.

[33] For perspective on the tangled questions of legal jurisdiction for Israelis and Palestinians alike, see Raja Shehadeh, "Human Rights and the Israeli Occupation," *CR: The New Centennial Review*, 8:1 (2008) 33–55; Lisa Hajjar, "Cause Lawyering in Transnational Perspective: National Conflict and Human Rights in Israel/Palestine," *Law and Society Review*, 31: 3 (1997) 473–504.

[34] Nathan J. Brown, "Judicial Review and the Arab World," *Journal of Democracy* 9:4 (1998) 85–99. Only Qatar, Oman, and Saudi Arabia lacked any judicial review in constitutional matters.

[35] Amr Shalakany, "'I Heard it All before': Egyptian Tales of Law and Development," *Third World Quarterly* 27:5 (2006) 833–853. In a very different legal setting, more 'Egyptianized' than 'Westernized,' Yemenis citing pre-Islamic indigenous and Greek sources as well as Quranic and Arabic texts refuted 'rejectionist,' Occidentalist contentions that human rights are an alien construct. Carapico, "Some Yemeni Ideas About Human Rights," in eds. Anthony Chase and Amr Hamzawy, *Alternative Voices on Human Rights in the Arab World* (Philadelphia: University of Pennsylvania Press, 2005) 137–152.

## POLITICAL AID AND LEGAL HARMONIZATION

After 1990, political aid projects intensified articulations of global and
Arab legal systems as well as regional harmonizations. Pedagogical pro-
grams most obviously enhanced legal multiculturalism. Bilingual legal
education and the huge multilateral effort to build a Palestinian law
institute are prime examples. Under the Euro-Med Justice II program,
the Euro-Mediterranean Network of Judicial Schools enabled the
Judicial Training Centers of Algeria, Egypt, Israel, Jordan, Lebanon,
Morocco, the Palestinian Authority, Syria, and Tunisia to partner with
European judicial schools and the European Judicial Training Network.
The Danish Institute for Human Rights and the ABA, among others,
exchanged faculty, consultants, and law students. Given its historical
influence, France spends most heavily on Arab legal systems, especially
in the Maghreb. There was a huge multinational investment in the Bir Zeit
University Institute of Law, established in 1993 within a university
endowed in the 1950s by wealthy Palestinians in the Gulf. The Ford
Foundation, the French and Qatari governments, the United Kingdom,
Belgium, Australia, UNDP, UNWRA, the European Union, Australian
Legal Resources International, USAID, the International Human Rights
Law Institute of DePaul University, the Arab-American Bar Association of
Chicago, the Open Society Institute of the Soros Foundation, and others
also got involved.

Some programs introduced novel articulations. Many new fields of
regulation applied to economic globalization: the explosion in media and
telecommunications; torts in shipping and insurance cases; standards of
inspection of agricultural products for export. Bringing regulation of such
matters into line with global norms is known in the business as harmonization. Actually, two kinds of harmonization, or concordance, were
applied simultaneously in Mediterranean countries. First, certain specific
national rules were synchronized with Euro-American procedures and
WTO guidelines. By 2010, all Mediterranean countries except Syria had
concluded EU Association Agreements that brought partners' regulatory
procedures closer to European economic expectations. Second, and
accordingly, Euro-Med Justice and other regional programs replicated
parallel projects, institutions, and Arabic-language materials among partner countries. There is global and regional harmonization, then, and extra
layering.

Euro-Med Justice and Euro-Med Police objectives were to coordinate
between and among the European Community and nine partners: Algeria,

Egypt, Israel, Jordan, Lebanon, Morocco, the Palestinian Territories, Syria, and Tunisia. Euro-Med Justice II aimed at "institutional and administrative capacity and good governance in the field of justice"; judicial proceedings; coordination in cross-border family disputes; criminal cooperation; and "reform of criminal and prison law in the Mediterranean Partner Countries with a view to facilitating the transposition of the relevant international instruments into the domestic law of the beneficiary countries and their implementation." It also sought "to create an inter-professional community of magistrates and law professionals in order to build an open and modern justice system that will uphold the rule of law and the effective implementation of human rights." Euro-Med Police II aimed "at strengthening police cooperation ... in the fight against all major types of organised crime such as terrorism, drug trafficking, human trafficking, weapons, nuclear, bacteriological and chemical substances, financial and cyber-crime etc."[36] This all seems to suggest a transnationalization of law on a scale between the national and the global.

Some countries harmonized more eagerly than others, and in some fields more than others. Tunisia won accolades for transposing international commercial statutes to align itself with market capitalism, but accepted only very limited technocratic or technological assistance in the judicial sector itself. Jordan not only signed the Universal Declaration, the civil and political rights covenants, declarations on women, children, and ethnic minorities, prohibitions against torture, and the Rome Statute establishing the International Criminal Court (ICC), but welcomed aid for national human rights institutions, the justice ministry, the judiciary itself, and other national entities.[37] The monarchy cooperated in the two big regional rule-of-law initiatives, Euro-Med Justice and the USAID-funded ABA program that worked on the Judicial Institute of Jordan, the National Centre for Human Rights, the Judicial Ethics Committee, and a Judicial Code of Conduct.

In the context of its asymmetric trade and aid negotiations with the European Union, and at the urging of the ABA and the World Bank, Amman adopted a Judicial Upgrading Strategy (JUST) according to a formula applied in several countries seeking trade agreements with the

---

[36] *Euro-Mediterranean Partnership Regional Cooperation: An Overview of Programs and Projects 2007/08*, European Commission, Brussels, 13–14. As an aside, it is unclear how the harmonization of Israeli practices with its Arab neighbors' was supposed to work.

[37] On the opening of the judicial system to external scrutiny, see the detailed evaluation by Zaha Al-Majali and Omar Qaddoura, "Jordan: The Independence and Impartiality of the Judiciary," Euro-Mediterranean Human Rights Network, Copenhagen, 2008.

EU. It covered corporate law, tax law, customs duties, legislation governing business competition, regulatory liberalization, intellectual property rights protection, and statistical standards. Also included under "Cooperation on Justice and Home Affairs" were bank transfer regulations to eliminate terrorist money-laundering and joint policing in areas including cyber-crime.[38] In a complementary program, the World Bank delivered a ten-week distance-learning course to familiarize jurists with World Trade Organization (WTO) norms and international law on such specific, modern issues as cross-border insolvency. Favorable trade and credit terms depend on following these prescriptions, and Jordan's adoption signified its perceived self-interest.

Under such circumstances, legal jurisdictions overlap. Even in a relatively compliant system, disjunctures between international law and domestic legislative capacity raised questions about which layer of law is applicable. Jordan, partner to so many international conventions, confronted these ambiguities. In 2008, amidst vigorous lobbying by local and international feminists, the elected Parliament defeated an amendment to its criminal code that would have placed so-called honor crimes on a par with other kinds of murder. This was a disheartening setback for Jordanian and international campaigns against leniency in cases of family violence, and even for the women in the royal family who had lent the amendment their prestige.[39] It also exposed ruptures between the principle of parliamentary discretion and treaty obligations to eliminate discrimination and violence against women. Does the rule of law (or promoting the rule of law) mean legislatures make laws, or that international treaties are binding on domestic law-makers? Meanwhile, in another kind of quarrel with different implications for the application of criminal law, the two houses of Jordan's Parliament split on a bill ratifying a bilateral extradition accord exempting Americans from Jordanian obligations under the Rome Statute to apprehend war criminals.[40] Coming from different directions, both cases addressed

---

[38] "Commission Staff Working Document Accompanying the Communication from the Commission to the Council and the European Parliament on Strengthening the European Neighborhood Policy, ENP Progress Report, Jordan," COM (2006), Brussels, December 4, 2006.

[39] For a detailed account of this campaign as a contest between modern and religious bodies of law, see Catherine Warrick, *Law in the Service of Legitimacy: Gender and Politics in Jordan* (Surrey, UK: Ashgate Press, 2009).

[40] Human Rights Watch (HRW), "*Jordan: Parliament Should Reject U.S. Impunity Deal: No Exemptions from International Justice for the Gravest Crimes*," London, December 7, 2005.

applications of international law, the role of the Jordanian legislature, and international expectations of compliance. These are questions of statutory domain.

The rule of law is a double-edged instrument, then. It can fortify metropolitan and/or municipal (domestic) law. People saw and expressed this. For instance, an assessment of justice assistance in Morocco collected statements from some Moroccans who complained about heavy programmatic concentration on European obsessions with migration, drug-trafficking, foreign direct investment, antiterrorism, and others who insisted that judicial upgrading programs only re-enforced the status quo power arrangement in the Kingdom.[41] These same issues carry over into projects supporting different kinds of human rights institutions and organizations, which in turn anticipate the politics of aid for women's machineries and NGOs considered later in this book.

## NATIONAL LEGAL DOMAINS

The provision of financing and technical assistance inevitably inflects power relations. Although it may be tempting to attribute anxieties over legal projects center to normative principles, the most noticeable vector of tension pitted state-strengthening projects against backing for non-governmental activists.[42] The European Union's two mechanisms for funding projects in the justice sector illustrate the difference: one under the MEDA framework works directly with state institutions, for instance by "twinning" justice ministries or exporting automation technologies; contrarily, the European Instrument for Democracy and Human Rights funds extra-governmental associations, sometimes deliberately evading official channels and permits.[43]

The state/non-state heuristic dichotomy has somewhat limited empirical utility, however. 'States' are not monolithic entities. They are collections of executive, bureaucratic, legislative, and judicial authority. Boundaries are fluid and contested. Consider the prospect of building a governing

[41] Anna Khakee, *Assessing Democracy Assistance: Morocco*, FRIDE Project Report, Madrid, 2010.
[42] Acuto, "Wilson Victorious?" argued that the backlash is not against democracy but against some democracy promotion techniques, some of the promoters themselves, and especially the distribution of resources to NGOs.
[43] Siân Lewis-Anthony, "The Initiatives in the Field of Judicial Reform in the Euro-Mediterranean Region," Euro-Mediterranean Human Rights Network, Copenhagen, July 20, 2009: 7.

authority where none existed beforehand. A 1999 UN document entitled *Rule of Law Development in the West Bank and Gaza Strip* identified fifteen separate "development points" for project interventions. Egyptian consultants advised the new Ministry of Justice on how to draft legislation. The rudimentary prosecutorial and penal systems, forensics, and law-enforcement agencies got basic coaching and some technology. The judicial system, then comprised of sixty-five judges, was provided some buildings, libraries, technical staff, and training. There was the Bir Zeit law institute, aforementioned. Elections and the National Legislative Council, also classified under the rule-of-law, drew a lot of experts. Foreigners trained Palestinians in national policy-development mechanisms and legal reform. A semi-autonomous Palestinian Independent Commission for Citizens Rights was created according to the Paris Principles of 1993 governing national independent human rights commissions. These categories might be considered 'state,' or municipal, but need also to be disaggregated among incipient parliamentary, judicial, and bureaucratic functions. Points beyond the state in civil society also garnered assistance: NGOs, the media, and the legal profession.[44] All these were alternate nodes of moral and legal authority. And the incipient Palestinian Authority was rudimentary compared with the heterogeneous legal-institutional environments in Egypt, Yemen and post-occupation Iraq.

Projects complicate these administrative and conceptual boundaries when international experts work inside the walls of existing judicial and legislative institutions in sovereign countries. Conventional development aid always seconded technocrats to the so-called executive 'line' ministries that deliver services, such as agriculture, education, public works, defense, or finance. This expert advice, known as 'technical assistance,' was now employed inside the other branches of government – judiciaries and parliaments – as well as in new executive institutions such as justice ministries or human rights councils.

Even technical advice to parliaments and judiciaries can influence performance and the distribution of power. Long after most other public institutions in Sana'a had been not only re-organized but physically re-modeled, re-located, or re-wired under foreign aid projects, the Ministry of Justice remained a quaint bastion of indigenous cut-stone architecture and pen-to-paper calligraphic records. This matters to the system of law.[45] It

---

[44] Rule of Law Development in the West Bank and Gaza Strip: Survey and State of the Development Effort, Gaza: UNESCO, May 1999.

[45] Brinkley Messick, *The Calligraphic State* (London: University of California Press, 1993).

follows that the injection of new technologies and competencies would change the character and operations of the judiciary. Excel and automated records do not merely record; they also define and enframe. A judge in Morocco, where they had been using typewriters, told evaluators, "They bought the computers but did not train people ... What they did not understand is that IT changes the power structure in an office."[46] Of course it does; documentation of legal knowledge makes a difference.

Foreign specialists in 'judicial services delivery' advised on processes such as digital inventories. They drafted practical legislation concerning procurement or public borrowing. The term technical assistance implies impartial, technocratic information, but most practitioners know it isn't really apolitical. The 'standard package' of legal sector assistance, comprised of drafting statutes and regulations, constructing, renovating, and equipping courthouses, purchasing computing, communication, and case management technology, training judges, magistrates, court staff, prosecutors and lawyers, supporting bar associations, and organizing international study trips for judges, court administrators, and lawyers looks like disinterested assistance, wrote one authority, but this "crypto-technocratic aura" obfuscates the "inherently political nature of rule of law promotion."[47] Another project veteran wrote that although work on reform and corruption inevitably introduced new resource flows and interrupted others, foreign experts "are all but forced to proclaim a 'myth of neutrality' that posits that judges and lawyers are dispassionate transmitters of impartial law."[48]

Legal sector development projects crisscrossed with national governance profoundly, then. Working inside judicial (and also parliamentary) institutions means penetrating deep inside the chambers of state power. Signified physically and socially by the presence of expatriates inside parliamentary office buildings, this transgresses conceptual and institutional frontiers between states and the international system. Moreover, the idiom of checks on presidential rule had implications for the balance of power that might flout central executive custody over governance, foreign affairs, legal jurisdictions, and, of course, foreign aid. Nevertheless it is also

---

[46] Khakee, *Assessing Democracy Assistance: Morocco*: 13–14.

[47] Magen, "The Rule of Law and its Promotion Abroad," 84, 96. Magen identified the categories of rule-of-law development as state-building; liberalization, reform, and human rights programs; transition that especially involves holding free and fair elections; and democratic consolidation.

[48] Blake K. Puckett, "'We're Very Apolitical': Examining the Role of the International Legal Assistance Expert," *Indiana Journal of Global Legal Studies* 16:1 (2009) 293–310: 295.

the case that technical assistance enhances municipal legal power by legislating novel fields of activity, creating new regulatory agencies, or improving the efficiency of administration and documentation. In this third sense, rule-of-law projects that partner with government institutions correspond to a conventional conception of 'aid' as that which strengthens 'state capacity.'

## NATIONAL HUMAN RIGHTS INSTITUTIONS

Not only are not all legal sector projects about human rights protection, but different kinds of human rights programs and institutions have different effects. The work of independent organizations such as Amnesty International, Human Rights Watch, and other monitoring organizations such as the Committee to Protect Journalists lead us to associate human rights advocacy with the denigration of state legal authority. Inter-governmental and parastatal democracy assistance is different. We have already seen that Arab governments, like other governments, attempt to marshal human rights talk for their own governance projects. Accordingly, not all political aid programs dealing with human rights are inherently adversarial; many fit into the conventional conception of 'aid.' Different projects fostered executive, judicial, and civic institutions, with different political implications.

One public-sector strategy favored by the United Nations since the 1993 World Conference on Human Rights in Vienna was to encourage "national human rights institutions" (NHRIs) to implement internationally recognized norms enshrined in what are known as the Paris Principles. True to the UN mandate to work with member governments, these were distinct from nominally non-governmental organizations mentioned earlier. At least nine Arab countries had established NHRIs by 2009, frequently but not always with overseas technical assistance.[49] One country-by-country evaluation showed that these highly politicized semi-autonomous parastatal institutions often enabled authorities to counter-balance private advocacy while claiming to be protecting rights. Along with France, the three Maghreb countries pioneered NHRIs before the Vienna conference. Morocco's won some international acclaim especially

---

[49] Investigating worldwide diffusion of NHRIs, "even" to Arab countries, Thomas Pegram, "Diffusion Across Political Systems: The Global Spread of National Human Rights Institutions," *Human Rights Quarterly* 32:3 (2010) 729–760, found three kinds of influences: (1) coercion including conditionality, (2) acculturation, and (3) persuasion.

for its "truth and reconciliation" work, whereas Tunisia's Higher Committee on Human Rights and Fundamental Freedoms was seen as a smokescreen for government abuses, and Algeria's, established soon after the military suspended parliamentary elections, seemed largely cosmetic. Egypt's parliament approved its National Commission while simultaneously refusing several independent rights groups' registration applications. Jordan and Qatar appointed royal family members to head their national institutions. With relatively more input from international experts and donors, the Palestinian Independent Commission for Citizens' Rights seemed the most active and substantial. Yemen and occupied Iraq (along with Afghanistan) established full-fledged Ministries of Human Rights.[50]

Expert appraisals of NHRIs were mixed. Bureaucratically, they paved avenues to officialdom, and served as clearing houses for special events, training projects, participation in international forums, public information materials, and other aid programs. As one German appraisal concluded, even if North African and Middle Eastern governments intended NHRIs to co-opt human rights activism, a side-effect was deeper governmental entanglement in rights conversations. Thus the establishment of national institutions appeared to shift "human rights as a bone of contention from one between international human rights NGOs and the government concerned to domestic struggles over policies, legislation and redress where the main players are state agencies, the NHRI, and domestic civil society."[51]

For sure, central executives sought to harness human rights, appropriate donor initiatives, and deploy documentary narratives. Independent Yemeni activists objected to the Ministry of Human Rights' selection of projects and entities for donors to fund, and its role in deflecting criticism away from the government and its security forces.[52] Likewise, the two independent Jordanian groups that won NDI funding to train and organize domestic observers in 2007 complained about restrictions imposed by the Ministry of Interior and the National Center for Human Rights.[53] Activists told consultants that Egypt's National Council for Human Rights

[50] Sonia Cardenas and Andrew Flibbert, "National Human Rights Institutions in the Middle East," *The Middle East Journal* 59:3 (2005) 411–436.
[51] Anna Würth and Claudia Engelmann, "Governmental Human Rights Structures and National Human Rights Institutions in the Middle East and North Africa," in *Islam and Human Rights*, ed. Hatem Ellisiesie (Frankfurt: Peter Lang Verlag, 2008) 239–256.
[52] See Edward Burke, *Assessing Democracy Assistance: Yemen*, FRIDE Project Report, May 2010: 9, 12–13.
[53] Jordan Election Observer, No: 12 (November 12, 2007), by the Electoral Support Unit at *al-Urdan al-Jadid* Research Center; *al-Hayat* Center for Civil Society Development, 2007 Parliamentary Election Observation, closing press statement, November 20, 2007.

(supported by the EC, Spain, Sweden, Norway, USAID, UNDP, and the Netherlands) was sometimes helpful, but in other ways insulated the presidency and constrained human rights projects.[54] Some said the ruling clique just appointed its own delegates to the National Council.[55] Moreover, after partly meeting its mandate to report violations, the Council was forced to scale back its operations in advance of the rigged parliamentary elections of 2010.

## TRANSNATIONAL CONFERENCES AND THE ARAB CHARTER

Projects to harmonize Arab legal systems with one another and/or with supranational jurisdictions, enhance municipal judicial authority, support national human rights institutions, or buttress independent national or transnational human rights agencies had diverse implications. Political aid sometimes followed conventional aid; at other times it eluded national bureaucracies. Whereas some assistance built central governance capacity, other projects backed freelance supra-national or sub-national advocacy networks. Under these non-governmental modes of grant-making beyond or within sovereign territorial and supervisory domains, bureaucratic, informational, and cash resources evaded customary bilateral and multi-lateral channels either by providing extra-territorial enclaves where dissidents expose official malfeasance or by sponsoring monitoring, legal counseling, educational outreach, and public interest litigation inside countries. In important ways, law was (at least partly) denationalized. As so many intellectuals and practitioners explained, foreign sponsorship was a mixed blessing for human rights organizations and legal services providers. The backlash against non-governmental funding will be explored in Chapter 4.

For decades, even while their governments stage-managed some human rights forums, independent Arab activists convened overseas to dodge restrictions on association, assembly, and speech. The Arab Organization of Human Rights held its founding conference in 1974 in Cyprus, and incorporated there a decade later, because no Arab capital would license it. Its draft statement on Human and Peoples' Rights in the Arab World,

---

[54] Kristina Kausch, "Defenders in Retreat: Freedom of Association and Civil Society in Egypt," FRIDE, Madrid, 2009: 12.

[55] Joshua A. Stacher, "Rhetorical Acrobatics and Reputations: Egypt's National Council for Human Rights," *Middle East Report* 235 (2005) 2–7.

with provisions criminalizing torture, outlawing martial law, and specifying environmental, welfare, and minority rights, was unveiled at a seminar at the International Institute for Higher Studies in Criminal Sciences in Syracuse, Italy. Sometimes changing hats, officers of the Egyptian Organization for Human Rights, the Palestinian Center for Human Rights, the Palestinian Society for the Protection of Human Rights and Environment, the Jordanian Society for Human Rights, the Lebanese Association for Human Rights, the Foundation for Human and Humanitarian Rights in Lebanon, the Moroccan Association for Human Rights, the Moroccan Organization for Human Rights, and the Tunisian League for Human Rights began regularly to attend the Paris meetings of *La Fédération internationale des ligues des droits de l'Homme.*

Their conversations re-opened discussions of the Arab Charter, the vague, impotent text adopted by the Arab League in 1994. Activists pressed for a constitution-like bill of rights. Two prominent think tanks, the Cairo Institute for Human Rights Studies and Lebanon's Association for the Defense of Rights and Liberties, won EU funding for a 2003 meeting under UN auspices called Towards An Effective Regional Protection of Human Rights: Which Arab Charter on Human Rights? Timed to coincide with the convening of the Arab League's Permanent Human Rights Committee, according to their web sites in 2005 it gathered representatives of three dozen Arab NGOs and eleven intergovernmental organizations with other legal and media experts, governmental and Arab League observers, and officers of the *Fédération internationale* and the Euro-Mediterranean Human Rights Network. The Beirut Declaration on the Regional Protection of Human Rights in the Arab World offered a revised Charter emphasizing national self-determination; affirming the universality of civil and political rights; insisting on the independence of the judiciary; denying exceptions based on cultural "peculiarities"; listing specific prohibitions against torture and states of emergency; and asserting the rights of women, children, ethnic minorities, and immigrants. The same two organizations got the European Human Rights Network to pay for conferences in Beirut, Cairo, and elsewhere, like one in 2004 that asked Is the Arab World Moving Forward on the Road to Democratic Reform and Respect of Human Rights? and devoted a session to The Human Rights Catastrophe in the Arab World.

In the best-case scenario for applied constructivism, international political aid helps Arab activists further the causes of justice and democratization. It helps forge normative consensus. Multicultural confabs release declarations meant to synchronize a trans-Arab legal regime with cosmopolitan legal principles and increasingly dense transnational institutional networks. It facilitates the formation of epistemic communities. I don't think this 'epistemic communities' perspective can be discounted. Not political aid strictly speaking, the intercontinental 2004 annual meeting of the *Union Internationale des Avocats*, a consortium of some 200 bar associations collectively representing 2 million barristers, held at the Fez Conference Center and the Jnan Palace Hotel around the theme of Lawyers of the World: A Single Code of Ethics? attracted a record North African and Arab turnout. Another meeting on The Role of the Judiciary in the Process of Political Reform in Egypt and in the Arab World, in Cairo in 2006, coordinated by the Cairo Institute, the *Fédération internationale*, and the Euro-Med Network for Human Rights, gathered about 120 judges, activists, lawyers, writers and academics from Morocco, Algeria, Tunisia, Sudan, Saudi Arabia, Bahrain, UAE, Syria, Lebanon, Yemen, and Egypt, along with scores of French, German, and American counterparts, officials from international institutions, foreign and Arab diplomats, and journalists. These are but two meetings of a vast network of intermittent extra-territorial conferences and inter-linked websites.

One might dismiss these conference declarations as so much hot air. Resolutions from that 2006 Cairo forum pillorying repression of the Egyptian Judge's Club and the Association of Tunisian Judges remained quite toothless, after all, and nonprofit advocacy organizations in quite a number of Middle Eastern countries faced retribution. National constitutions and official rhetoric already promised judicial autonomy, fair trials, and other principles routinely breeched; there was no shortage of oratory on human rights. On the other hand, some hoped that through sheer repetition such declarations would be gradually and incrementally codified and internalized until an ethical consensus coalesces around which Arab educators, journalists, and opinion entrepreneurs may appeal. I am also suggesting that these organizations circulate cosmopolitan legal language directly addressing Middle Eastern conditions, in modern standard Arabic, in refined translation from English and French, but laced with specifically regional concerns about military occupations, self-determination, and social justice. These concerns are popularized via lectures, PowerPoint presentations, declarations, and newspaper columns. Conferees trade experiences: Yemenis learn about Moroccan family law, or compare notes on NGO laws or *Shari'a*-based arguments against corporal punishment. Then they share these ideas among informed publics back home, acting as norm entrepreneurs and interpreters. This is not mere 'spread'; it is 'articulation.' A Creolized patois about both national and individual rights gained currency in the larger Arab public sphere.

As we will see later, many think tanks with legal expertise went after international grants or contracts to sustain their projects. This enabled them to enlarge and upgrade their operations. Groups in the Maghreb, Egypt, Jordan, the Palestinian territories, Lebanon, and Yemen issued reports with diction and citations that began to approximate those of Amnesty International, Human Rights Watch, and the United Nations. Beyond enabling professionals to embarrass governments in international arenas, foreign funds went toward legal counseling, education, and defense to endangered individuals or classes: battered women, political prisoners, laid-off workers, and others. As documented in dozens of reports and assessments, foreign aid permitted human rights defenders to upgrade and intensify their work in Cairo, Amman, Sana'a, Ramallah-Jerusalem, Rabat, and other Arab capitals – at least up to a point.

What happened next was complicated, however, as scholars analyzing disputes and lawsuits over foreign snooping and funding in Egypt revealed. According to one study, with international financial backing, professional Egyptian human rights organizations including the Center for Human Rights Legal Aid, the Center for Women's Legal Aid, the Land Center for Human Rights, the Human Rights Center for the Assistance of Prisoners, EOHR, the Cairo Institute, and the Arab Center for the Independence of the Judiciary and the Legal Profession were able to use public interest litigation to test laws and even constitutional principles governing labor union elections, judicial oversight of national elections, restrictions on associational freedoms, land tenure, torture, and other fields in a "productive synergy": hundreds of suits and counter-suits were pressed in Egyptian courts.[56] Yet when the Mubarak regime cracked down on strikers and labor actions, one legal aid worker told a foreign researcher that international donors "just disappeared" . . . in order "to protect their broader programs."[57] Later, when the Center for Trade Union and Workers' Services, a previous winner of the French Republic Prize for Human Rights, was closed and its leader sentenced for provoking labor strikes, Egyptian comments on pleas by the French embassy, the International Trade Union Confederation, and the International Labor

---

[56] Tamir Moustafa, "Got Rights? Public Interest Litigation and the Egyptian Human Rights Movement," in eds. Chase and Hamzawy (2005) 153–173.

[57] Neil Hicks, "Transnational Human Rights Networks and Human Rights in Egypt," in eds. Chase and Hamzawy (2005) 64–88: 83–84. Instead of pressing for associational rights and autonomy, Hicks reports, USAID supported an NGO Service Center to work with legally registered NGOs.

Organization ranged from "helpful" to "minimal" and an example of "occasional diplomatic support behind closed doors."[58]

If international agents supported human rights defenders, this support fell short when push came to shove. Foreign agencies didn't side decisively with jurists organized through the Judges' Club, who pressed their constitutional duty to review the 2005 elections and constitutional autonomy from the Ministry of Justice.[59] Europe impassively watched the crushing of the judges' revolt and the kangaroo trials of two prominent jurists who blew the whistle on corruption. This was in part because of structural and institutional features of its inter-governmental foreign policies, according to one analysis, complicated by fears of an interruption in ongoing trade negotiations. Moreover, the strong Egyptian-U.S. alliance weakened Europe's relative leverage. Finally, the EU's investment in law enforcement agencies was divorced from its human rights programs.[60] Despite its avowed human rights policy, then, it seemed that Europe merely offered Arab activists opportunities to brazen out their own governments at their own peril. If anything, different agencies and commentators suspected that the aggregate effect of Western pressures on friendly Arab governments was detrimental for human rights and independent human rights defenders.

Across the MENA region, then, many people concluded that the injection of some new material, symbolic, and networking capital into ongoing struggles over legal practices, mottos, and institutions did less to influence human rights outcomes than to enable intra-professional inter-cultural dialogues. Conference declarations and reports issued jus cogens language and human rights principles in legal Arabic and carried the collective weight of a large cadre of legal practitioners. Immaterial to actual performance, perhaps, they nonetheless facilitated further development and circulation of a distinctly modern legal-Arabic language featuring fundamental constitutional principles ranging from self-governance to individual, social, economic, and criminal justice. Counterfactually, the wealth of Arabic-language declarations and model constitutions, expertise among bilingual practitioners, and networks of Arab rights defenders and jurists might have been tapped for the Iraq project. Instead, Arabic documents and the wider corpus of international legal expertise were stunningly

---

[58] Kauch, *Defenders in Retreat*, 18–19.

[59] On struggles over judicial prerogatives, see Nathalie Bernard-Maugiron, "Judges as Reform Advocates: A Lost Battle," *Cairo Papers in Social Science* 29:2/3 (2006) 60–84.

[60] Sarah Wolff, "Constraints on the Promotion of the Rule of Law in Egypt: Insights from the 2005 Judges' Revolt," *Democratization*, 16:1 (2009) 100–118.

under-utilized in a situation where they might have been valuable: occupied Iraq.

## CONSTITUTING IRAQ

In comparison either with projects in sovereign states or with multilateral
legal reconstruction efforts in other post-conflict situations, the American
role in writing a new constitution for Iraq, re-organizing its beleaguered
judiciary, and setting a war crimes tribunal in motion were unprecedented
in the post-colonial era. These activities also diverged from the accumulated wisdom of experts in international law and optimistic constructivist
hypotheses.

The constitutional project was in many respects the showpiece of the
American political project in Iraq. Now in post-conflict situations such as
Cambodia or Rwanda, and new nations such as Bosnia, Eritrea and East
Timor, there is a potentially valuable, perhaps indispensable, role for
impartial legal expertise in drafting constitutional documents.[61] UN,
European, and Canadian international and comparative law specialists
who had worked in those places had drawn what they considered crucial
lessons about engaging stakeholders in building substantive consensus, the
importance of a transparent and unhurried process, the advantages and
limitations of foreign intercessions, and the obligation to get a constitution
in place before holding elections.[62] These were largely ignored.

Americans were ill-equipped for rebuilding Iraq's courts system, as an
advisor explained, because the U.S. federal government lacked either any
bureau with technical expertise in delivery of justice services or a pool of
justice and policing specialists to tap in a case like Iraq.[63] Among 500 or
600 American legal consultants who traveled to occupied Iraq, some were
excellent (judging by their writings), but many were very young and
unqualified. Only a handful spoke Arabic, and fewer still were educated
in legal Arabic. Furthermore, and importantly, Americans were less

[61] Louis Aucoin, "The Role of International Experts in Constitution-Making," *Georgetown
Journal of International Affairs* 1 (2004) 89–95, cautions against dismissing the whole
enterprise as a U.S.-based cottage industry. The U.S. Institute of Peace issued Special
Report 132 entitled "Iraq's Constitutional Process: Shaping a Vision for the Country's
Future" in February 2005 based on a USIP-UNDP study in 18 post-conflict situations that
emphasized crucial input of citizens at every stage and the utility of technical experts.
[62] Jamal Benomar, "Constitution-Making after Conflict: Lessons for Iraq," *Journal of
Democracy* 15:2, l (2004) 81–95; Peter Kurrild-Klitgaard, "Blood, Ba'ath, and Beyond:
The Constitutional Dilemma of Iraq," *Public Choice* 119:1–2 (2004)13–30.
[63] David H. Bayley, "U.S. Aid for Foreign Justice and Police," *Orbis* 50:3 (2006) 469–479.

familiar than European and Arab specialists with Iraq's post-colonial version of Napoleonic civil law courts. Yet the high-profile American advisors to the early stages of drafting the Transitional Administrative Law (TAL), and thereby the Iraqi constitution, who wrote books about their experiences did not mention or seem to consider that Arabic-educated legal scholars well-versed in public international law had been studying existing Arab constitutions, putting universal standards into contemporary legal Arabic, and drafting a Human Rights Charter for the region in Arabic.[64] Along with two Iraqi-American law professors and consultants from the Public International Law and Policy Group (a Carnegie-affiliated think tank) and the International Institute for the Rule of Law (a division of the US Institute of Peace, USIP), they worked mainly in English with English materials to draw articles from the U.S. constitution and U.S. Bill of Rights and the Universal Declaration.

An example of why this matters is illustrated by the concept of 'federalism.' Washington determined in advance that Iraq would be a federal republic in order to preserve the autonomy enjoyed in Kurdish areas since 1991, and the TAL designated two levels of federalism beneath the central government: regions and provinces. The word 'federal' was written in Arabic as '*fadarali*' in the early drafts debated by Iraqis on the drafting committee. This transliteration from English was familiar to Arab political scientists and news junkies as a descriptor of the relatively decentralized U.S., German, and Canadian systems of government. It was not however a common Arabic expression with particular symbolic or substantive resonance. Therefore, later drafts and ultimately the Iraqi constitution rendered the notion of federalism into Arabic as '*ittihadi*,' a neologism derived from the common word *ittihad*, meaning federation or union, also used in constitutional documents to refer to the national government. However, the adjectival form, *ittihadi* (not listed in the English-Arabic, Arabic-English, legal Arabic, or Iraqi Arabic dictionaries I checked) was also an unfamiliar term unlikely to inspire the patriotic connotation that 'federal' conveys to Americans. It was closer to the complex multi-tiered asymmetric regional self-governance and representation in Canada, where, in addition to provincial governments, distinct geographic regions populated by linguistic minorities exercise special autonomy. One feature of this constitution, as an expert on Arab

---

[64] See Diamond, *Squandered Victory*, and Noah Feldman, *What We Owe Iraq: War and the Ethics of Nation Building* (Princeton: Princeton University Press, 2004).

constitutions observed, was that provincial governments were given greater autonomy than elsewhere in the region, where they are typically overseen by an executive Ministry of Local Administration.[65] On the other hand, a historian of the British mandate in Iraq suggested that the term 'federal' as used in the TAL and subsequent constitutional proposals might have a negative connotation for Iraqi Arabs, who saw in the Anglo-American division of Iraq in 2003 parallels to colonialism, giving rise to "fears that it was intended to establish the basis for a permanent, decentralized federal structure."[66] Another historian observed that the federal option was rejected by most Sunni Arabs and many Shi'a in Central Iraq, and that the document was notably vague on the relationship between local and central government.[67] My point here is that linguistic choices matter a great deal to the indigenization of constitutional and legal principles.

Wording was not the only, or main, trouble, however. High-level consultants later described a messy, politicized, counter-productive process. As discussed in the next chapter, the tight TAL-driven deadline for writing and ratifying a constitution in the summer of 2005 was problematic.[68] USIP's rule of law program officer gave a step-by-step account of how the "pressure-cooker approach" produced a sub-optimal outcome.[69] A paper on Iraqi courts enumerated many elements the constitution ratified in October 2005 left to subsequent legislation, including judicial independence and competence.[70] An initially optimistic consultant later bewailed a "post-sovereign paradigm of constitution-making" characterized by "pathologies" whereby Americans played double roles of broker and party in the negotiations; moreover, he said, the exclusionary results of the January 2005 elections necessitated

---

[65] Nathan J. Brown, "The Final Draft of the Iraqi Constitution: Analysis and Commentary," The Carnegie Foundation for International Peace, September 16, 2005: especially comments on Chapters 4 and 5. Brown remarked elsewhere on other drafts and provisions.

[66] Toby Dodge, *Inventing Iraq: The Failure of Nation Building and a History Denied* (New York, Columbia University Press: 2003) 165.

[67] Charles Tripp, *A History of Iraq* (Cambridge: Cambridge University Press 2007) 300–301.

[68] Nathan Brown, "Iraq's Constitutional Process Plunges Ahead," Carnegie Policy Outlook, Washington, July 2005.

[69] Jonathan Morrow, "Iraq's Constitutional Process II: An Opportunity Lost," USIP Special Report No. 155, Washington, December 2005.

[70] Matthew T. Simpson, "Iraqi High Court Authority: A State-Practice Review of the Source of High Court Authority and an Assessment of 2005 Iraq Constitution," Islamic Law and Law of the Muslim World Paper No. 07–01, 2007.

FIGURE 1. Iraqis work October 3, 2005, at a Baghdad printing house on printing sheets for ballot papers for the October 15, 2005, referendum on a draft constitution. Photo: Karim Sahib/AFP/Getty Images. Used with permission.

special bargaining outside formal parameters, and the railroading through of the referendum defied the premises of the process.[71] One

---

[71] Andrew Arato, "Post-Sovereign Constitution-Making and its Pathology in Iraq," *New York Law School Law Review*, 51:3 (2007) 534–555. See also Arato, "Sistani v. Bush: Constitutional Politics in Iraq," *Constellations* 11:2 (2004) 174–192, on constitutional development and unmet demands from prominent Iraqis for substantial citizen input.

of the Iraqi-American law professors most closely involved, Feisal al-Istrabadi, called the process insufficiently organic and driven by American partisan issues; it left neither time nor space for Iraqi political elites to forge a common vision; in the final analysis, he contended, the extreme federalism in the constitution enflamed ethno-sectarian tensions among Kurds, Sunni Arabs, and Shi'a.[72] Another consultant to the drafting process later said it had "failed miserably" on both procedural and substantive grounds.[73]

If the drafting process was sub-optimal, however, the advertising campaign for what the referendum ballot deemed "the constitutional project" was impressive. Most of the materials were produced by the Independent High Electoral Commission with technical assistance from the United Nations and probably the Americans. Visually striking billboards and posters urged citizens to vote for the constitutional project. One showed an attractive Iraqi woman in a headscarf above a caption in Arabic about a "guarantee of your legitimate rights" (*tadamun huqik al-shar'a'i*). Several pastel-hued line drawings with Arabic and/or Kurdish captions showed ballots being put into boxes. One read "yes, yes, yes." Another poster depicted various Iraqi regions and ethnicities as petals on a multicolored flower. Within the constraints of print reproduction, I selected two of these for the clarity of their presentation in black and white. The first shows hands on a poster with a copy of the constitution on the top and the ballot to be marked either 'yes' or 'no' at the bottom, over the logo of the Independent High Electoral Commission. Although it is actually an AFP photograph of ballot print-shop workers producing the poster, it seems to my American eye to convey many hands swearing on the constitution. The second poster is written in Kurdish, and says to a minority group seeking self-determination something like 'break your shackles by voting for the constitutional project.' Personally I see very clear messages in both images, but I cannot infer how these graphics or the whole exercise of a yes-or-no referendum registered with women and men, Kurds and Arabs, or other demographic groups in Iraqi society.

---

[72] Feisal Al-Istrabadi, "A Constitution without Constitutionalism: Reflections on Iraq's Failed Constitutional Process," *Texas Law Review* 87:7 (2009) 1627–1655.

[73] Zaid al-Ali, "What Egypt Should Learn from Iraq," *Open Democracy*, April 21, 2011.

FIGURE 2. A 2005 Iraqi poster for the constitutional referendum reads in Kurdish "break the shackles of the past, choose tomorrow." Photo: Ayub Nuri. Used with permission.

## LEGAL LAYERING

Language, imagery, and symbolism are one thing. Institutional practices and innovations are another, especially if they carry the force of law. Prior to the Coalition intervention, wrote one of the many legal advisors who left shaking her head, "Iraq had maintained a comprehensive and complex justice system, and had secured a high level of competence and capacity amongst justice system staff, albeit with few resources."[74] Rather than fixing the system they broke, the evidence is that the invaders overlaid new institutions on top of it and interspersed a few Anglo-American precepts onto the compound structure codified in the 1969 Iraqi law derived from Britain's 1918 Baghdad Penal Code. There were already a supreme Court of Cassation, provincial Courts of Appeals, Courts of First Instance, Administrative Tribunals, felony and misdemeanor criminal courts, juvenile courts, traffic courts, and civil personal status, labor, and commercial

[74] Cyndi Banks, "'Reconstructing' Justice in Iraq and the Rule of Law," paper presented to the ISA Conference 2008, San Francisco: 9.

courts. Islamic law influenced personal status codes, and rules of evidence, but otherwise it was a secular system. Unlike the Anglo-American jury system, courts were organized on the French model, wherein panels of judges gather evidence and reach verdicts. Military and security courts martial operated outside the civilian justice system, and independent tribal judges adjudicated disputes in rural areas.

Sweeping CPA (Coalition Provisional Authority) edicts on the eve of nominal independence in June 2004 instituted new layers of sacrosanct extra-legislative law. In the commercial sphere, denationalizations of the public sector not only privatized state companies but erased distinctions between native and foreign businesses such that American firms operated inside Iraq while also enjoying extra-territorial legal status.[75] For present purposes, the upshot was that Iraq's courts were now to be governed by a statutory hodge-podge mixing the 2005 Constitution, Iraq's 1979 Judicial Organization Law, the TAL, and relevant CPA Orders. Making sense of this oddly composite system, important elements of which were not negotiated, articulated, or indigenized, was no mean feat.[76]

Beyond the American military's arrogation of judicial and policing functions, new municipal civilian institutions were superimposed over this existing patchwork of overburdened, now physically wrecked courts lacking even telephones. Baghdad's Judicial Institute was renamed the Iraqi Judicial College, the Police Academy for training officers was replaced by a less prestigious Police College, the Ministry of Justice was reorganized and downsized, prisons were removed from the Ministry of Interior's purview, and the Revolutionary Court and extra-judicial State

---

[75] On Bechtel and other security firms see Timothy W. Luke, "Unbundling the State: Iraq and the 'Recontainerization' of Rule, Production, and Identity," *Environment and Planning* A 39:7 (2007) 1564–1581. Deborah D. Avanti, "The Privatization of Security: Lessons from Iraq," *Orbis* 50:2 (2006) 327–342, explains the ambiguous jurisdictions for contractors not covered by the Uniform Code of Military Justice, the Geneva Conventions, domestic American law, or Iraqi law.

[76] A 53-page descriptive appraisal was presented by the ABA Judicial Reform Index for Iraq, Iraq Legal Development Project, Washington, July 2006. Four comprehensive reports written in Arabic by Iraqis for the World Bank were translated into English: Medhat Mahmoud, "Judicial System in Iraq: A Review of the Legislation Regulating Judicial Affairs in Iraq," paper commissioned by the World Bank for the Iraqi Judicial Forum, The Judicial System in Iraq: Facts and Prospects, Amman, Jordan (2–4 October 2004), and, for the same seminar, Saad Abdeljabbar Al-Alloosh, "Overview of Judicial Control of the Constitutionality of Laws in Iraq and Its Prospective Role in Safeguarding Rights and Public Freedoms"; Akram Nash'at Ibrahim, "Modernizing Iraqi Penal Code to Serve and Protect Human Rights"; and Hadi Aziz Ali, "Civil Courts Procedures in the Service of Litigants, Human Rights Protection, and Judicial Performance Improvement."

Security Courts were disbanded. A new Ministry of Human Rights was authorized to investigate crimes of the Ba'ath era. A High Judicial Council, a Federal Supreme Court to hear constitutional issues, a Central Criminal Court specialized in terrorism cases, the Iraqi Special Tribunal, and an extra-judicial "de-Ba'athification bureau" with an American-run Judicial Review Committee were also invented. An Iraqi Justice Integration Commission was given the task of involving citizens in the legal reconstruction effort. An autonomous Judicial Association was formed. The Iraqi Bar Association, created in 1933, was de-Ba'athified. Police and court records were digitalized. There was a massive effort to upgrade policing. These and other radical, top-down innovations implemented mainly by an array of U.S. military officials and private contractors with little regard to antecedent arrangements significantly altered power relations, as one consultant observed, and resulted in disharmonies, tensions, and failures.[77]

The investment in reconstruction of the pre-existing system or even training future jurists paled by comparison. Once considered among the Arab region's finest, Iraq's three law schools had been decimated by years of fiscal starvation, surveillance, censorship, sanctions, and finally looting, leaving fewer than fifty demoralized and overburdened law professors all told.[78] In 2004, some faculty flew to Cairo, Rome, and Syracuse to hear lectures by international and Egyptian jurists and law faculty. DePaul University's School of Law, Case Western University, and some other American law schools won USAID grants to work with the Colleges of Law at Baghdad University, Suleymania University, and Basra University. There were other visits by American, Arab-American and occasionally non-American law professors and experts. Yet by 2010, Iraqi higher education had barely recovered, and reportedly only 200 professors from all academic faculties combined had studied in the United States.[79] The whole effort seemed rather modest and bilateral compared with Bir Zeit and the Euro-Med law school partnerships.

International agencies stepped in to retrain over 600 sitting judges apparently vetted for continuation on the bench. While the invasion was still underway, also, the U.S. Justice Department announced on its web site

---

[77] Cyndi Banks, "'Reconstructing' Justice in Iraq and the Rule of Law," *Hague Journal on the Rule of Law*, 2: 2 (2010) 155–170: 5.

[78] Haider Ala Hamoudi, "Toward a Rule of Law Society In Iraq: Introducing Clinical Legal Education into Iraqi Law Schools," *Berkeley Journal of International Law* 23:112 (2005) 112–136.

[79] Karim Altaii, "Send In the Professors,"*New York Times*, April 8, 2010.

that expatriate Iraqis were invited to a two-week Colloquium for Iraqi Jurists on the International and Domestic Applications of Rule of Law Principles intended to "provide Iraqi judges and lawyers with training on International Law obligations they will need to take into account in a future Iraq," especially in "conventions and customary international law, human rights and due process, international standards of ethics, and the basis of judicial administration." A program launched in The Hague held regular sessions in Prague, funded by the British and Swedish aid agencies with collaboration from the Stockholm-based International Law Assistance Consortium (ILAC), the Czech government, the International Association of Prosecutors, the International Bar Association, and the ABA's institute in Prague. U.S. Supreme Court Justices Anthony Kennedy and Sandra Day O'Connor and Lord Woolf, Chief Justice of England and Wales, addressed these meetings. With Swedish funding, ILAC and the Human Rights Institute of the International Bar Association invited Iraqi judges and prosecutors to Dubai for trainings by Australian, South African, Tunisian, Dubai'i and UN legal practitioners. The EU allocated 10 million euros for a JUST LEX project to train 520 judges and hundreds more senior police and magistrates. Other European and UN programs ensued. Yet by 2011, Iraqi jurists and barristers were curiously under-represented in donor-funded pan-Arab legal conferences of the sort described earlier.

American legal scholars and journalists picked up on ill-conceived plans to graft some American notions onto the pre-existing legal system. Unfamiliar with the Napoleonic tradition, military personnel, in particular, imported mismatched substantive and procedural elements such as a 'model plan' for private counsel based on fee structures and attorney pool systems run by U.S. public defender offices.[80] *The Atlantic Monthly* ran a comedy-of-errors story of a colonel whose personal initiative to apply the Maryland traffic code in Baghdad was stymied by sloppy translations that confused rules for buses and cars in stipulations like "No talking to the driver."[81]

More seriously, but also strangely, a point was made of respecting Iraq's existing 1969 Criminal Code, with amendments to toughen it by extending maximum and imposing minimum penalties for kidnapping, rape, vehicle

---

[80] Jim Edwards, "Rebuilding Iraq's Judicial System from the Ground Up," *New Jersey Law Journal* 3 (2003), a commentary on the rule-of-law sector evaluation report by 13 U.S. lawyers in May 2003.
[81] William Langeswiesche, "Welcome to the Green Zone: The American Bubble in Baghdad," *The Atlantic Monthly* (November 2004) 61–88.

hijacking, and looting. The CPA also retained the 1971 Egyptian-style edition of the Iraqi Criminal Procedure Code while interspersing pieces of the American adversarial system of defense and prosecution and principles of habeas corpus. Amidst so many decrees annulling or replacing previous statutes it was unclear whether this was a default decision, a curious concession to Iraqi's judiciary, or an explicit design related to other American objectives.

What a fascinating confluence. Two American law review articles analyzed Iraqi jurists' interpretations of the amended law under circumstances of belligerent occupation and civil strife. Authors of the first study asked eighty-two Iraqi judges who took an Anglo-American training course in Prague to rule on hypothetical evidence about American soldiers accused of torturing foreign and/or Iraqi terrorists. Judges most apprehensive about escalating violence passed the most severe sentences, the authors concluded, whereas in a "negative case of the diffusion of Anglo-American legal regimes" the "less worried" judges "were freed by an indeterminate law to hand down more lenient punishments for torture."[82] The author of the second paper, a disaffected American military lawyer, blamed low conviction rates or relaxed sentences handed down by U.S.-appointed judges on the Iraqi Central Criminal Court against terror suspects apprehended by American soldiers on judges' sympathies with the rebels, their mechanistic training in the civil law tradition, the two-eyewitness *Shari'a* rule, the absence of juries and cross-examinations, failure to apply American-mandated minimum sentences, and the fact that the proceedings and inquisitors' notes were in Arabic, with translators in short supply.[83] Notwithstanding their contrasting portrayals of the integrity of Iraqi judges and the guilt or innocence of the accused, authors of both articles pointed to the problematic superimposition of some new rules and procedures; and also to the politicization of justice in the context of an insurgency against a foreign army. Both surmised that judges were inevitably influenced by political contexts and events. A *New York Times* reporter painted an even bleaker picture of courts overwhelmed by thousands of suspects detained by American forces, fifteen-minute trials

[82] John Hagan, Gabrielle Ferrale, and Guillermina Jasso, "How Law Rules: Torture, Terror, and the Normative Judgments of Iraqi Judges," *Law and Society Review* 42:3 (2008) 605–643. The cases were hypothetical because U.S. soldiers were immune from prosecution in Iraqi courts.

[83] Michael J. Frank, "Trying Times: The Prosecution of Terrorists in the Central Criminal Court of Iraq," *Florida Journal of International Law* 18:1 (2006) 1–133. While observing that judges were being assassinated by rebels, this author called them liars, Ba'athists, lazy, and corrupt.

conducted without legal defense, erratic sentencing, and frequent acquittals.[84]

## THE TRIAL OF SADDAM HUSSEIN

The vexing question of where, how, and under what system of laws to bring Saddam Hussein and some of his henchmen to justice was answered summarily in December 2003 when the Coalition Provisional Authority promulgated the Statute of the 'Iraqi Special Tribunal' to be organized by Americans and some Iraqi-Americans but ultimately run as an Iraqi court. This decree was given constitutional status in the 2004 Transitional Administrative Law. Then it was annulled in 2005 by Iraq's Transitional National Assembly on the grounds that the constitution barred special tribunals (of which there had been far too many under the previous government). The Assembly renamed it the 'Iraqi High Tribunal,' and removed provisions in the TAL allowing for the appointment of two international jurists.[85] This indigenization eschewed the mechanisms of the International Criminal Court and international laws criminalizing war crimes and mass executions. Emphatically it retained the Iraqi death penalty for murder.

The High Tribunal and the Dujail trial were marked by novel problems of jurisdiction and a peculiar amalgamation of American directive and Iraqi law. The crime was the slaughter of Iraqi Shi'a in 1982, during the war with Iran. The governing statute was the toughened version of the 1969 Iraqi Criminal Code, allowing for imprisonment and execution by hanging or firing squad. The trial was paid for and supervised from the CPA's Regime Crimes Liaison Office and staffed by Iraqi judges given a crash course in habeas corpus by U.S. Justice Department experts.[86] Legal scholars, including one who joined the defense team, argued that the unilateral creation of the Tribunal by the United States in the context of occupation defied international law.[87] One legal analysis depicted a bizarre kind of legal pluralism,

[84] Michael Moss, "Iraq's Legal System Staggers beneath the Weight of War,"*New York Times*, December 17, 2006, a lengthy investigative piece; see also the three-part *Times* series by Moss and David Rohde, beginning on May 21, 2006, with "Misjudgments Marred U.S. Plans for Iraqi Police," depicting a clumsy, scaled-down, ineffectual effort to train the Iraqi police forces.

[85] Guenael Mettraux, "The 2005 Revision of the Statute of the Iraqi Special Tribunal," *Journal of International Criminal Justice* 5:2 (2007) 287–293.

[86] Binoy Kampmark, "The Trial of Saddam Hussein: Limits and Prospects," *Contemporary Review* 288 (2006) 192–200, labeled the structure of the court an "American creation."

[87] Curtis F. J. Doebbler, "An Intentionally Unfair Trial," *Journal of International Criminal Justice* 5:2 (2007) 264–271.

nearly bereft of multilateral and international law features but hewn to the cruelly shared Iraqi and American use of capital punishment.[88]

Whatever their competence in Iraqi law, few if any Iraqi jurists inside Iraq or returning from exile were knowledgeable about recent developments in international criminal justice, the newly established International Criminal Court (ICC), ad hoc tribunals for Rwanda and the former Yugoslavia, or jurisprudence on matters of command responsibility; nor were they familiar with multijurisdictional criminal trials, war crimes, crimes against humanity, or genocide.[89] One scholar speculated: "Advisors with experience of this area of law and of handling complex international trials could have been appointed. Arabic texts of the decisions of international courts and legal texts could have been made available to all parties, and researchers and law clerks could have assisted the judges, prosecutors and defense counsel ... without prejudicing the independence and the domestic nature of the court."[90]

Most consultants and legal experts remarked on the abnormalities of the tribunal. In defense of the tribunal, one of the five Case Western law professors who trained some of the jurists compared the Dujail trial with other inherently messy "internationalized-domestic tribunals" in Sierra Leone, the former Yugoslavia, and Rwanda.[91] Yet he and his team also acknowledged that the tribunal was not consistent with the ICC's "complementarity regime" of domestic war crimes tribunals, in part because "it is a misnomer to refer to the Iraqi High Tribunal as a 'domestic' court" when behind the scenes, inappropriately, the occupying power "played a crucial role in drafting the Court's Statute, collecting evidence to be used by the prosecution, and providing both security and financing to the Court."[92] Such an unorthodox structure gave the impression that it was meant to undermine the ICC, evade international law, and avoid having

---

[88] Asli U. Bali, "Justice under Occupation: Rule of Law and the Ethics of Nation-Building in Iraq," Symposium: Nation-Building in the Middle East, *Yale Journal of International Law* 431 (2005) 431–473: 30.

[89] Eric Stover, Hanny Megally, and Hania Mufti, "Bremer's 'Gordian Knot': Transitional Justice and the US Occupation of Iraq," *Human Rights Quarterly* 27:3 (2005) 838–839.

[90] De Bertodano, "Were There More Acceptable Alternatives to the Iraqi High Tribunal?": 299–300. See also Melissa L. Dougherty, "A Comparative Analysis of International Tribunals: The Formation of an Iraqi Judiciary to Try Sadaam Hussein," Bepress Legal Series, Working Paper 588, April 9, 2005.

[91] Michael P. Scharf, "The Iraqi High Tribunal" [A Viable Experiment in International Justice?], *Journal of International Criminal Justice* 5:2 (2007) 258–263.

[92] Michael Scharf et al., "Ten Lessons from the Saddam Trial," report generated from the October 7, 2006, Cleveland Experts Meeting, Case Western Reserve University,http://www.law.case.edu/saddamtrial/index.asp?t=1. The team regretted that no non-Iraqi Arab

American officials called upon to testify, wrote one expert.[93] An observer from the International Center for Transitional Justice said that the Dujail trial, intended as the first and easiest of fourteen trials for mass murders under Saddam Hussein, fell short because judicial impartiality was compromised by political interference; the right to a full defense and other fair trial standards were breached; and evidentiary and analytical lapses prevented exposure of the full extent of crimes and evidence thereof.[94] Responding to the guilty verdict, the UN High Commissioner for Human Rights and the United Nations Working Group on Arbitrary Detentions reiterated their concerns that due process had not been observed. When appeals were dismissed, the UN Special Rapporteur on the Independence of Judges and Lawyers urged Iraq not to carry out the death sentence until procedural flaws were redressed. The UN also protested the grotesquely inappropriate conditions of the execution and the broadcasting of video in violation of international norms.[95] Almost everyone involved was dismayed to see how political and counter-procedural it was. No other single episode covered in this book more fully underscores my basic argument – that professional consultants and practitioners recognize that 'political aid' is political and paradoxical.

No longer was the American monologue about leading an international criminal justice movement launched at Nuremburg believable. Uncle Sam neglected to give Iraq a model constitution or exemplary courts. Although American story-tellers could spin tales about Iraqi judicial sovereignty and the normalcy of execution, overseas audiences, including anti-death penalty agitators in Italy and their allies among the most ecumenical elements of Arab judicial communities, reacted with shock and revulsion.

Pictures of a corpse dangling from a rope evoked other widely distributed images of Abu Ghraib prisoners on dog-leashes or hooded and wired. There was ample evidence of American resort to cruel and unusual punishments. The trial and execution did not represent the rule-bound highground departure from Saddam Hussein's government's own special

judges were named to the Tribunal because a distinguished regional jurist might have enhanced perceptions of judicial independence.

[93] José E. Alvarez, "Trying Hussein: Between Hubris and Hegemony," *Journal of International Criminal Justice* 2 (2004) 319–329. Even while disputing "legal absolutist" arguments advanced by Human Rights Watch, Alvarez concluded that the tribunal fell short of legal standards.

[94] Miranda Sissons and Ari S. Bassin, "Was the Dujail Trial Fair?" *Journal of International Criminal Justice* 5:2 (2007) 272–286.

[95] UN Assistance Mission for Iraq (UNAMI) Human Rights Report, November 1–31, December 2006: 21–22.

tribunals many Americans expected in the early days of the occupation. Instead it gave solace to regional henchmen prone to assassinating opponents after summary tribunals, and enabled Saddam's admirers in the region to portray him as a nationalist martyr. Five or six years later when other Arab dictators were deposed by popular forces, this weak legal precedent proved unfortunate: there might have been a model for bringing Ben Ali, Mubarak, Qadhafi, and Salih to justice. Even at the time, advocates of international law were reminded that human rights and international law are not 'made-in-America' brand-names: the United States lags behind global legal and normative standards in adhering to the death penalty for domestic crimes, refusing to sign documents such as the Convention for the Elimination of Discrimination Against Women, and opposing the Rome Statue and the International Criminal Court.

## LEGAL PLURALISM AND GLOBALIZATION

In addition to the aberrant, disruptive instance of post-invasion Iraq, this chapter has traced how political aid intersects with domains of state authority and/or traverses the 'national' boundaries of North Africa and the Middle East. It has shown that some projects, even if they seem to infringe on the conceptual domains of sovereignty or to defy the political status quo, can augment the bureaucratic and regulatory capacities of security states and their appropriations of human rights norms. Yet other projects, especially support for independent liberal reformers who 'shame and blame' those same client administrations, provoke a backlash. These themes carry over into later chapters on women's advocacy and NGO financing, which shift the focus from American policy to the domestic politics of Arab countries.

Law is dynamic. Legal jurisdictions are permeable. Over the centuries, Arab regimes absorbed European principles and practices into 'indigenous' legacies and converged on a more-or-less common notion of 'law and order.' In the late twentieth and early twenty-first centuries, legal experts and democracy brokers brought selected legal, economic, and strategic phrases and formulas to composite judicial environments already shaped by evolving international conventions. The influences of 'political aid' were probably more incremental than transformational, and more quarrelsome than inspirational. Still, one of the salient trajectories in this chapter has been further confederacy of Arab and some European practices; another has been the widening, deepening, and increasing sophistication of intermediate layers between national and global domains where the lingua franca is modern standard legal Arabic laced with English and/or French. One does not have to believe in democratic alchemy to see this as an interesting development: an actualization, in extra-territorial conference spaces, of an otherwise transient historically derived epistemic community of modern Arab advocates and practitioners. This community is not merely, as regional iconoclasts often insist, a translation service for a 'West' obsessed with narrowly defined bourgeois liberties. Rather, or in addition, it worked, with some external financial backing, to forge consensus around constitutional principles reflective of the gamut of international human rights principles, including protections from torture or arbitrary arrest, gender equality, intellectual and associational freedoms, and the rights of indigenous and colonized peoples. This struggle, far from complete, was noteworthy in part because it addressed a regional layer of legal consciousness that defied simplistic juxtapositions between Western and Islamic conceptions of justice.

The next three chapters wrestle with different aspects of this problematic: the contradictions between constructivism and power politics are exemplified in international involvement in elections; the paradoxes of liberal idealism surface in programming and institution-building for women's empowerment; and the state-non-state conundrum comes to the fore in 'foreign funding' for 'civil society organizations' defined as CSOs. As in the justice sector, political development projects were often contested and paradoxical, as participants are all too well aware.

# 2

# Electoral Representation

After the Cold War, game-changing elections in several former Soviet republics and Warsaw Pact countries seeking membership in the European Union were encouraged and celebrated by North Atlantic leaders. In the West, these elections were applauded as signs of the democratic will of the people but equally of the triumph of liberal ideals, Western military power, global capitalism, and a new more peaceful world order. There were inspirational examples elsewhere as well: the election of former political prisoner Nelson Mandela in post-apartheid South Africa springs to mind. As newsworthy, photogenic events marked by ceremony, celebrity, choreography, and – sometimes – a suspenseful crescendo and unpredictable denouement, breakthrough multiparty elections sparked 'big bang' theories about seamless political transitions from authoritarianism to democracy. In those exuberant years, it seemed obvious that the global hegemon, the NATO alliance, world centers of finance, and voters freed from the yoke of dictatorship all benefited from the ballot-box elixir. Elected leaders of advanced democracies instinctively prefer dealing with democratically elected governments, optimists reasoned, and would therefore extend moral support, technical assistance, and various incentives for one-party regimes to hold competitive electoral campaigns and peacefully yield power at the behest of voters. This vision is the poster child of 'democracy promotion.'

During this euphoric period, too, a growing cadre of experts honed the relatively new science of electoral design and administration; refined methodologies for observation and verification; and crafted transnational codes of conduct. An especially rigorous standard was set for admission to the European Union. A global democracy bureaucracy

parlayed specialized assessment rubrics, and teams of international consultants, volunteers, and public personalities participated in the routines
and celebrations of national elections. Often their well-publicized press
conferences on Election Night granted a kind of international stamp of
approval; now and then, they declared a vote to be fraudulent.
Appearances by Jimmy Carter, other respected retired politicians, or
sitting European parliamentarians conveyed a Western interest in the
performance of democratization, but also did seem a fairly reliable indicator that minimal standards were met. Political scientists and activists
working in Arab countries began encountering or being invited to join
teams from the European Union, the United Nations, the Carter Center,
NDI, the International Foundation for Electoral Systems (IFES),
Elections Canada, and other organizations. Increasingly (though not
consistently), these or other professional organizations published the
authoritative accounts of electoral cycles, from voter and candidate
registration through the announcement of results. These industry reports
offered insights into whether, when, and how international consultants
and observers participated in various Arab elections. This chapter cites
these reports in order to understand evolving transnational assessment
rubrics, or what might be considered the rules of the game. The question
then becomes: to what extent were these rubrics and rules applied in
different situations?

The overall argument that democracy promotion is inherently political
is almost too easy to apply to American engagement in Arab politics. The
conditions for Western enthusiasm about democratic change inside the old
Evil Empire of the Soviet bloc (or parts of the Third World where friendly
dictators had lost their usefulness) did not obtain in the Middle East.
Instead, everyone talks about hypocrisy, double standards, and inconsistencies. In the solipsistic study of Uncle Sam's foreign policy, the usual
metaphor is that strategic reason overrides messianic zeal. From a Middle
Eastern perspective, even this telling seems to exaggerate American good-
will. Compiling well-known stories, this chapter contrasts publicity for a
few elections that seemed to fit a triumphal Western chronicle with other
cases of backing for unelected dynasties or military commands that export
oil, make peace with Israel, support NATO military operations, comply
with the World Trade Organization, or hold Islamist parties at bay. Unlike
the proto-typical Communist country, where strategic considerations,
economic interests, democratic ideals, and technical expertise all coincided
to push for ballot-driven regime change, in the Middle East they often
seemed ill-disposed. This point is widely acknowledged. One explanation

for the persistence of Arab authoritarianism was Western support for the status quo.[1]

Independent scholars generally are less familiar with mechanical aspects of what is arguably the central task of applied transitology: the design, administration, and/or verification of campaign and voting procedures. Relying on industry transcripts, therefore, this chapter juxtaposes a techno-cratic account of the work of an incipient transnational elections regime with the 'high politics' of Western interactions and elections in Palestine, Iraq, and several sovereign countries. It documents the sometimes dry details of what consultants, trainers, and monitors do and write about what they do. It traces the rise and, one might say, fall of a transnational consortium of experts forging mechanical standards, sharing knowledge, and applying increasingly sophisticated observing techniques. It compares their uneven inroads in the Arab region: in self-governing countries, where incumbent strongmen wanted foreign consultants and spectators to ratify the status quo, and under unusual circumstances in Kuwait, Palestine, and Iraq, where world powers showcased their support for electoral self-determination.

It was often said that the United States and its allies sacrificed demo-cratic ideals to keep undemocratic Arab governments safe and secure. In the early days of democracy promotion, a former Cold Warrior legendarily asked and answered a rhetorical question: "Do we seriously want to change the institutions in Saudi Arabia? The brief answer is no: over the years we have sought to preserve those institutions, sometimes in prefer-ence to more democratic forces"[2] More than two decades later, Secretary of State Condoleezza Rice told an audience at the American University in Cairo, "For 60 years, my country, the United States, pursued stability at the expense of democracy in the region, here in the Middle East, and we achieved neither." Scholars and policy-watchers amplified and annotated these points. Even before 9/11/2001, Arab political reform looked like an "afterthought" relegated to the level of "low policy" and tempered by fears that Arab voters would not favor pro-American candidates.[3] Indeed a prolific progressive iconoclast declared that American policy was deter-mined to "deter" Arab democratization.[4] At the zenith of democratic

[1] Eva Bellin, "The Robustness of Authoritarianism in the Middle East: Exceptionalism in Comparative Perspective," *Comparative Politics*, 36: 2 (2004) 139–157.
[2] James Schlesinger, "The Quest for a Post-Cold War Foreign Policy," *Foreign Affairs* 72:1 (1993) 17–28: 20. The author was a former Secretary of Defense and CIA director.
[3] Amy Hawthorne, "Do We Want Democracy in the Middle East?" *Foreign Service Journal* (February 2001) 43–49.
[4] Noam Chomsky, *Deterring Democracy* (London: Verso, 1991).

messianism after the invasion of Iraq, Pentagon fears that aggressive pressure for elections could undermine regional allies fostered a "survival strategy" of "controlled liberalization" for other countries in the region.[5] Discrepancies between oratory and actions fanned widespread Arab mistrust of U.S. motives.[6] "At the same time that the United States asked governments to reform," one pollster averred, "it also asked them to support policies in Iraq, the war on terrorism, and the Arab-Israeli issue that the vast majority of their publics passionately opposed."[7] Well-meaning electoral reform programs might not only fail to counter terrorism but could disturb U.S. interests in protecting Israeli security, oil and gas flows, and the stability of friendly regimes, a self-styled realist warned.[8] Amidst fears of Arab popular opinion, talk about democratization looked to a prominent Palestinian-American scholar like a cynical cover for imperial designs, backstopping of undemocratic allies, and outright military intervention.[9] The Carnegie Endowment's top expert called the "gleaming rhetorical edifice" around the export of freedom "a myth" eclipsed by economic imperatives and the war on terror.[10] With America's reputation damaged by abuses of detainees at Abu Ghraib and Guantanamo prisons, skepticism and backlash in the Arab world, and the reluctance of European and other international democracy supporters to be associated with the United States, he added later, the Obama administration equivocated between supporting human rights and investing in stability while specifically backing off from pressing either elections or the independence of civic associations.[11]

European policy observers similarly saw a scrimmage between virtuous intentions and pressing interests concerning trade, migration, and security

---

[5] Tamara Kofman Wittes, "Arab Democracy, American Ambivalence," *The Weekly Standard*, February 23, 2004, 34–37. See also Marina Ottoway, "Promoting Democracy in the Middle East: The Problem of US Credibility," Carnegie Endowment for International Peace Working Papers, Democracy and Rule of Law Project, No. 35, Washington, March 2003.

[6] Katerina Dalacoura, "US Democracy Promotion in the Arab Middle East since 11 September 2001: A Critique," *International Affairs* 81:5 (2005) 963–979: 972.

[7] Shibley Telhami, "Exporting Democracy to the Middle East," *Dissent* (Spring 2007) 57–58.

[8] F. Gregory Gause, "Can Democracy Stop Terrorism?" *Foreign Affairs* 84:5 (2005): 62–76.

[9] Rashid Khaladi, *Resurrecting Empire: Western Footprints and America's Perilous Path in the Middle East* (New York: Beacon Press, 2004): 46.

[10] Thomas Carothers, "The Democracy Crusade Myth," *National Interest Online*, June 6, 2007.

[11] Thomas Carothers, *Democracy Policy under Obama: Revitalization or Retreat*, Carnegie Report, Washington, January 2012.

in the Mediterranean 'neighborhood.' Given a perceived choice between democratization and primary concerns, it seemed, "The EU will always give higher priority to security."[12] Rarely was serious financial assistance "conditional" on holding "open" elections, a respected authority wrote: political conditionality was the "dog that didn't bite."[13] While Europeans liked to hope a democratic Middle East would become less prone to instability and violence, decision-makers, in the short-run, deduced a zero-sum trade-off between democratization and security, and opted for the latter.[14] These accounts all reference the idealism/rational-actor conundrum from the 'high' viewpoint of Western great powers.

These thoughts are helpful to bear in mind. However, studies of foreign policy objectives do not tell us much about activities and outputs nearer to the ground. Below the radar of international relations, a global regime located in Stockholm, Ottawa, and Berlin, as well as in D.C., with branches in Cairo, Beirut, Amman, and other Arab cities, offered a technical, legalistic, professionalized, codified, and methodologically refined proficiency in the design, management, and documentation of elections. Its training component had rather widespread effects: tens of thousands of poll-workers, volunteers, and college students took short courses and received field manuals in Arabic familiarizing them with the basic investigative tools for monitoring national election laws and transnational standards. Compared with other sectors, it is worth noting, work on elections is episodic and contingent, often compressed within a period of months, weeks, or even days. Here the universalization of sensible rubrics with wide appeal and short-term task orientation would seem conducive to constructivist predictions about the spread of epistemic communities of

[12] Gorm Rye Olsen, "The European Union: An Ad Hoc Policy with a Low Priority," in ed. Peter J. Schraeder, *Exporting Democracy: Rhetoric vs. Reality* (Boulder: Lynne Rienner, 2002) 131–145: 133. The EU's aims in the late 1990s were to "seize back" the peace process grabbed by the United States; offset the threat of instability and fundamentalism; expand markets for industrial exports; and enhance "hub-and-spoke trade relations," according to Paul Rivlin, *Economic Policy and Performance in the Arab World* (Boulder: Lynne Rienner, 2001) 169–185.

[13] Richard Youngs, "Democracy Promotion: The Case of European Union Strategy," Brussels, Center for European Policy Studies Working Document No. 167; October 2001: 37. Sabine C. Zanger found little statistical correlation between EU funding and indicators for human rights and democratic practices: "Good Governance and European Aid: The Impact of Conditionality," *European Union Politics* 1:3 (2000) 293–317.

[14] Richard Gillespie, "A Political Agenda for Region-building? The EMP and Democracy Promotion in North Africa," Institute of European Studies University of California at Berkeley, Paper 040530, 2004.

'democrats.' This would be the sanguine argument that in this iconic sector, 'the West' or 'the international community' does promote competitive, transparent elections.

Even optimistic theories about international regimes should recognize that instituting or altering political processes is a halting, combative task with incremental, often uneven results. The extent of international involvement varied considerably (across countries and over time) from high involvement in a few Arab elections to none in others. Years can go into the design and preparation of 'first' elections, as in Palestine and Iraq, and only in those two places did international agents determine that elections would be held, when, and how. Elsewhere, sovereign authorities sometimes invited technical consultants to give input on mechanics; trainer-trainers to hold classes for candidates, poll-workers, and domestic monitors; and/or teams of international monitors to watch the actual vote. By and large, however, incumbents staging elections cherry-picked projects that served their governance interests, and rejected the rest as adversarial "meddling." The Mubarak administration waved away international expertise or monitoring, for instance, and then the SCAF permitted international teams of trainers and observers to participate in the 2011/12 parliamentary balloting, only to shut down some (but not all) of the sponsoring organizations. In a roundabout way, the authoritarian backlash against international technical assistance, training, and monitoring is a compliment to IRI, NDI, and other agencies claiming to counterpoise tyranny.

On the other hand, critical theorizing about what monitors, trainers, and experts do could suggest that legibility projects render the inner workings of a polity readable and thus theoretically manageable. In other words, funders hoped to instill in the political society the capacity to auto-police, self-discipline, and then release the data to imperial powers. Around the turn of the twenty-first century, therefore, one's expectations might have been that foreign experts advised client governments in Egypt, Tunisia, Yemen, Algeria, and other countries to display enough of the trappings of competition and transparency to justify continuing Western support and perhaps to pacify Arab electorates. If so, one might have predicted technically adept electoral design, administration, and verification in Palestine, and especially in Iraq, conducive to Western interests, and that Mubarak would welcome help in manufacturing credible electoral victories. Additionally, if political aid in the crucial field of elections served American hegemony, then Washington's official pronouncements and experts' findings would usually match. Finally, methodologically sophisticated reconnaissance missions ought to have yielded reliable political intelligence capable of predicting (if not controlling) political events. Critics of American interventionism naturally expected that in Iraq the highest levels of the U.S. state apparatus, USAID, and parastatal or nongovernmental groups funded by USAID or NED would manufacture the appearance of consent to a government serving American imperial interests.[15]

Yet another theory is that all this is mere simulacra, a choreographed performance of democratization. Accounts of the multilaterally orchestrated balloting pursuant to the Dayton Accords among warring nationalities in the former Yugoslavia used words like "gunboat" or "Potemkin" democracy,[16] or referred to "Beltway Bandits" or "Marriott Brigades."[17] Industry insiders cautioned against "flying carpets bearing wise men for a weekend."[18] Long-term consultants cast doubt on jet-set photo-ops and congratulatory statements issued from airport departure lounges before poll-watchers, national or foreign, had time to compile their data. By the end of the 1990s, American policy-makers were exhorted to eschew the counsel of "elections nuts" pushing quick post-conflict elections as an easy "exit strategy."[19] Later experts decried the tendency to "convey the impression, exacerbated by fleeting media coverage in places like Ukraine, Indonesia, and Iraq, that democracy is mainly about electing government officials."[20] Prescient of the Iraq experiment, a comparative study applying a 'ballots-to-bullets' hypothesis – that fierce competition in situations where rules are poorly routinized may provoke sore losers to resort to

[15] William J. Robinson, "What to Expect from U.S. 'Democracy Promotion' in Iraq," *New Political Science* 26: 3 (2004) 441–447.

[16] Ted Galen Carpenter, "Jackboot Nation Building: The West Brings 'Democracy' to Bosnia," *The Mediterranean Quarterly* 11:2 (2000) 1–22; David Chandler, *Bosnia: Faking Democracy after Dayton* (London: Pluto, 1999); Gary T. Dempsey, "Fool's Errands: America's Recent Encounters with Nation-Building," *Mediterranean Quarterly* 12:2 (2001): 57–80.

[17] David Corn, "Beltway Bandits," *The Nation* 257:18 (November 29, 1993): 648; Kevin F. F. Quigley, "For Democracy's Sake: How Funders Fail – and Succeed," *World Policy Journal* 13:1 (1996) 109–119.

[18] Graham Allison and Robert Beschel, "Can the United States Promote Democracy?" in ed. Charles Wolf, Jr., *Promoting Democracy and Free Markets in Eastern Europe* (Rand: prepared for the Agency for International Development, Santa Monica, 1991) 98.

[19] Thomas Carothers, *Aiding Democracy Abroad: The Learning Curve* (Washington: The Carnegie Endowment for International Peace, 1999) 86–87, 135.

[20] Don Pressley and Lawrence Groo, "Streamlining U.S. Democracy Assistance," *Georgetown Journal of International Affairs* 1:2 (2005) 113–121: 120.

armed strife – gave caution about the wisdom of "experts from role-model states" pushing complex systems of electoral representation.[21]

During the Cold War era of CIA-instigated coups, balloting in frontline client states seemed choreographed to rally American public opinion around military adventures in Vietnam and Central America. Framed in terms of a battle between democracy and communism, nearly any election, or any anti-communist result, could be portrayed as democratic; voter turnout could be spun as popular acclaim for American hegemony. These were dubbed "demonstration elections."[22] It has also been argued that all development brokers construct theatrical scenarios with dramatic plot sequences, casts of stars, and thousands of 'extras'[23]; if so, election projects, with victory and defeat, photogenic moments, and millions of extras, offer special drama and spectacle. Teams of international observers systematically gathering data, dispensing technical expertise, and training local monitors can make the event look a lot like natives performing democracy for election tourists. In the Arabic-language media, as American democracy brokers in Egypt were reminded in 2011/12, some people portrayed international experts and monitors and their local counterparts as spies seeking intelligence with which to control political outcomes.

Good stagecraft is not the same as effective socio-political engineering, however. Grand plans by national governments can fall short of radically transformational objectives, after all.[24] This could well be true for applied transitology, too. All donor programs are policy experiments; they may not work as intended.[25] Agricultural aid does not necessarily produce a cornucopia, unless perhaps of agricultural bureaucracies.[26] In the political

[21] Jack Snyder, *From Voting to Violence: Democratization and Nationalist Conflict* (New York: Norton, 2002) 350–353.

[22] Edward S. Herman and Frank Brodhead, *Demonstration Elections: U.S.-staged Elections in the Dominican Republic, Vietnam, and El Salvador* (Boston: South End Press, 1984).

[23] David Craig and Doug Porter, "Framing Participation: Development Projects, Professionals, and Organizations," in ed. Melakou Tegegn, *Development and Patronage* (UK: Oxfam, 1997) 50–57: 54.

[24] James C. Scott, *Seeing Like a State: How Certain Schemes to Improve the Human Condition Have Failed* (New Haven: Yale University Press, 1998).

[25] Dennis A. Rondinelli, *Development Projects as Policy Experiments: An Adaptive Approach to Development Administration* (London: Methuen & Co., 1983). Roger C. Riddell, *Foreign Aid Reconsidered* (Baltimore: Johns Hopkins University Press, 1987); Robert Cassen and Associates, *Does Aid Work?* (Oxford: Claredon Press, 1987).

[26] Yahya M. Sadowski, *Political Vegetables? Businessman and Bureaucrat in the Development of Egyptian Agriculture* (Washington: The Brookings Institution, 1991).

sphere, it is one thing to enframe and choreograph an event; it is quite another to get people to stick to their scripts. As one perceptive critic wrote, just because the "democratic offensive" is "meant to be an element in the politics of domination ... doesn't automatically make it happen."[27] Or it might look that way to Americans, for instance, but not to Iraqis. It is worth asking, as mentioned earlier, what the 'performance' of an election signifies to different participants, and how various actors make meaning of campaign rituals, get-out-the-vote billboards, celebrations of Voting Day, the act of marking a ballot, or declarations of who won.[28]

This chapter sequentially compares international involvement in a series of Arab elections during two decades marked by both stability and tumult. It needs to consider several dimensions. One is the 'high' politics of North Atlantic military and diplomatic relations intended to stabilize pliant allies and occasionally destabilize challengers. The second trajectory is the evolution of a transnational elections regime distinguished by its specialized procedures and reflected in its declarations and the spread of a norm of international monitoring. Finally, our main concern is with the ground level, where those techniques are (or are not) applied to specific electoral events. To understand when, where, and how foreigners participated in Arab elections, in turn, we must consider the ordinary or exceptional circumstances under which elections were held, whether power is transferred, and so on, as well as the extent of international involvement in design and administration and, finally, whether transnational agencies verified the face validity of the process. This tangle of inquiries can be tamed methodologically by focusing on the 'outputs' of political aid in the elections sector: these are, inevitably, reports issued before, during, and especially right after a national vote takes place. Comparing the reports for different elections – in Lebanon, Iraq, and Palestine, for instance – helps us to understand that the 'double standards' do not pit geostrategic pragmatism against fuzzy sentimentalism; instead, they juxtapose unilateral impulses against codified rules and empirical rubrics. The contrast suggests that internationally supported standards for the conduct and verification of elections cannot be dismissed as a tool of American imperialism.

---

[27] Jochen Hippler, "Democratisation of the Third World After the End of the Cold War," in ed. Hippler, *The Democratisation of Disempowerment: The Problem of Democracy in the Third World* (London: Pluto Press, 1999) 1–32.

[28] Wedeen, "Conceptualizing Culture," 721.

## THE EARLY 1990S

The first post–Cold War decade was the era of worldwide 'elections mania.' Even in the first few years, however, wildly discordant responses to landmark elections in Algeria, Kuwait, and Yemen established a pattern of extreme G-7 ambivalence about formal processes of Arab elections. "Caught up in the contradiction between global principle and regional application," wrote one scholar, "the United States is accused of meddling, by undemocratic ruling elites who feel undermined by Washington's democratic evangelism, and of hypocrisy, by indigenous liberal-democratic reformers and human rights advocates."[29] America faced a "democracy conundrum" posed by the difficulty of "balancing between its principles – support for free and fair elections – and its particular interests."[30] The "double negative whammy" was that voters might favor anti-American parties.[31]

In the first test, Algeria, Northern powers welcomed a veritable military coup d'etat in lieu of an Islamist victory at the polls. Domestic foment during the late 1980s enticed Algeria's ruling party to schedule competitive multi-party municipal and legislative elections in two stages in the winter of 1991/92. Yet entrenched military forces blocked a run-off vote that the right-wing Islamist opposition seemed certain to win, effectively annulling the results of the first round and throwing the country into constitutional and political crisis. Washington and Paris didn't flinch. The argument advanced – that if Islamists won an election it would be "one person, one vote, one time," meaning that once installed the Islamists would never relinquish office – was utterly spurious: no secular Arab ruling party ever yielded power to the opposition, either; moreover in this case, secular generals opted for civil war. The nonchalance of France and other NATO governments toward the imposition of martial law was striking.[32] One commentator pointed out that the assertion that the coup was the "lesser of two evils" was belied by the horrific years of bloody civil strife

[29] Michael C. Hudson, "To Play the Hegemon: Fifty Years of U.S. Policy Toward the Middle East," *The Middle East Journal* 50:3 (1996) 329–343.

[30] Richard W. Murphy and F. Gregory Gause, "Democracy and U.S. Policy in the Muslim Middle East," *Middle East Policy*, V:I (1997) 59–60. See also Catharin E. Dalpino, *Deferring Democracy: Promoting Openness in Authoritarian Regimes* (Washington: Brookings Institution Press, 2000).

[31] Howard J. Wiarda, *Civil Society: The American Model and Third World Development* (Boulder: Westview, 2003) 121.

[32] For further details, see William W. Quandt, *Between Ballots and Bullets: Algeria's Transition from Authoritarianism* (Washington: Brookings Institution, 1998).

that ensued.[33] Another labeled the response a "classic case of Western confusion about and disinterest in Arab democratization."[34] A third described a "wait-and-see policy that demonstrated to the Arab world the lack of sincerity in Washington's global advocacy of democratization."[35] Reversing recently adopted "conditionality" rules to cut off aid under such circumstances, the European Council, following Paris's lead, actually increased military and development aid to Algeria and encouraged all G-7 donors and global financial institutions to do likewise.[36] These reactions set a precedent for the next two decades of Western involvement in Arab electoral politics.

Huge publicity heralded elections in Kuwait after the tiny oil-rich monarchy was liberated from Iraqi occupation by an American-led military coalition in 1991. The 1992 National Assembly elections attracted a pool of what a long-time Kuwait-watcher dubbed "democracy tourists," though evidently not any official monitoring delegations (then still in their infancy).[37] Because Kuwait had been holding parliamentary elections since the 1960s, voting signified not a breakthrough but a restoration of sovereignty. Although only elite men got to exercise the franchise in a nonpartisan contest for a rather impotent legislature, the event was hailed from Washington as a beacon of the 'new world order.' Foreshadowing the spotlight on post-Saddam Iraqi elections, speech-makers and columnists celebrated that Kuwait was free to have an election, not that the election itself was free. Disputing the official line about how the foreign military presence unleashed pro-democracy forces, country experts wrote that "it was more an opportunity lost, as the U.S. government chose to support some of the most antidemocratic tendencies on the part of the ruling elites and seemed oblivious to the pro-democratic opposition traditions in Kuwait."[38] Accordingly, America's response when the Emir subsequently suspended parliament was muted. Later rounds of balloting were not

---

[33] Vickie Langohr, "An Exit from Arab Autocracy," *Journal of Democracy* 13 (2002) 116–122: 119.

[34] Sadiki, "To Export or Not to Export Democracy to the Arab World," 67.

[35] Bradford Dillman, "Round Up the Unusual Suspects: American Policy toward Algeria and Its Islamists," *Middle East Policy* 8:2 (2002) 126–143.

[36] Olsen, "The European Union," 140–141.

[37] Mary Ann Tetreault, *Stories of Democracy: Politics and Society in Contemporary Kuwait* (New York: Columbia University Press, 2000) 101.

[38] Jill Crystal and Abdallah al-Shayeji, "The Pro-Democratic Agenda in Kuwait: Structures and Context," in ed. Bahgat Korany, Paul Noble, and Rex Byrnen, *Political Liberalization and Democratization in the Arab World: Arab Experiences* (Boulder: Lynne Reiner Publishers, 1998) 101–125.

significantly advised or observed from abroad. In any case, oil-rich
Kuwait, a net donor of economic development assistance, was not prime
territory for political aid, either.

Official international monitoring was piloted in April 1993 when newly
unified Yemen held a multi-party, universal adult-suffrage vote after an
invigorating campaign. This was a 'first' election that seemed like a breakthrough (but later became evidence of a 'ballots-to-bullets' hypothesis).
District representation for a lower house of parliament had already been
negotiated to preserve existing geographic constituencies in what had been
North and South Yemen. International experts did not design the system of
representation, but they did assist in setting up the Supreme Elections
Committee and arranging the myriad tasks of organizing voter and candidate registration, situating balloting stations, devising a system for tallying votes, and so forth. Foreign agencies imported voting booths, ballots,
and ballot boxes, and trained thousands of poll-workers and domestic
monitors. It was also the first time official international delegations monitored an Arab election. Jimmy and Rosalind Carter led an NDI/Carter
Center task force, there was a large European deputation, lots of embassies
put their staffs on the road, and (less formally) scores of visiting technicians, academics, and journalists watched.

I was living in Sana'a and witnessed these events. Official U.S. and
European delegates and independent journalists and scholars fanned out
around the main cities to watch voters at men's and women's stations show
their registration cards, enter a curtained booth, come back out, put a piece
of paper in a box, and ink their thumbs. It was not as scientific as it would
later be: congratulatory statements were a bit premature, and some reports
seemed naively ideological.[39] Still, the inexperienced Supreme Elections
Committee benefited from technical advice, foreign witnesses did seem to
enhance the performance, formal monitoring reports were issued, and
the whole experience stood up reasonably well to nascent transnational
standards. But with diplomatic relations still strained by Yemen's vote
against Security Council authorization of the 1991 military operation
to dislodge Iraqi forces from Kuwait, Washington was not impressed.
The visiting American ambassador-at-large sniffed that "one election
does not a democracy make." Yemen's example should not be considered

---

[39] Showing its Cold War bias, IRI's "background briefing" effused about the grassroots
popularity of the North's ruling party while dismissing the Socialist Party: "1993 National
Elections in the Republic of Yemen: Political Background Briefing," International
Republican Institute (January 1993) 7–10.

a "blueprint" for neighboring countries, he told Sana'a audiences; if anything, Yemen should emulate the Kuwaiti model.[40] These remarks were certainly more about geopolitics than what had happened in Yemen.

## THE POLITICS OF ELECTIONS MONITORING

The early examples of Algeria, Kuwait, and Yemen anticipated subsequent antipathies between the partly ideological strategic preferences of Western powers and incipient transnational standards. The expanding specialized elections establishment fawned new agencies, refined assessment methodologies, and gathered cross-national electoral data. Global franchises and partnerships sprang up. Increasingly sophisticated technical advice to government officials, political parties, and NGOs promised to improve administration of elections.

Within a few years, an international election regime developed certifiable rubrics for organizing and validating elections. Via European Community admissions criteria, the EU Elections Unit and other organizations such as the Network of Europeans for Electoral and Democracy Support amassed considerable savoir faire in the facilitation of high-quality elections. Major initiatives originated with the International Institute for Democracy and Electoral Assistance, established in Stockholm in 1992 as an inter-governmental think tank and well known by the acronym International IDEA. The Canadian capital of Ottawa became quite a hub for election-related research and activity. The United Nations, whose experiences with trusteeship and peacekeeping caused it to develop world-class capabilities, created an electoral assistance unit in 1992 to coordinate and support outside or domestic poll-watchers, administrative and technical advice, help with voter registration, training of election officials, overall logistics, procurement of election materials, synchronization of international financial arrangements, and computerization of electoral rolls. The Organization for Security and Cooperation in Europe (OSCE) and even the Arab League and the African Union sometimes fielded teams of witnesses. In the United States, NDI, IFES, and the Carter Center were staffed with professional elections experts.

Technocratic documentations recorded the work of an incipient transnational regime. The expressed aim of elections assistance is to

---

[40] David Mack, talk at the American Institute for Yemeni Studies, April 21, 1993, which I attended; cited in Ahmed Noman Almadhagi, *Yemen and the United States: A Study of a Small Power and Superpower Relationship, 1962–1994* (London: Tauris, 1996) 153.

institutionalize administrative arrangements, normative expectations, and formal processes through a combination of technical assistance and monitoring. An international metric evolved from the 1990 Copenhagen document of the OSCE and the Inter-Parliamentary Union's 1994 Criteria for Free and Fair Elections. In 1999, Elections Canada hosted the first meeting of the Global Electoral Organization Network and helped found something called the Partnership for Electoral and Democratic Development.

Gradually, worldwide, the presence of international monitors became a marker of electoral transparency; their official reports constituted a kind of international stamp of approval. Their activities were unmistakably political from the perspective of the governments being aided and/or evaluated. Some incumbents refused any "foreign interference." Citing "sovereignty" or "Western imperialism," rogue republics of Saddam Hussein's Iraq, Sudan, Libya, and Syria, with their ersatz voting rituals, vilified monitoring as espionage. The affluent Western allies Saudi Arabia, the United Arab Emirates, Bahrain, Qatar, and Oman hid behind dynastic traditions, not even holding façade elections until the twenty-first century. Kuwait's ruling dynasty felt that its domestic electoral record was too solid to need expatriate advice or verification.

Even some client regimes dependent on conventional foreign aid, notably Mubarak's Egypt, wouldn't accredit international monitoring delegations. By contrast, for more than a decade Yemen's Ali Abdallah Salih was happy to have them certify that his party kept winning. It was often a matter for negotiations. When USAID/Rabat and IFES proposed to send technicians, trainers, or monitors, "it was apparent that the Moroccan government was not interested in an organization coming in to their country and telling them how they should, or should not, conduct their elections," and they did not want to be categorized with least-developed countries such as Angola or Cambodia.[41] Wary of diplomatic repercussions, election specialists trod gingerly. IFES's report on the 1998 elections complementing "Morocco's continued democratic process" caused a team member to question whether the appraisal was "honest evaluation or whitewash."[42] Later the NDI team invited to document the September

[41] Thomas C. Bayer, *Morocco Direct Legislative Elections June 25, 1993: Report of the IFES Monitoring and Observation Delegations* (Washington: IFES, 1993) 9, 32. In neighboring Tunisia, an Arab was bumped from an IFES team because only American citizens were invited: Jeff Fischer and Clement Henry, *Pre-Election Technical Assessment, Tunisia, December 15-December 22, 1993* (Washington: IFES, 1993) 3.

[42] Henry Munson, Jr. "International Election Monitoring: A Critique Based on One Monitor's Experience in Morocco," *Middle East Report* 209 (1998) 37–39.

2007 vote reiterated modestly its intent to demonstrate "the interest of the international community" and to offer constructive policy recommendations: "The delegation does not seek to interfere in the election process, nor does it intend to, or could it, render a final assessment of the election process."[43]

Even as more Arab countries held elections, presidential dethronements and even parliamentary party turnovers were unheard-of. If anything, researchers found that as Arab citizens were voting in relatively more frequent, competitive, and transparent parliamentary, local, and even presidential elections, officials learned to gerrymander representation and tinker with electoral laws.[44] To the extent that domestic and/or foreign monitors unmasked time-honored habits of interference and outright fraud, indeed, it seemed that electoral system engineering actually increased and/or became more sophisticated.[45] Arab regimes became more "proficient at containing and disarming democracy promotion – if not exploiting it for their own purposes."[46] By this time, elections seemed increasingly as semiotic performances of the power of incumbency rather than mechanisms for the orderly transfer of power.

It seemed possible, then, that political aid projects would tighten the grip of incumbent clients. In a good example of 'authoritarian upgrading,' Algeria played on the interests expressed by France, Spain, and the EU in its stability. Human Rights Watch reported that "The lackluster and silent monitoring of the 1995 Algerian presidential elections by the

---

[43] NDI, Statement of the International Pre-Election Delegation to Morocco's 2007 Legislative Elections, Rabat, August 15, 2007: 1.

[44] Marsha Pripstein Posusney explains proportional, multi-member district, and/or winner-take-all systems in "Multi-Party Elections in the Arab World: Institutional Engineering and Oppositional Strategies," *Studies in Comparative International Development*, 36:4 (2002) 34–62. Ellen Lust-Okar and Amaney Ahmad Jamal, "Rulers and Rules: Reassessing the Influence of Regime Type on Electoral Law Formation," *Comparative Political Studies* 35 (2002) 337–367, found that single-party Arab regimes tended to prefer single-member district-based systems likely to consolidate majorities, whereas monarchs leaned toward at-large party-list systems of proportional representation that dispersed seats representation among a wide range of parties.

[45] Marsha Pripstein Posusney, "Behind the Ballot Box: Electoral Engineering in the Arab World," *Middle East Report* 209 (1998) 12–15.

[46] Steve Heydemann, "Upgrading Authoritarianism in the Arab World," The Saban Center for Middle East Policy, Analysis Paper No. 13 (Washington: The Brookings Institution, October 2007). For variations on this concept, see Daniel Brumberg, "Democratization in the Arab World? The Trap of Liberalized Autocracy," *Journal of Democracy* 13:4 (2002) 56–68. Andreas Schedler refered to "electoral authoritarianism" in "The Menu of Manipulation," *Journal of Democracy* 13:2 (2002) 36–50.

Arab League, Organization of African Unity, and the United Nations enabled the authorities to boast of the international presence without having to face thorough monitoring or public reporting by the observers."[47] No foreign officials investigated numerous complaints about the 1996 Constitutional referendum, which reformed the electoral process in a way that made it more manageable, nor the October 1997 municipal elections, but for the parliamentary elections of June 1997, the UN coordinated efforts by more than 100 eyewitnesses from some 20 countries.[48] Algiers denied visas to outside observers in advance of its 1999 presidential elections, when six of the seven candidates withdrew before voting began. By 2004, delegates from the Arab League, the African Union, the EU, OSCE, and the UN witnessed the landslide victory of a pro-Western, business-friendly president. In 2009, international monitoring groups declined invitations to witness another astounding presidential re-election.

Whether or not international monitoring teams were present, however, their methodologies were introduced indirectly inside or beyond sovereign jurisdictions. Even as Jordan declined official international observer delegations, for instance, Amman hosted an event called The Arab Summit for Monitoring Elections in the Arab World. Under the influence of International IDEA, and with help from NDI and the *Friedrich Ebert Stiftung*, the prominent think tank called *al-Urdan al-Jadid* issued studies on Jordanian and Palestinian elections and developed a proposal for gender quotas that was accepted for the 2003 elections. Importantly, too, Arab intellectuals were invited to join international delegations observing regional balloting experiences. Individual Egyptians, Algerians, Moroccans, and Jordanians watched how Yemeni, Lebanese, or Palestinian elections were conducted, and in the process got trained, offshore, in the basic rubrics of monitoring. When they got back home, they gave media interviews. Later they offered short courses for students or volunteers in how to detect transparency and/or fraud. Finally, Arabic-language press coverage of regional elections – most conspicuously the Palestinian elections of 1996 and 2006 – cited reports and press releases from international monitors.

---

[47] HRW, "Algeria: Elections in the Shadow of Violence and Repression," April 1999.
[48] HRW, Human Rights and Algeria's Presidential Elections: A Human Rights Watch Background Paper, April 1999. The West's largely positive reaction, according to Hugh Roberts, "Algeria's Contested Elections," *Middle East Report* 209 (1998) 21–24, had little to do with the actual voting process.

## PALESTINIAN ELECTIONS OF 1996

In the heady years after the end of the Cold War, 'electricians,' so to speak, helped engineer, verify, and publicize extraordinary breakthrough elections in South Africa, Bosnia, Russia, Nicaragua, and Palestine, Central and Eastern Europe, and elsewhere. Democratic peace, which boiled down to the idea that elected governments do not make war against each other, seemed to be on the march. Even amidst this burst of triumphalism, the 1996 election was an astonishing multilateral undertaking to constitute an 'interim governing authority,' the Palestine Authority, a state-like apparatus linking two territories that heretofore existed in a veritable black hole in the Westphalian system.

The assumption seemed to be that an election would yield sovereignty, democracy, and peace in one fell swoop. The 1993 Oslo Accords between Israel and the Palestine Liberation Organization, the exile group already recognized by the Arab League and the UN General Assembly as the "legitimate representative" of the Palestinian people, specified elections to a National Council as a major step in negotiations that might lead, in phases, to Palestinian statehood. More about peace-making and nation-building than selection of leaders – since it was a foregone conclusion that PLO leader Yasser Arafat and his Fatah party would win – it functioned as a performance of democratic idealism for the international community and, for Palestinian voters in the West Bank and Gaza, evidently, of national self-determination.

The election was an enormous technical and diplomatic challenge met by a vast transnational investment of time and money but shaped, too, by American unilateralism. The unparalleled election would have been unimaginable a few years earlier. Designing, negotiating, and implementing a representative system took hundreds of international experts some years. Since proposals for 'dry run' local votes came to naught, it was really the first election for the Occupied Territories. Intercontinental specialists compared the advantages of district-based and party-list plurality systems. Although Israel ruled out voting by exiles and refugees, the unicameral National Council was deliberately designed to include equal numbers of national-constituency and district-based seats on the premise that eventually the legislature might represent Palestinians living elsewhere under the national constituency. The Oslo Protocol on Elections established criteria for credentialing of inter-governmental, non-governmental, and domestic monitors; and designated the EU as the coordinator of support from Canada, Egypt, Japan, Jordan, Norway, the Russian Federation, South

Africa, the United States, the Islamic Conference, the Movement of Non-Aligned Nations, the Organization of African Unity, and the United Nations. Australia, China, Cyprus, Malta, Switzerland, and Turkey also sent delegations.[49] The EU's Election Unit alone devoted hundreds of specialist-months to drafting the electoral law, making administrative arrangements, and directing public education, and it sent 35 long-term observers who were joined by a former Swedish Minister of Justice, 300 European, and 600 other official observers for the actual balloting.[50] Consultants flew in from Australia, Canada, and around the planet to help with creation of the electoral commission, constituency demarcation, voter registration, candidacy rules, time-tables and budgets, ballot design, campaign ethics, security, placement and staffing of voting stations, and a host of other preparatory tasks to election-day activities and counting procedures.[51]

All this multilateralism was entangled with old-fashioned geopolitical showmanship. European Community spokesman Chris Patten said in June 2002, "We know that a well-governed Palestinian State that follows democratic principles and operates in a predictable and transparent way on the basis of market economy rules is the best security guarantee for its neighbours, and in particular for Israel." The EU was the designated lead actor and financier; Australia, Norway, Canada, France, England, and the United Nations were also major players. Yet the others fumed that Uncle Sam stole the limelight. A European Parliament panel concluded that Europe needed to add "political content" to its vital technical assistance, "which would guarantee the European Union recognition of the efforts made and not merely thanks for having provided the money needed for printing the ballot papers." The Americans "once again were able to present themselves as the instigators of Palestinian democratisation."[52]

---

[49] An authoritative account was offered by The National Democratic Institute for International Affairs and the Carter Center, *The January 20, 1996, Palestinian Elections* (Washington: NDI, 1997).

[50] Alicia Martin Diaz, *The Middle East Peace Process and the European Union*, European Parliament Directorate General for Research Working Paper, Political Series POLI-115EN, Brussels, May 1999.

[51] For painstaking documentation by IFES and other contractors, see, for instance, Keith Klein and Adila R. Laidi, Pre-Election Assessment West Bank and Gaza (Washington: IFES, May 10, 1994); and Hania Bardawil, *IFES West Bank and Gaza Resource Centers' Voter Education Project in Advance of the January 20, 1996, Palestinian Legislative Council and Ra'ess Elections, December 1995-January 1996 Final Activity Report*, Washington, 1996.

[52] Diaz, *The Middle East Peace Process and the European Union*: 38, 68.

Initially congratulating itself for the performance, the White House became frustrated when the democratic peace equation failed to add up to a final Palestinian–Israeli settlement. The Agency for International Development's Democracy and Governance web page still enthused in 2000 that with its support for about 1,500 domestic and 30 foreign monitors and civics lessons reaching some 80,000 voters, "The elections were widely acknowledged to have been free and fair, and provided a strong popular mandate for democratic governance." To policy-watchers it had "appeared that American principles *and* American interests were served" by the victory of Fatah and Arafat in 1996.[53] USAID had followed up with $6 million to contractors and grantees such as Associates in Rural Development (ARD) and NDI for strengthening the Palestine Legislative Council; $2 million for IFES to advise local elections; and state-of-the-art electronics to record legislative proceedings and votes. Working with a local think tank, the Center for Palestine Research and Studies, and consultants from the accounting firm of Arthur Anderson, ARD won several contract extensions to work inside the Palestinian legislature.[54]

Soon these programs came under fire back home in the United States.[55] The outbreak of the second *Intifada* and the expiration of the Oslo Accords that had been the legal basis of the Palestinian Authority stalled the nation-building effort as Israeli forces encircled the PA premises in Ramallah. In early 2002, urging a fresh vote to break the stalemate and encourage the "peace camp," the EU budgeted for another round amidst Israeli accusations that it was "funding terror."[56] An American Pre-Election Assessment cautioned against recklessly "premature" balloting,

[53] Murphy and Gause, "Democracy and U.S. Policy," 60–61.

[54] David Schenker, *Palestinian Democracy and Governance: An Appraisal of the Legislative Council* (Washington: Washington Institute for Near East Policy, 2000), 108–109. See also the series of reports including *Performance Measurement Report #2, Palestinian Legislative Council Report (Final)*, submitted to USAID/West Bank and Gaza, ARD (Associates in Rural Development), Inc., Burlington, Vermont, March 1999.

[55] Funding a non-sovereign entity was difficult for USAID's interstate assistance bureaucracy, as explained by Sara Roy, "U.S. Economic Aid to the West Bank and Gaza Strip: The Politics of Peace" *Middle East Policy*, V-IV:4 (1996) 50–77; and Scott Lasensky, "Underwriting Peace in the Middle East: U.S. Foreign Policy and the Limits of Economic Inducements," *Middle East Review of International Affairs* 6: 1 (2002).

[56] "European Commission approves EUR 5.45 million to support Palestinian reform, plus EUR 2.5 million for election observation mission," IP/02/1901-Brussels, 17 December 2002; Charmaine Seitz, "The Palestinian Elections That Never Were," *Middle East Report Online*, January 24, 2003. Europeans "only scurry around sending emissaries to see Sharon and Arafat, they make ringing declarations in Brussels, they fund a few projects and more or less leave it at that, so great is the shadow of the U.S. over them," wrote Edward Said, "Palestinian Elections Now," *Counterpunch*, June 17, 2002. See also

however, citing insufficient "political time" needed for negotiating rules of the game and "technical" time required for "voter and candidate registration and registration verification; training of election officials and monitors; design, purchase, and delivery of election materials and equipment; and political campaigning."[57] It noted, too, the danger that elections would merely rubber-stamp the existing Fatah leadership. Soon thereafter, an Elections Reform Support Group comprised of representatives of Denmark, Germany, Greece, Ireland, Italy, Japan, the Netherlands, Norway, Spain, Sweden, the UK, the United States, the European Commission, the office of the European Union Presidency, and the United Nations constituted itself. But American concurrence would await Arafat's death several years later. The second Palestinian elections took place a decade after the first, under very different circumstances and with very different outcomes. In the meantime, the chronology takes us first to more routine rounds of voting in sovereign countries and then to the aberrant case of Iraq.

## THE NEW MILLENNIUM

The international elections regime garnered momentum into the twenty-first century, even in the Middle East. In 2000, the UN Commission on Human Rights specifically cajoled one-party states such as Iraq and Egypt to open competition to opposition parties. International IDEA developed Codes of Conduct for Political Parties Campaigning in Democratic Elections and for the Ethical and Professional Observation of Elections and Guidelines for Determining Involvement in International Election Observation. In conversation with International IDEA and other specialized organs, the United Nations issued Principles for International Election Observation and a Code of Conduct for International Election Observers on October 27, 2005. (This was scarcely two months before the Iraqi elections for a permanent legislature.) The rationale for standardized reference points, said a former Canadian Prime Minister, was that "when international election observation missions gather information methodically, comprehensively, and accurately, and analyze it objectively

---

Etgar Leflovits, "Government's 'Arafat File' shows how EU money was used for terror," *Jerusalem Post*, May 6, 2002; Stephen Castle, "Angry EU Denies Claims that Funds Reached Bombers," *The Independent*, May 7, 2002; Chris Patten, "A Road Map Paid for in Euros," *The Financial Times*, 17 July 2003.

[57] Palestinian Elections: A Pre-Election Assessment Mission Report prepared jointly by IFES, IRI, and NDI, August 2002, Washington: 9.

and impartially, the reports they produce will be credible and legitimate in the eyes of both the participating governments and the international community."[58] About two dozen democracy brokers and multilateral institutions from around the world signed on.

Standardized rubrics attempted to address early allegations of partiality, infringement of sovereignty, and snap judgments by devising increasingly precise observable indicators of equal access to the media by all candidates, ballot tampering, undue presence of armed forces around polling stations, and a range of potential procedural violations. Thus the verification became more than just a judgment call. "Sound-bite pronouncements" now seemed to experts a "symptom of inexperience" with the complexities and formal methodologies of evaluation.[59]

Arabic-language manuals were handed out to tens of thousands of poll-watchers, even in some countries that barred foreign monitors. Increasingly, intellectuals, activists, journalists, and university students familiarized themselves with universal standards. While some kingdoms' and party-states' legerdemain in emulating conventions without actually relinquishing power was notable, so, increasingly, was other countries' failure to meet even minimal criteria. Moreover, close coverage of regional elections and monitors' reports in satellite stations including *al-Jazeera* and *al-'Arabiyya* and pan-Arab newspapers, especially *al-Hayat*, familiarized wider audiences with cosmopolitan rules of engagement. Transnational conventions became more familiar; a huge industry with bilingual franchises across the region acquired proficiency in appraising plausible elections. This might be read as the technocratic substitution of external for domestic legitimization; but on the other hand, alumni of short courses on monitoring also constituted a kind of epistemic community that crossed ideological spectrums and national boundaries. Also, cell-phones made it possible for citizen watchdogs armed with a simple questionnaire to compile reports efficiently even where there were no foreigners around.

September 11, 2001 impelled new transnational programs for Arab liberalization. Americans approached the formerly off-limits democracy-deprived monarchies on the Arab side of the Persian Gulf. First-time elections in several GCC countries may have been a direct consequence of American or Western prodding, as Washington asserted, but the role of external agencies inside these self-sufficient polities was minimal. The centerpiece was an NDI/IRI/IFES partnership known as the Consortium

---

[58] Quoted, ibid. Palestinian Elections: A Pre-Election Assessment: 7.
[59] Carothers, 1999, *The Learning Curve*: 134.

for Electoral and Political Processes Support (CEPPS) that opened a Gulf Regional Campaign School to train female and male candidates from Bahrain, Kuwait, Oman, Qatar, the United Arab Emirates, Saudi Arabia, Yemen, and, of course, Iraq. (It was expected to be a model for other Regional Campaign Schools to be opened in the Levant and the Maghreb.) CEPPS spent more than $1 million on consultants and trainers for first-time parliamentary elections in Bahrain and Qatar in 2002 and 2003.

But the Gulf's absolute monarchies remained diffident; these activities were very fractious. In Bahrain, NDI/CEPPS conducted a $400,000 USAID-financed "party strengthening" program, a roundtable on the electoral law, meetings with lawmakers, a Political Organization Leaders' Summit, an assessment of political organizations, and several consultancies between 2003 and 2006 – only to be censured for interference. Amidst a bureaucratic obstacle course and media mudslinging, NDI's country team leader was expelled, at least twice. It was observed that the organization had been accused of both whitewashing and tarring Bahrain's electoral process.[60]

## A FIRST-HAND ACCOUNT: YEMEN 2003

I was once a monitor and was trained in the methodology. For a decade, Ali Abdallah Salih's government had hailed virtually all forms of political aid and democratic publicity, and Yemen unexpectedly became a model for Arab elections and a showcase for democracy brokers' expertise. NDI continued to work with the Supreme Elections Committee (SEC) on regularly scheduled elections. Hundreds of monitors were trained. Courses for parties and partisan and non-partisan female and male candidates were open to all legal organizations, regardless of ideological leanings or democratic credentials: the ruling General People's Congress; the Socialist Party that formerly governed South Yemen; the ultra-conservative Islamist-leaning *al-Islah* (Reform) Party, one of whose founding fathers was prominently listed on the American list of al-Qa'ida terrorists; several Nasirite parties; two branches of the Ba'ath; and two Zaydi-oriented parties, one more liberal than the other although the Yemeni government dubbed them both "royalist." The syllabus covered Yemeni electoral

---

[60] Dina Bishara, "Arab States: Rough Sledding for U.S. Party Aid Organizations," *Arab Reform Bulletin*, 5:6 (2007); Marisa Katz, "Rhetoric v. Reality: Democratease," *The New Republic* June 6, 2005.

law, international electoral conventions, the basics of campaign management, and the monitors' checklist. Here, the etiquette of neutrality also
served an operational goal of putting international consultants and
information-gatherers in direct contact with a wide spectrum of elites.

As a serendipitous member of NDI's delegation to observe Yemen's
April 2003 election, I thought the SEC, its international advisors, and the
American and European monitoring missions had all done their homework.[61] Technical assistance to the Supreme Elections Committee helped
professionalize administrative procedures. The monitoring protocols had
become more refined with geographical sampling, observational checklists, and cell-phone trees. Well-briefed domestic, in-country, and visiting
monitors coordinated their efforts. The short-term observer delegation,
comprised of a couple of dozen people, including several of us "country
specialists," some experienced monitors, quite a few Mediterranean
Arabs, and activists from Turkey, South America, and elsewhere, met in
Sana'a for two days of briefings by NDI, expert, and Yemeni speakers.
Then we were assigned, in pairs, one Arabic speaker per pair, with an
interpreter and a driver, to randomly sampled cities. I went with a Turkish
feminist to al-Mukallah, a steamy Southern town facing the Indian Ocean,
with cell phones and English and Arabic copies of Yemeni laws and
international monitoring instructions in hand. On Election Day we drove
around to visit as many urban and rural polling stations as possible with a
checklist for observations. It was interesting and fun and tiring.

Local volunteers are the real observers at every polling station: in
Yemen, one observer representing each candidate on the local ballot plus
non-partisan independent local monitors sit from when polls open at 7:00
a.m. until at least when the station closes twelve hours later, and usually
into the night as paper ballots are counted. Most had the same training and
manuals we had. We were to spot-check their presence and observations.
In one lush oasis town outside al-Mukallah, a monitor wearing a white
National Democratic Institute Observer banner across her head-to-toe
black veil drew me aside and said, "My colleagues and I want to say we
hate what your country is doing to Iraq, but your delegation is welcome."
Most Americans in the Arab world have heard similar statements, but she

---

[61] The University of Richmond had awarded me a faculty travel grant to watch the May 2003
parliamentary elections as part of this research on what international agencies were doing.
Because the invasion of Iraq was underway as I made travel plans, however, and to quell
the worries of my mother and colleagues about my safety, I contacted the National
Democratic Institute to enquire about their security provisions. NDI graciously invited
me to join its team.

explained that poll-watchers had debated at some length the distinction between American foreign policy and NDI training. Her admonition is my thesis.

We watched local monitors inspect and sometimes quibble over every checkmark and doodle on paper ballots for hours into the evening. Quite a few times they asked our opinions – was this a vote, or a random stroke? It was more folksy than contrived. Back in Sana'a the next day we learned of several incidents: the NDI team heard gunfire near a polling station in Aden; soldiers milled around outside some others; an international delegation was turned back from a military checkpoint north of Sana'a "for their own safety." Moreover, spokespersons for the leading opposition parties, the Socialists and Islah, respectively, came to the Sheba Hotel to file complaints about suspected infractions. Every incident, grievance, and detail of a pretty well-run election was enumerated in the lengthy NDI and EU reports. On the afternoon before our departure the NDI and European delegations had an audience with the Yemeni president. An Italian parliamentarian lectured him on women's rights, but the state-run media's footage showed dignitaries congratulating him on his party's electoral success. I concluded that the incumbent General People's Congress had won 'fair and square' by campaigning on the premise that only the ruling party can deliver patronage.[62]

About eight years later I attended some elections monitoring training sessions facilitated in Arabic in Cairo by Egyptians who had learned the tricks of the trade as volunteer monitors in Yemen, Palestine, or Lebanon.

## UNEVEN SPREAD EFFECT

The same monitoring methodology was applied in Lebanon in 2005 after the so-called Cedar Revolution against Syrian occupation restored long-standing electoral traditions. Lebanon is an Arab exception because instead of a strong executive it is governed by a peculiar constitutional system, designed by the French, drawing somewhat on Ottoman precedents, in which religious communities (principally Maronite, Sunni, and Shi'a) are separately represented, with top posts designated for the major sects; and in that its electoral system survived assassinations, civil wars, and foreign invasions. On technical grounds, its believable elections could be construed as the oft-sought "model for the region." The EU observation

---

[62] Carapico, "How Yemen's Ruling Party Secured an Electoral Landslide," *Middle East Report Online*, May 16, 2003.

mission, comprised of 26 long-term data-collectors, 62 short-term monitors, and additional representatives of the European and Spanish parliaments was given the task of providing "an impartial, balanced and informed assessment of the entire election cycle." Again the team included plenty of Arabs from neighboring countries. Together they observed opening, polling and counting procedures in 1,308 polling stations. On hand, too, were a Francophone team organized by former UN Secretary General Boutros Boutros Ghali, a U.S. Congressional delegation, and more than 400 domestic poll-watchers. The EU's 71-page report was packed with details, explanations, and charts, but refrained from pointing thumbs up or down. The summary began: "The elections were well managed and took place in a peaceful manner within the existing framework." Minor procedural shortcomings indicated the "the need for better preparations." This cautious, technical diction signaled that Lebanon passed snap inspections at 1,300 hundred polling stations, meeting a minimal standard while still needing technical assistance and continued monitoring.

The machinery for designing and/or verifying elections were not applied in either of the countries of greatest American interest at the time, however: Egypt and Iraq. The Mubarak regime blocked a constitutional effort by the relatively independent Egyptian judiciary to exercise their authority to monitor the 2005 elections, and totally barred official foreign observers. Iraqis saw neither the scale nor the professionalism of the 1996 Palestinian elections; observer reports like those on Yemen and Lebanon were not issued.

The most populous Arab state had been the lynchpin of American policy toward Israel's neighbors since the Camp David Accords. Cairo had an imposing, heavily fortified USAID compound, a vast donor community of resident and visiting development experts and democracy brokers, and conferences, workshops, forums, and think-tanks galore. Yet it remained a one-man, one-party police state under continual emergency legislation since Anwar al-Sadat's assassination by Islamist radicals in 1982. President Husni Mubarak and his ruling National Democratic Party won preposterous majorities, evaded inspection, repressed credible opposition candidates, and denied the Egyptian judiciary its constitutional right to validate elections.[63] Following 9/11, Mubarak styled himself as a commandant in the war on radical Islamist terror. But heavy-handed tactics embarrassed the White House. Having postponed a scheduled

---

[63] On the legal issues and the role of the Judges' Club, see Mona El-Ghobashy, "Egypt's Paradoxical Elections," *Middle East Report* 238 (2006) 20–29.

visit in protest against the leading opposition candidate's arrest, Secretary Condoleezza Rice, in her American University in Cairo address, not only admitted that Washington had "turned a blind eye to the absence of democratic forces, to the absence of pluralism in the region," but insisted that Egypt's parliamentary elections "must meet objective standards that define every free election," including freedom to assemble and campaign openly, the absence of violence or intimidation, and "unrestricted access" by international election monitors and observers.

These explicit instructions were ignored by the recipient of $1.8 billion annually in official American aid: about $50 million for good governance, some for socio-economic development, and far more in arms transfers and military training. Pending presidential and parliamentary elections in 2005, another million dollars went toward NGO poll-watcher workshops. Yet despite momentum from the Egyptian judiciary and civic activists, officially neither domestic nor outside monitors were able to perform their duties.[64] After Mubarak scored an incredible eighty-eight percent of officially tally, the White House issued what a leading Republican champion of American democracy promotion bemoaned as "formulaic" and "muted" criticisms of "bloody repression."[65] American, French, and European Union leaders congratulated Mubarak on his victory and hailed the fact of holding multi-candidate presidential elections at all a "historic departure." Rice talked about enabling domestic and international monitors, equal access to the national media, internationally accepted electoral norms, freedom of expression, protection against intimidation, and American support for continuing "progress."[66] Faced with vanilla criticism, Cairo threatened to suspend the International Republican Institute's work on parliamentary elections a couple of months later. Leading democracy brokers fumed over disagreements among the State Department, the White House, embassies abroad, and the Egyptian

---

[64] For the controversies, see Gihan Shahine, "Monitoring Plans Undeterred," *al-Ahram Weekly* No. 757, 25–31 August 2005 and "An ISO Certificate of Democracy," *al-Ahram Weekly* No. 743, 19–25 May 2005; Magda El-Ghitany, "Observing, Not Monitoring," *al-Ahram Weekly* No. 744, 26 May-1 June 2005; and Amr El-Choubaki, "Monitoring the Monitors," *al-Ahram Weekly* No. 757, 25–31 August 2005.

[65] Joshua Muravchik, "A Democracy Policy in Ashes," *Washington Post*, June 27, 2006; Jeffrey Azarva, "U.S. Silence on Egypt Betrays Democracy Activists," *The Baltimore Sun*, June 15, 2006.

[66] Jeremy M. Sharp, "Egypt: 2005 Presidential and Parliamentary Elections," CRS Report for Congress, September 21, 2005:5–6, and Yoram Meital, "The Struggle over Political Order in Egypt: The 2005 Elections," *Middle East Journal*, 60: 2 (2006) 257–279.

government.[67] Before the Mubarak administration's final fraudulent 2010 elections, discussed later, the Egyptian constitution was amended to eliminate judges' responsibility to monitor. There were ironies here besides the oft-noted hypocrisy of the United States in turning a blind eye to electoral fraud. One is why Mubarak's military government, client and ally of Washington, did not take what might have been competent technical assistance to upgrade one-party domination with a more plausible performance of consensual rule.

## REPRESENTING IRAQI REPRESENTATION: 2005

Civilian tools and expertise were available to design and administer elections in post-conflict situations and also to help validate the outcome. If there were ever a time for the highest possible quality of electoral engineering, this was it. Nonetheless, a top-notch marketing campaign notwithstanding, the CPA and the UN together failed to provide a well-designed persuasive system for federal parliamentary representation for Iraq. Instead, potential voters and overseas audiences were treated to a triple-shot performance of the big bang fable of democratization. In January, October, and December of 2005, headlines declared that votes were being prepared for, held, then counted. Consciously or not, Anglophone coverage mostly conveyed the impression that Iraqis or other Arabs had never cast ballots before, evoked a kind of mystique around the act of going to a polling station, and subscribed to the seemingly obvious assumption that Americans and Englishmen know how to hold an election. Given the stakes for the United States, the expertise available, and what I observed in Yemen and read about Palestine, I personally expected first-class election engineering in Iraq.

Instead, the process was neither as well prepared nor as well documented as the Palestinian elections of 1996 or 2006, or several Yemeni elections. There were lots of flaws and irregularities in design, execution, and documentation. Sending voters to the polls at all flew in the face of sensible norms not to schedule balloting when the safety of candidates, voters, and international monitors cannot be protected. Actual performance fell short of criteria applied to Yemen, Rice's advice to Egypt, routine documentation in Lebanon, or even Central American demonstration elections. Well-reasoned academic and expert-practitioner admonitions

---

[67] Lorne Craner, "Will U.S. Democratization Policy Work?" *Middle East Quarterly* 8:3 (2006) 3–10.

about quick electoral fixes and plebiscitary ethnic censuses were whisked aside. Expedience of timing, design, and evaluation overrode the good advice of professionals.

Much of this story is known. After two years of stalling, the Coalition Provisional Authority (CPA) mandated three rounds of balloting in 2005 on scarcely a year's notice. This required extraordinarily swift execution of painstakingly intricate tasks. The CPA squelched early community-level initiatives for local elections in 2003 and 2004, proposals for a national conference to forge an elite consensus, and expert advice to optimize local and popular representation.[68] Instead, willy-nilly, a North Carolina contractor and a development brokerage company were hired to designate hundreds of local officials.[69] In some places, American commanders installed mayors or governors. In Baghdad City, U.S. soldiers vetted candidates for the neighborhood councils, which in turn choose district councils, which in turn elected the City Council.[70] At the national level, CPA head L. Paul Bremer III asked the special UN envoy (the Algerian diplomat who had organized Afghanistan's pre-election national conference) to appoint an Interim Governing Council. Bremer reasoned that "elections would take up to a year to organize. Then the Iraqis would need time to write their constitution, which in turn would have to be submitted for approval by the public in a referendum." This would take two years, he asserted at the time, in an estimate consistent with the Palestinian arrangement.[71] These

---

[68] Christoph Wilcke, "Castles Built of Sand: U.S. Governance and Exit Strategies in Iraq," *Middle East Report* 232 (2004). Larry Diamond, "Building Democracy after Conflict: Lessons from Iraq," *Journal of Democracy* 16:1 (2005) 9–23: on decisions and reversals, 10–12; on the need to "hold local elections first" 18.

[69] Ali A. Allawi, *The Occupation of Iraq: Winning the War, Losing the Peace* (Yale University Press, New Haven: 2007) 110: Bremer "had no intention of agreeing to the formation of a provisional government"; 224–226 on American pressures for UN envoy Lakhdar Brahimi to recommend against early elections. See also William Booth and Rajiv Chandrasekaran, "Occupation Forces Halt Elections throughout Iraq," *Washington Post*, June 28, 2003. On the contracting firm Research Triangle Institute see the International Crisis Group, *Iraq: Can Local Governance Save Central Government? ICG Middle East Report No. 33, 27 October 2004*. Chemonics issued progress reports, i.e., *Chemonics, Democracy and Governance.* "Building Democracy in Iraq," October 7, 2003.

[70] A philosophical contrast between Hannah Arendt's notion of governance by the people and arbitrary CPA and RTI decisions was offered by Gail M. Presbey, "Challenges of Founding a New Government in Iraq," *Constellations* 12: 4 (2005) 521–541. A British diplomat administering four southern provinces reflected thoughtfully: Hilary Synnott, "State-building in Southern Iraq," *Survival*, 47:2 (2005) 33–56.

[71] L. Paul Bremer III, *My Year in Iraq: The Struggle to Build a Future of Hope* (New York: Simon and Schuster: 2006) 210, main quote, "two year" time frame repeated on 212. On

maneuvers put the United States in what the CPA's constitutional consultant called the "'delay elections' camp."[72] And along with such other measures as press censorship, they fed the counter-narrative in the Arabic press about suppressing democratic aspirations and fomenting sectarian strife. In retrospect, almost everyone saw these decisions as politicized, if not the geo-strategic shrewdness of an astute rational actor.

Against so many expert recommendations to have a constitution in place before holding elections, the CPA hired three Americans to draft a constitution-like Transitional Administrative Law (TAL) by June 2004. Vague on electoral arrangements and the nature of the federalism it espoused, the TAL nonetheless mandated deadlines subsequently held to be sacrosanct: a transitional assembly elected by January 31, 2005; the constitutional referendum held by October 15; and a permanent parliament in office by the last day of 2005. This breakneck schedule precluded the political and technical time everyone knew was necessary. It further defied the common-sense legal principle that elections cannot be held amidst violent turmoil.[73] But the TAL deadlines drove the election law, issued by Bremer as Order 96 of June 2004 amidst a phenomenal flurry of end-of-term edicts, specifying a system recommended by the UN's top elections expert as the "most expedient."[74] The same week, the UN formally created the Independent Electoral Commission for Iraq, given the primary task of barring Ba'ath Party candidates.

Electoral architecture structures representation in important ways. There were two rounds of legislative elections in Iraq in 2005. The first

tasks of getting an electoral law and voter lists, see 217. Elections in June 2004, he wrote, 225, would be "doable" but "rough and ready."

[72] Noah Feldman, *What We Owe Iraq: War and the Ethics of Nation Building* (Princeton: Princeton University Press, 2004) 116, and on transformative potential of elections and the "undemocratic nature of the occupation" 111, the longer story, 92–129. See also Peter Baker and Robin Wright, "In Iraq, Bush Pushed for Deadline Democracy," *Washington Post*, December 11, 2005; Rajiv Chandrasekaran, *Imperial Life in the Emerald City*, 244–248; and Kenneth Pollack et al., "A Switch in Time: A New American Strategy for Iraq," Saban Center Analysis 7, Brookings Institution, Washington, February 15, 2005.

[73] HRW warned that campaign violence would discredit the process, in "Iraqi Elections: Human Rights Concerns: Questions and Answers from Human Rights Watch," January 21, 2005.

[74] Perelli defended the timetable to reporters in a Coalition Provisional Authority Press Conference with Carina Perelli, Head of the UN Electoral Assistance Mission to Iraq, Baghdad, Iraq, April 15, 2004; see also Colum Lynch, "U.S. Troops' Role in Iraqi Elections Criticized by U.N. Official Assails Distribution of Material," *Washington Post*, January 27, 2005; Colum Lynch, "Report Cites Mismanagement in U.N. Elections Office," *Washington Post*, March 31, 2005.

utilized the most streamlined, undifferentiated of all available systems of representation; in the second round, a very complicated system replaced it. In the first round, in January, the expedient decision was to create a single national constituency for a unicameral transitional legislature elected from closed party lists. It had numerous sub-optimal ramifications. The presumed virtue of the at-large constituency system for the 275-member Transitional National Assembly (and, similarly, for eighteen Governorate Councils and the semi-autonomous Kurdistan National Assembly) was that all votes nationwide for a single chamber of parliament were tallied together. In other words, all national legislators were to represent not localities or governorates but the whole of Iraq. This is a mathematically simple formula: one person, one vote, one count. It is a single national constituency, not a federal system. The CPA had argued that a more federal system of geographic representation would necessitate a technically difficult and time-consuming census or sophisticated mapping. Even if existing district boundaries were unsuitable, and redrawing them was technically problematic, however, there were not practical barriers to provincial representation for seats in the Assembly (or for an upper chamber in a bicameral parliament). Voters got different color-coded ballots for the Governorate Councils that were counted in each province; color-coding could have been used for provincial seats in the national legislature, too. The idea of nationwide rather than regional representation was complemented by the extraordinary effort to establish extra-territorial polling stations in Iran, Jordan, the United States, and around the world to enable Iraqis abroad to exercise their citizenship.[75]

This design skewed the regional and communal distribution of seats. In particular, the at-large constituency system turned out to exacerbate ramifications of the election boycott in three central governorates the Americans called the Sunni Triangle. (By contrast, geographic constituency representation in a federal system is not affected by differential voter turnout rates in different provinces.) In the end, the under-representation of communities who were not convinced that casting votes would give them fair representation led to prolonged behind-closed-doors post-election bargaining and ultimately to inter-sectarian violence.

[75] Possibly this system was designed to sweep former exiles appointed by the UN at the behest of the CPA back into office: Tareq Y. Ismael and Jacqueline S. Ismael, "Whither Iraq? Beyond Saddam, Sanctions and Occupation." *Third World Quarterly*, 26: 4–5 (2005) 609–629: 626–627; Pollack, "A Switch in Time," 87–89; and Patrick Clawson, "Forward Progress," *New Republic Online*, December 15, 2005.

At-large national-constituency systems with low thresholds for representation tend to promote large numbers of small parties, whereas single-member geographic constituencies favor fewer larger parties. In Iraq in January 2005, nearly 100 different, mostly newly-founded parties entered the contest. The designers of the system for the January elections further opted, partly to protect candidates' physical safety, for what is known as a 'closed' party-list system that lists parties but not their candidates' names. This meant that the identities of the 7,000 candidates running for office were not disclosed. During the foreshortened campaign, therefore, voters were given ballots listing the names and pictorial logos of 99 parties but not the names of candidates.[76] Among other things this made it nearly impossible to tell whether women's names were represented on party lists as mandated by the announced gender quota. Compounding these architectural deficiencies, a three-day curfew was imposed before the vote. This alone would have cast serious doubt on elections in Yemen (or Nigeria, or most other countries). Moreover, after voters went to the polls, three months passed before a government was named, evidently after ex post facto negotiation within and among parties over who had won what. Safety was compromised, and the connection between going to the polls and naming a government was far from transparent.

To be sure, some multinational know-how was brought to bear by European and United Nations personnel advising from the Green Zone or Amman; Canadian, Japanese, and German out-of-country training for elections officials; and other nations' facilitation of expatriate voter-registration. The European Commission donated costs for 35 UN staffers, three European elections specialists, and other kinds training and advice. But neither the UN, citing its role in preparing the elections, nor the EU, citing security concerns, nor the OSCE, fresh from its leading role in the Ukrainian elections, was prepared to send anyone into the maelstrom.[77] In December 2004, Elections Canada, together with the United Nations and the Independent Electoral Commission of Iraq, convened an Ottawa

---

[76] Some argued that the voting was deliberately manipulated: Carl Conetta, "The Iraqi Election "Bait and Switch: Faulty Poll will not Bring Peace or U.S. Withdrawal," Project for Defense Alternatives Briefing Report #17, January 25, 2005; Seymour M. Hersch, "Did Washington Try to Manipulate Iraq's Election?" *The New Yorker*, July 25, 2005.

[77] Mark Turner and Roula Khalaf, "UN Diplomats Warn over Iraqi Election Monitoring," *Financial Times*, January 20, 2005, reported "Monitoring is a big problem. 'There won't be any international observation mechanism,' said one UN diplomat. 'The UN is not willing. No one is willing. No one wants to send their people there.'" Peter Beaumont, "Fresh Doubts over Iraq Elections," *The Observer*, December 5, 2004, quoted UN envoy Lakhhdar Brahimi's reservations about polling amidst so much violence.

forum to establish an International Mission for Iraqi Elections (IMIE) led by a steering committee of elections officials from Canada, the UK, Indonesia, Mexico, Panama, Albania, other Eastern European countries, Yemen, and the Arab League.[78] With money from the Federal Foreign Office, the *Friedrich Ebert Stiftung* nurtured a network of Iraqi non-governmental organizations, coordinated by two NGOs called *Tammuz* and *Shams*, and held seminars for 120 Iraqis in Amman, Jordan. With this indispensable training, domestic monitors did their best.

International monitors were scared off, however. Amidst near anarchy, IMIE fielded only one foreigner to observe in-country balloting by 14 million Iraqis.[79] No established professional organizations published formal reports that I could find. A domestic Election Information Network (EIN, an acronym that sounds like the Arabic word for "eye"), acknowledging NDI, UN, and EU assistance, issued via cell-phone trees messages from its 10,000 members who checked eighty percent of polling places throughout the day, and concluded, according to its web site on January 31, 2005, that "despite problems which can be considered modest under the circumstances, the election appears to have been conducted without systemic flaws and in accordance with basic international standards."

Topping this, London's Department for International Development (DFID) glowed that "On 30 January, ordinary Iraqis bravely took to the polls to cast their votes in the first democratic elections in Iraq for over 50 years. This was an historic occasion, marking a highly significant stage in Iraq's political process. The high level of participation demonstrated that the majority of Iraqis support the political process, even in the face of violence and intimidation."[80] So, in a way, the performance conveyed to Anglophone audiences a 'significant' breakthrough. On the other hand, an opinion writer in *al-Ahram Weekly* ridiculed "the congenital defect of a sloppy election conceived by, and under, military occupation and lacking even the façade of any international body that might guarantee its legitimacy."[81]

---

[78] Elections Canada Press Release, "Establishment of an International Mission for Iraqi Elections," December 20, 2004.

[79] Robin Wright, "No Foreign Observers to Monitor Iraq Vote," *Washington Post*, January 22, 2005, reported that the EU and the Carter Center declined to send observers. Barbara Slavin, "In Iraq, Setting Election Date the Easiest Part," *USA Today*, November 23, 2004, reported that whereas the U.N. deployed 266 personnel for the Afghan elections, there were only ten U.N. staffers a month before Iraq's, expected to increase to twenty-five in December.

[80] "Elections in Iraq," Department for International Development, Iraq Update Issue 6, February 2005.

[81] Sinan Antoon, "Democracy and Necrology," *al-Ahram Weekly* No. 727, 27 January-February, 2005.

FIGURE 3. An Iraqi shows a ballot marked "YES" before casting it in a polling station in Mosul, October 15, 2005. The photographer's caption continues: "Armed men with assault rifles warned civilians that a polling station would be attacked, and handed out leaflets depicting a donkey (ass) voting in front of a figure of Uncle Sam in a bid to disrupt the voting process." Photo: Mujahed Mohammed/AFP/Getty Images. Used with permission.

After selecting from a list of 99 choices in January, Iraqis got to vote yea or nay in the October 15 constitutional referendum. With the TAL clock ticking, transitional appointees belatedly designated a parliamentary constitutional drafting committee, which in turn got a scant couple of months to do its work.[82] There was inadequate time for public deliberation; IFES was printing the official version of the text a week before the plebiscite, while other drafts were still in circulation. Security precautions scuttled most of the planned mass meetings and public debates. As noted in the last chapter, however, the multimedia public relations campaign was well-designed to present voters with a simple choice: 'yes' to the constitutional project; or 'no'. Figure 3 shows a sample ballot in Arabic and Kurdish marked with the correct response, 'yes.' Recall also the other pro-constitutional posters mentioned and/or illustrated in the previous chapter.

British and American officials and English-language media celebrated that the majority of those who cast ballots checked the 'yes' box, signifying

---

[82] For details, see *Unmaking Iraq: A Constitutional Process Gone Awry* International Crisis Group Middle East Briefing No. 19, 26 September 2005.

support for a new constitution. Verification of the vote did not stand up to
the advertising, however. The Next Century Foundation, an American
group identifying itself as "the only international observers operating at
large in the interior of Iraq," fielded a team of about twenty soldiers and
civilians. Its blog posts on November 3 and December 10 noted minor
irregularities, but deemed the exercise honest, fair, credible, and an accurate reflection of the views of the Iraqi people. Perhaps, but they did not
explain their methodology. The Tammuz Organization for Social
Development and other Iraqi NGOs fielded thousands of volunteers and
issued memos on the tallying process, and my purpose is not to discredit
those efforts. As discussed in the chapter on law, however, it was unclear if
the constitution or the referendum held for most Iraqis the momentous
import inferred by the British and American governments and media.

Still seemingly determined to set off the big bang that would ignite Iraqi
democracy and give them an "exit strategy," authorities scheduled a third
round of balloting for 2005.

This time, tacitly admitting design flaws in elections for the transitional
legislature, experts recommended a revised representation system for the
new National Assembly balloting. This happened on short notice in
advance of the TAL's deadline and the vote scheduled for December 15.
Hoping to counteract the deleterious effects of a potential boycott, UN
consultants drew up – and the transitional assembly adopted – a new two-
tiered system with 230 provincial seats and 45 national-constituency seats
representing, inter alia, overseas voters. Also, a robust gender quota
requiring one female for every two males on party candidate lists, recommended by International IDEA, the United Nations, and the TAL, was
given greater force for this round. Seats in the single-chamber legislature
were to be apportioned to party lists according to a mind-boggling two-
step mathematical formula.[83] One advisor to Iraq's electoral commission

---

[83] According to Adeed Dawisha and Larry Diamond, "Iraq's Year of Voting Dangerously,"
*Journal of Democracy* 17: 2 (2006) 89–103, "the seats in parliament were filled in two
steps. First, the number of votes cast in each province (formally called governorates) was
divided by the number of allocated seats to produce the 'governorate quota.' Any party
that achieved the quota was entitled to one seat, and additional seats were allocated in
multiples of the quota. This process was repeated in every province to fill the 230 district-
based Assembly seats. The remaining 45 seats were then distributed first among the parties
and entities that did not win seats on the provincial level but were able to accumulate votes
nationally equal to or higher than the 'national electoral quota.' This quota was arrived at
by dividing the total number of votes in the country by the number of Assembly seats,
(275). Only one party was able to earn a seat through this compensatory process. The
remaining 44 seats were then distributed among all participating parties in accordance

FIGURE 4. Iraqis walk by a billboard representing a sample ballot in Baghdad, December 10, 2005, and other campaign banners. Photo: Mohammed Hato/AP Photo. Used with permission.

labeled it a "strange pseudo-compensatory hybrid" system.[84] In contrast with the extremely simple system for electing in January the transitional parliament, the new architecture proved difficult to explain to voters, even with full-color maps and illustrated diagrams. This time, the ballot offered voters a dizzying array of more than 200 choices among parties, coalitions, and individual candidates. Figure 4 shows men walking by a billboard-sized "sample ballot" and a smaller campaign banner. Many other full-color posters, brochures, diagrams, illustrations, and billboards explained the confusing process.

In addition to publicity, cash, expertise, and publicity were invested in procurement, outreach, and training. IFES obtained election supplies from a Canadian company; polling station kits and ink from a Danish firm, DCS Group, which equipped the Palestinian election too; and tamper-proof ballot boxes, ballots, and counting devises from specialized companies

---

with their respective national vote shares. Expatriate voting, which took place in 15 countries, was designed to claim a portion of these seats. The Independent Electoral Commission of Iraq (IECI) announced on October 29 that 228 political parties, coalitions, and other entities had registered to compete in the elections," 95–96.

[84] Jarrett Blanc, "Rules do Matter: What the Iraqi and Palestinian Elections Tell Us," IFES, March 1, 2006.

around the globe. According to a bulletin on its web site, "Building on the successes of the January national and provincial elections, USAID coordinated with the Independent Election Commission in Iraq (IECI) and supported Iraqi civil society groups reaching out to voters" with comprehensive voter mobilization and public awareness campaigns. Infomercials, public service announcements, and *al-Hurra*, the broadcast voice of America in Iraq, pitched the constitution and the elections. IRI brought in Republican public relations talent to set up a press center in Baghdad and teach American-style campaign strategies to candidates and their managers. As British Prime Minister Tony Blair had done before the January elections, American Secretary of Defense Donald Rumsfeld and Vice President Dick Cheney each flew to Baghdad with reporters and camera crews in tow. A big to-do was made of purple fingers as an indicator of societal acclamation.

More local watchdogs were posted than in January, thanks in part to monitor-training workshops by USAID, NDI, IFES, and the *Ebert Stiftung* in Amman. EIN, the coalition of Iraqi NGOs, issued observations from its 14,000 poll-watchers on Election Day. Trainings and trainer-trainings, widely available Arabic-language manuals, and the cell-phone trees activated for communications, constituted a veritable "epistemic network" or "community of democrats" in which Iraqis joined tens of thousands of Arabic speakers between the Mediterranean and the Indian Ocean trained to recognize the hallmarks of a properly-run election.

International monitoring was still ad hoc, however, compared with Lebanon or Palestine. IMIE, the organ created in Ottawa a year earlier, deployed nearly 400 people to witness overseas voting in 15 countries.[85] About 850 foreigners were reportedly accredited as domestic observers by Iraq's electoral commission, among them two Members of the European Parliament, one Romanian MP, and representatives of IMIE, the National Democratic Institute, an American group called the Arabic Center for Independent Judges and Lawyers, an Egyptian organization called INSAN/Movement for Peace and Disarmament, the UK's Next Century Foundation, Norwegian People Aid, the German Valley Organization, and Baghdad-based diplomats from Denmark, Canada, Italy, Japan, Netherlands, Romania, Sweden, UK, and the United States. According to a Foreign Office news release, they were able to visit polling stations in

---

[85] International Mission for Iraqi Elections, "IMIE Releases Preliminary Statement on Iraq OCV," December 16, 2005; on the post-facto monitoring, Patrick Quinn, "International Team to Review Iraq Results," *Washington Post*, December 30, 2005.

Baghdad, Basra, and Kurdistan.[86] IMIE conceded that they were "recruited mainly from in-country international organizations and embassies" and that the "absence of a more extensive international observer presence" in light of safety issues "put a special burden on ... domestic monitors."[87] In the end, indeed perhaps prematurely, and contrary to industry conventions, the head of the 50-person UN team, citing some 120,000 Iraqi poll workers and watchers nationwide, reassured web site visitors that voting had been "transparent and credible." But this was the defense of the architect, not the finding of the inspector.

Actually the process was rife with irregularities and violence. I am not saying that it was fixed, but rather substandard. The massive deployment and involvement of (Anglo-American) military forces in everything from the designation of local leaders to the distribution of propaganda ought to have been red flags, as were credible reports of intimidation by various security forces.[88] In response to numerous complaints, and amidst calls for a boycott of the new parliament by a coalition of several dozen disgruntled Iraqi parties, IMIE sent two Arabs, a Canadian, and a European to Iraq in late December to investigate.[89] Other rumors of malfeasance circulated, even in the United States.[90] Also, although unlike in January this time the results were tallied at the provincial level, which was an improvement, the failure to hold the scheduled concurrent elections to Provincial Councils threw the constitutionality of the exercise into doubt. In the event, on account of the anonymity of party-list candidates and the complexity of

[86] Amidst many sketchy accounts and now-defunct internet links, a more complete account was Jeff Fisher's "Council of Representatives Election Composite Report, Iraq, December 15, 2005 Final Report," IFES Center for Transitional and Post-Conflict Justice, Washington, February 20, 2006, a signed 21-page analysis that examined turnout, complaints, and other factors (but not sampling or procedural notes).

[87] IMIE Assessment Team Final Report, January 19, 2006: 5.

[88] United Press International, "Coercion Marred Iraqi Elections," December 20, 2005; Jonathan Finer, "In Iraq, Signs of Political Evolution," *Washington Post*, December 8, 2005, wrote: "Television and radio airwaves are replete with slick advertisements costing anywhere from $1,250 per minute on al-Sumariya, a Lebanon-based satellite station focused on Iraq, to $5,000 per minute on *al-Arabiya*, a network based in the United Arab Emirates."

[89] International Mission for Iraqi Elections, "IMIE Releases Preliminary Statement on Iraq OCV," December 16, 2005; Patrick Quinn, "International Team to Review Iraq Results," *Washington Post*, December 30, 2005.

[90] See the controversial report of The Project on Defense Alternatives, "Masque of Democracy: Iraqi Election System Still Disfavors Sunni Arabs, Favors Kurds." PDA Briefing Memo #35, 10 December 2005. See also Omar Fekeiki and Jonathan Finer, "Iraqi Political Parties Threaten a Boycott, Coalition Demands New Elections," *Washington Post*, December 23, 2005.

apportioning seats among 220 parties and organizations according to an advanced-math formula, individual winners' names were not posted until twelve weeks later. Five months after votes were cast, the new government was formed. In the next chapter I will quote quite a few Iraqi women skeptical about this process.

In other words, instead of engendering faith in a system of representation, this supposedly decisive electoral exercise ushered in months of behind-the-scenes horse-trading. It looked to the authors of the 1984 book entitled *Demonstration Elections* like a bad remake. Citing strife, the closure of *al-Jazeera* in Baghdad, and other campaign-season irregularities, one of them characterized the "calculated use of voter turnout as a measure of approval of the election and occupation itself, with the opposition of rebels serving as the dramatic counterpart of the contest. If people voted despite that rebel opposition it supposedly demonstrated the populace's support of the official candidates – and of the occupation – and rejection of any opposition."[91] The multimillion dollar advertising campaign to brand Iraq's elections as a shining example and the special figurative significance Americans vested in pictures of Iraqis with purple forefingers looked inane to Yemenis and Algerians who had inked their digits only to face civil war and the re-assertion of military-backed ruling parties.

In Iraq, then, although the semantics and optics of free-and-fair elections appealed to American and British leaders and electorates, standard rubrics for electoral assessment were suspended. Instead, ad hoc arrangements amidst inauspicious circumstances made the performance a far cry from the "model for the region" the White House claimed. For all the expertise in electoral design, one would have expected higher quality engineering when Western professionals had a chance to devise an Arab democracy from scratch. Instead, the Iraqi electoral arrangement assumed some of the peculiarities of the French-designed Lebanese sectarian system, matched an Arab narrative about divide-and-rule neo-colonialism, and fueled sectarian strife. The international stamp of approval in the form of long dry technical documentation was missing. Let us not entertain fantastic conspiracy theories that circulated in the Arabic media about American designs to hand Iraq over to pro-Iranian Shi'a zealots. Nonetheless, I submit

---

[91] Quoted, Edward S. Herman, "The Election in Iraq: The U.S. Propaganda System is Still Working in High Gear," ZNet Iraq, February 13, 2006; also, Frank Brodhead, "Reframing the Iraq Election," ZNet Iraq, January 21, 2005.

that because of disruptures between short-term American self-interest and professional rubrics, 'the international community' failed to provide the detailed factual certification that might counter such rumors. Also, whereas British and North American reporters and readers may have put Iraq's December elections on a different page from Palestinian balloting weeks later, it is not unreasonable to assume that some Jordanians or other Arabs following the news would connect the two events. Although similar in that in both cases foreign powers determined whether and when votes would be cast, the contrast in the monitoring effort and the reactions from Western officials was quite remarkable.

## AN ELECTORAL TURNOVER: PALESTINE 2006

The next month there was a watershed in the Palestinian Territories: a ruling party narrowly lost a hotly contested election. This had not happened in the Arab world for decades. Under a revised system combining district and at-large representation, the Islamist pariah party, Hamas, won 74 of 132 seats over the now-Western-backed Fatah. Then the United States and other Western powers and pundits repudiated extraordinarily transparent results. Here was the long-dreaded "double negative whammy": the conclusion of by-the-book procedures instituted by a massive transnational nation-building program was unsatisfactory to Israel and NATO. The disjuncture between the foreign-policy pronouncements of North Atlantic leaders and universal protocols for verifying the procedural aspects of elections were thrown into sharp contrast.

Standards of impartiality had already been breached by the time the vote was taken in January 2006. After Arafat's death in November 2004, Washington finally threw its weight behind Palestinian elections. Further, the United States unabashedly backed the presidential bid of a chief Oslo negotiator, Mahmud Abbas, Arafat's heir. On the advice of Associates in Rural Development, the consulting firm that worked inside the Palestinian legislature, and its subcontractor, Strategic Assessments, USAID launched a media promotional drive touting the accomplishments of the PA under Fatah.[92] In a similar vein, spokesman Javier Solana threatened to withhold

---

[92] Scott Wilson and Glen Kessler, "U.S. Funds Enter Fray in Palestinian Elections: Bush Administration Uses USAID as Invisible Conduit," *Washington Post*, January 22, 2006, emphasize the departure from traditional USAID transparency directives in publicity crediting the PA, not USAID, for popular projects.

the considerably larger package of EU aid to the PA in the event of a Hamas victory.[93]

There was no gainsaying the unusually transparent result. It was reported that 800 visitors including former American, Swedish, and French leaders, two Congressional delegations, and 27 European Parliamentarians joined more than 17,000 domestic volunteers to watch 1.3 million voters cast ballots. A total of 185 EU observers who sampled more than 800 polling stations in 14 of the 16 electoral districts published a 7-page preliminary statement noting that delegates were kept out of two districts in Gaza, that disturbances in the lead-up "at times threatened to prevent the holding of elections," and that Israeli forces obstructed some stations in East Jerusalem. But they described an overall orderly process during the campaign, registration, voting, and counting. The 48-page final report analyzed relevant legislation, voter and candidate registration, access to media, campaign procedures, the role of women, voting procedures, the tallying and release of results, individual complaints by defeated candidates, and methods of data collection to substantiate its opening statement called the elections "successful" and "open and fairly contested."[94] The European Parliament's spokesperson called them "extremely professional, in line with international standards, free, transparent and without violence" and even "a model for the wider Arab region."[95] The 85-member NDI/Carter Center team deemed the process consistent with the Declaration of Principles for International Election Observation, cosmopolitan norms, and Palestinian law.[96] Jimmy Carter used the words orderly, peaceful, honest, fair, and safe, and acknowledged the clear voter preference for Hamas candidates.[97] Unlike in Iraq, there were lots of

---

[93] Nathalie Tocci, "Has the EU Promoted Democracy in Palestine? And Does It Still?" *CFSP Forum*, 4: 2 (2006) 7–10.

[94] European Union Election Observation Mission West Bank and Gaza 2006, Statement of Preliminary Conclusions and Findings, "Open and well-run parliamentary elections strengthen Palestinian commitment to democratic institutions," Jerusalem, January 26, 2006; and the press release of the Members of the European Parliament, "MEPs oversee historic Palestinian election," January 30, 2006.

[95] European Union Election Observation Mission West Bank and Gaza, "Statement of Preliminary Conclusions and Findings," Jerusalem, 26 January 2006.

[96] Preliminary Statement of the NDI/Carter Center International Observer Delegation to the Palestinian Legislative Council Elections, 26 January, 2006. An analysis for IFES noted that the unusual "mixed" system may have contributed to the Hamas victory: Jarrett Blanc, "Palestinian Election Analysis: How Hamas Won the Majority," *IFES Features*, February 20, 2006.

[97] "Palestinian Elections: Trip Report by Former U.S. President Jimmy Carter," The Carter Center, January 30, 2006.

FIGURE 5. Members of a European Union mission observe Palestinian security forces voting early in the Palestinian Legislative Council elections at a polling station January 21, 2006, in Gaza City. Photo: Abid Katib/Getty Images. Used with permission.

photographs of European and international monitors on hand for the exercise. One such picture appears in Figure 5.

Defying normal conventions, world powers encouraged the losing party, Fatah, not to honor the results. The Middle East 'Quartet' of the UN, the United States, the EU, and Russia issued a contorted statement calling the election "free, fair and secure," yet "at odds" with "the building of a democratic State."[98] Washington urged other Quartet members to deny aid to a Hamas-run government, and having heretofore advocated a strong Prime Minister to counter Arafat's presidential powers, sought to fortify the executive by training and arming a Presidential Security Guard.[99] A former U.S. diplomat used the words "erratic" and

---

[98] Secretary-General SG/2103 PAL/2041, "Statement on Palestinian Elections by Middle East Quartet," January 26, 2006.

[99] The genuine legal conundrum was analyzed by Aaron D. Pina, "Palestinian Elections," Congressional Research Service Report for Congress, February 9, 2006, and Tim Youngs, "The Palestinian Parliamentary Elections and the Rise of Hamas," Research Paper 06/17, House of Commons Library, London, 15 March 2006. It was a mistaken, vacillating policy, according to Keir Prince, "Palestinian Authority Reform: Role of the International Community," *Arab Reform Bulletin*, 5:9 (2007).

"convolutions" to characterize this policy.[100] An Arab-American intellectual compared Abbas's putsch to Pinochet's U.S.-backed coup against the
elected Allende government in Chile.[101] The European Union scrambled
for ways to extend humanitarian assistance that would bypass the Hamas-
led government, eventually stranded in Gaza while Western powers sought
to shore up a rump PA in the West Bank. Canada, a major donor,
suspended its financial commitments. Instead of being urged to accept
the outcome of a transparent ballot, Fatah was encouraged to make war
on Hamas.

This backward conditionality flouted the ethos of fair play encoded in
election observation manuals and training. Since these matters were covered closely in the Arabic language press, informed publics noted dispar-
ities between Iraq and Palestine in the right of exiles to vote, the
smoothness of the process, assessment against conventional benchmarks,
outside inspection of polling stations, overall security, the clarity of the
voter preferences, and, of course, the reactions from Washington, London,
and Ottawa. Later, a European researcher admonished that the EU had
lost "credibility as a normative actor" due to its boycott of the Hamas
government, partisan backing of Fatah, and subsequent failure to push for
scheduled elections to go forward.[102]

Thanks largely to international assistance, the 2006 Palestinian parliamentary elections were so correctly executed that they yielded a milestone
defeat of an incumbent party to its campaign rivals. This was historic for
the Arab region. Nonetheless, Europe and North America defied procedural norms by openly supporting Fatah during the campaign and the
ensuing armed confrontation. If monitoring were supposed to ensure that
all parties, including the losers, would submit, then the effort had malfunc-
tioned. Perhaps Washington and Brussels rejected the Hamas victory on
principled grounds, because, as they said, it is a terrorist organization that
refuses to recognize Israel. Nonetheless, because of the scope of the international monitoring process, everyone recognized that they were a legal
party successful in a competitive contest against a discredited and corrupt
incumbent ruling party.

---

[100] Philip C. Wilcox, Jr., "U.S. Policy and Palestine: Reform and Peace are Interdependent,"
*Arab Reform Bulletin*, 4:9 (2006).
[101] Joseph Massad, "Subverting Democracy," *al-Ahram Weekly*, No. 851, 28 June–4 July
2007.
[102] Daniela Huber, "Is the EU losing credibility in Palestine?" FRIDE Policy Brief No. 50,
Madrid, June 2010.

## THE END OF ELECTORAL EXPERIMENTATION

Culminating over ten years of great expectations for electoral makeovers, 2005/2006 seemed at the time the year of elections, a potential watershed even in the arid Middle East. In retrospect, it was the crest of the wave. Erstwhile Northern enthusiasts now cautioned that the dénouement, as in Algeria, Yemen, Palestine, and Iraq, can bring Islamist gains, internecine violence, or both; or they can merely ratify the status quo as at other times in Egypt, Yemen, Jordan, Morocco, and Algeria. Country by country, results were disheartening to those who had put great stock in the promotion of elections. Professionals in the European Election Coordination Group, among others, were engaged in soul-searching over the anomalies between elections observation and terrorism lists, the expense of fielding foreign monitors, the tensions between promoting elections and promoting regime change, and trade-offs between fostering free competitive elections and other EU foreign policy goals.[103]

Double standards won out, as anyone watching closely could attest. Palestinian legislative elections and a separate round of local and municipal elections, both scheduled for 2010, were cancelled by the Fatah-run PA executive with what a prominent Palestinian intellectual called "the willing participation of the United States and European governments in the abrogation of the democratic process."[104] The Rand Corporation, a nominally private think tank that generates advice for the American military, attributed Washington's "deferral of domestic experiments" and the "declining cachet for democratization" to belated recognition that "the wrong people can win."[105] According to the UNDP's *Arab Human Development Report*, after the Hamas victory the United States shifted its attention away from democracy back toward pressuring Jordan and Egypt to support American-sponsored peace talks with Israel.[106]

Only two countries' elections passed muster in the next half-decade, with lackluster results: Morocco and Lebanon. Morocco crept closer to

[103] European Parliament's Committee on Foreign Affairs and Committee on Development *EU Election Observation: Achievements, Challenges*, EU EOM paper, Brussels, June 2008.
[104] Mustafa Barghouthi, "The Slow Death of Palestinian Democracy," *Foreign Policy*, July 21, 2010.
[105] Frederic Wehrey et. al., *The Iraq Effect: The Middle East after the Iraq War*, Rand Project Air Force, Santa Monica, 2010: 102–103.
[106] UNDP, *Arab Human Development Report 2009: Challenges to Human Security in Arab Countries*, United Nations Development Program, New York, 2009: 75–76.

compliance in 2007 with the monitoring regime even while concentrating power in the hands of the new king. There was ample assistance from the European Instrument on Democracy and Human Rights and German and American agencies.[107] NDI sent pre-election experts and deployed volunteers from 19 different countries to visit 375 polling stations and train 2,000 domestic observers fielded by an NGO called the *Collectif Rabat* accredited at the eleventh hour; true to form, NDI's report combined criticisms with procedural recommendations including prompt posting of precinct level results and electoral code amendments guaranteeing full access by domestic and international observers.[108]

For Lebanon's parliamentary contest in 2009, NDI sent a 44-member team "to demonstrate the interest of the international community in the development of the democratic political process and governance in Lebanon and to present an accurate and impartial assessment of the political environment" and published an official report three weeks after polling.[109] Ninety people joined the EU Election Observation Mission (EOM), which issued a 33-page, 15-chapter well-footnoted final report covering the major points in the Declaration of Principles: the legal and administrative framework; the campaign environment; voter and candidate registration; the roles of the media, civil society, and women; the election-day experience; access to polling stations by people with disabilities; counting and the announcement of results, complaints and appeals; and recommendations. It noted public trust in the electoral process, the neutrality and professionalism of the Ministry of Interior in its administration, a well-maintained security environment, and the posting of results outside polling stations for an extra measure of transparency.[110]

Even as Morocco and Lebanon aspired to keep pace with international standards, other allies eschewed good advice on how to conduct credible elections. Yemen misspent its reputation for relative concordance with monitoring norms on a grandiose multi-million dollar spectacle of

---

[107] Sylvia Bergh, "Morocco: A Centrally Steered Semi-Authoritarian State?" in Netherlands Institute for Multiparty Democracy, *Beyond Orthodox Approaches: Assessing Opportunities for Democracy Support in the Middle East and North Africa*, NIMD/Hivos, The Hague, 2010: 24.

[108] NDI, Final Report on the Moroccan Legislative Elections, September 7, 2007: 23.

[109] NDI, Final Report on the 2009 Lebanese Parliamentary Elections, NDI, Washington, March 1, 2009.

[110] European Union Election Observation Mission to Lebanon, "Final Report on the 7 June 2009 Parliamentary Elections," EUEOM, Brussels, 2009.

presidential power.[111] While the military government then suspended electoral processes, rounded up dissident journalists, repressed protests, and generally reversed the halting post-unification process of constitutional democratization, the United States rapidly scaled up its heretofore modest economic and military package to fortify the state security apparatus's capacity to go after al-Qa'ida's Arabian Peninsula branch.[112] Notwithstanding the suspension of elections and legitimate stakeholder pleas, one expert admitted, European reports seemed to validate the ruling party's landslide victory.[113]

Jordan, so compliant with many international legal conventions, also regarded electoral scrutiny as adversarial. In 2007 there was quite a scuffle to get even domestic monitors certified at the Ministry of the Interior and the national human rights council. Although transnational democracy brokers supported domestic observer activities, evidently they did not even apply for accreditation themselves. A couple of years later, the king decided to dissolve parliament and postpone the next scheduled round of elections. In 2010, polling was marked by violence and a resounding victory for incumbent power-holders. NDI's preliminary press release on the November 9 elections noted numerous allegations of vote-buying, frequent reports of voters turned away from polling stations, confusion over "virtual" sub-districts, the abnormally high number of illiterate voters, the presence of plain clothes security personnel inside polling centers, and the boycott of the elections by the kingdom's largest organized political party; but found reason in the twelve seats set aside for women and the precedent set by the presence of international monitors to call the exercise an "improvement."[114]

Monitoring was flawed, then, and influenced by politics. It reproduced simplifications about very gradual, guided transitions to pro-Western "democracies." Yet, at the same time, international scrutiny did signal relatively greater transparency. Stalwart ally Husni Mubarak flunked the minimal test while scoffing at lessons that might possibly have saved his

[111] Wedeen, *Peripheral Visions*, analyzes the performative aspects of a patently bogus election.

[112] Sheila Carapico, "Special Operations in Yemen," The Middle East Channel, *Foreign Policy*, Thursday, May 13, 2010; Carapico, "Kill the Messengers: Yemen's 2009 Clampdown on the Press," The Middle East Institute, *Viewpoints* No. 11, June 2009: 6–7.

[113] Richard Youngs, "How to Revitalize Democracy Assistance: Recipients' Views," FRIDE Working Paper 100, Madrid, 15/06/2010:11, adding: "'So much for listening to local actors' was the justifiable response from Yemeni civil society."

[114] NDI, "Jordan Elections Show Clear Improvement over 2007 Polls, NDI Observer Mission Says," November 10, 2010.

dynasty. By the same token, Western democracies did not push too hard. After facing a credible opposition candidate for the presidency and some Muslim Brotherhood victories in the relatively competitive contests in 2005, the ruling National Democratic Party parliamentary majority revised constitutional provisions for judicial oversight of elections, presidential term limits, and presidential campaigns. Presumably grateful for Cairo's sweeping counter-terrorism policies, Washington greeted the constitutional amendments as "reforms."[115] Europeans acknowledged that despite resources heaped on the elections sector, the international community had unhesitatingly accepted manipulated polling results.[116] In reply to direct calls from American leaders for transnational observers of its 2010 parliamentary ballot, Cairo sneered that citizens in an advanced democracy like Egypt would object to this as a transgression of sovereignty.[117]

Egypt's fraudulent November 2010 balloting did not trigger the supposed conditionality. It was a patently bogus performance: the absurdly short campaign season featured closures of independent news media, mass arrests, and other naked displays of executive power. In the run-up, amidst the roundup of a thousand Egyptian activists, the *Washington Post* admonished the Obama administration to make an explicit connection between "Mubarak's domestic repression and the more than $1 billion in U.S. aid Egypt receives every year, much of it directed to the military," and called for an end to "the State Department's practice of allowing Egypt to exercise a veto over which civil society groups receive U.S. aid."[118] Reports from international satellite stations, newspapers, human rights groups, and the blogosphere provided many signs that polls failed to open, monitors and voters were turned away, ballot-boxes arrived at polling stations

---

[115] On 'realpolitik,' see Anthony Shadid, "Imagining Otherwise in Egypt: Opposition Campaign Embodying Bush Vision Now Lies in Pieces," *Washington Post*, March 18, 2007; Jackson Diehl, "Rice's Rhetoric, in Full Retreat, *Washington Post*, January 22, 2007. On the constitutional reforms, see Andrew Exum and Zack Snyder, "Democracy Demotion in Egypt: Is the United States a Willing Accomplice?" Policy Watch #1212, March 23, 2007.

[116] Youngs, "How to Revitalize Democracy Assistance," 4, 8; Annie van de Pas, "Egypt: Engaging in a Pyramid Power System," Netherlands Institute for Multiparty Democracy, *Beyond Orthodox Approaches: Assessing Opportunities for Democracy Support in the Middle East and North Africa*, NIMD/Hivos, The Hague 2010.

[117] Michele Dunne and Amr Hamzawy, "Does Egypt Need International Election Observers?" The Carnegie Endowment Middle East Project, October 15, 2010.

[118] "Mr. Obama vs. Mr. Mubarak," *Washington Post*, November 26, 2010. Note that months later, when the State Department stopped allowing Egyptian bureaucrats to veto NGO funding, all hell broke loose.

already stuffed, and plainclothes thugs beat up citizens. Nonetheless, NDP candidates, including women running in the super-districts, claimed a landslide. After the ruling party secured an astounding 209 out of 211 seats in the first round, another *Washington Post* editorial lamented "timid and painstakingly balanced comments" from low-ranking Obama administration spokespersons. The *Post*'s editorialists speculated that colossal electoral deceit and American acquiescence could destabilize Egypt.[119] By this time, American policies were so consistently and obviously political that they no longer seemed paradoxical.

In the interim, Mesopotamia proved the graveyard of great expectations for the transformative effects of balloting. Iraq held elections in 2009 for provincial councils and again in 2010 for the national parliament, still with a fair amount of UN and U.S. assistance. Posters and billboards in Arabic (not shown) attempted to explain to voters how the process worked. The March 2010 plebiscite utilized the mathematical formula for geographic and compensatory seats from December 2005 amidst ongoing instability. NDI's regional director wrote in an op-ed column listing indicators that the process was free, fair, genuinely competitive, and well-monitored by domestic groups, including the Iraqi *Shams* (to which NDI provided support), concurring with declarations by UN official overseers that irregularities were not of a magnitude to distort the results.[120] Even assuming that he was correct, it is not clear that the oblique formula leading from the elections to formation of a government convinced Iraqis that they were deciding on a national future.

This was an important event in the evolution of what its Anglophone champions referred to as Iraq's fragile democracy. At such times, the international community, through the certified elections observation process, is expected to 'demonstrate its interest' and perhaps verify the face validity of the exercise with the kind of formal documentation supplied for Lebanon and Jordan. Yet the 2010 Iraq elections were also not duly monitored. From what I could gather, it was pretty much like 2005. According to various overlapping reports on the internet, the EU, UN affiliates, the United States, Canada, Australia, and the Organization of the Islamic Conference collectively promised to send more than 350 international observers; more than 600 were accredited; an EU Electoral Assistance Team of 16 electoral and logistics experts was stationed in

---

[119] "Who's Afraid of Egypt?" *Washington Post*, December 5, 2010.
[120] Leslie Campbell, "Iraq's Election Was Free and Fair," *Foreign Policy.com*, March 30, 2010.

Baghdad, Erbil and Basra; the U.S. State Department assigned in-country personnel as observers; the Next Century Foundation issued a report on June 23, 2010; and the International Election Monitors Institute sent 6 former legislators from Sweden, the United Kingdom, Canada and the United States to observe and lend legitimacy to the process. There were up-beat press releases before, on, and just after polling day. A barrage of advertising affirmed Western engagement with the democratization of Iraq. Nonetheless, NDI and EOM did not post full-fledged reports.

Actually, Iraq's 2010 balloting could not be verified. It was too dangerous to deploy teams according scientific sampling, and impossible to testify to a calm orderly campaign environment, the partisan neutrality of ex facto de-Ba'athification, or procedural plausibility and transparency. I found neither reports nor photographs documenting the presence of neutral foreign monitors. When President Obama declared from the Oval Office in a speech marking the official August 31, 2010, end of the American combat mission that "This year also saw Iraq hold credible elections that drew a strong turnout" and "A caretaker administration is in place as Iraqis form a government based on the results of that election," he was giving positive spin to an inconclusive election that did not really 'take.' By year's end there were new faces in parliament but the same men were in charge. In 2011/12 the arrangement seemed to be collapsing. My hunch would be that the women quoted in the next chapter who were not sanguine about elections, quotas, or other promises of democratic representation in the first few years after the U.S.-led occupation probably did not develop great faith in Iraq's parliamentary system by the end of the decade.

The two main story-lines traced in this chapter are as follows. First, over the course of nearly two decades the transnational expertise for designing and appraising electoral performances were refined tremendously, and basic principles of monitoring and validation were taught and transmitted to many thousands of activists in the region. Second, neither incumbent autocrats nor the leaders of Western democracies honored the rules of the game. No wonder Arabs became distrustful in their estimations of American and/or Western commitments to regional democratization, and experts tried to downplay the mystique of elections. Electorates and democracy brokers themselves became dispirited.

So much the hallmark of democracy promotion, election-related projects were special: short-term, events-driven, newsworthy activities with nation-wide spread, relatively high potential impact, and global geo-strategic import. This might be why or because Uncle Sam made such a show of supporting elections, as if to convince Americans of our virtuous commitment to Arab democratization. There are a couple of problems with this. First, 'electioneering' is not an American brand but a transnational enterprise. Second, American policies – regardless of who is in office – deviate from norms for free and fair elections. Therefore this chapter has insisted on distinguishing professional programs from White House rhetoric. American might and the transnational governance regime really are two distinct phenomena in global politics, and in the Middle East they have often been at odds. Strains between unilateralism and multilateralism apparent in the U.S.-led military operations in Iraq resurfaced in Iraq's electoral architecture as well as in the high tribunal. The international expertise was available to leave Iraqis with a more carefully designed system of parliamentary representation that would better withstand a regional and international litmus test. It was not deployed. Counterfactually, one might speculate that unequivocal application of emergent transnational expectations would make voters more likely to see elections as a way of choosing political representatives. The central contradiction of power politics has been its love-hate relationship with majority rule.

Another paradox that cropped up repeatedly in this chapter also bedevils other sectors. It is seductive to analyze selective publicity, foreign observation, documentation rituals, pabulums of guided transitions, and mapping exercises as neo-colonial moves to render restive Arab politics decipherable and governable. This is a theoretically and analytically compelling hypothesis. However, it is also empirically and ethically challenged by the data. Two decades of electoral experimentation did not yield a viable politics of domination in the Middle East. So the same evidence that 'promoting' elections is a display of strength simultaneously casts doubt on teleological assumptions of superpower omniscience and invincibility. The normative drawback of describing this as a device for post-colonial Western domination is that ossified national security establishments use that argument as propaganda to rationalize despotism. No wonder some Arab and other intellectuals see the projects described in this chapter as part of a system of imperial governmentality. By the same token we need to be able to analyze the anomalies of political aid without reproducing distinctly regressive and/or xenophobic polemics. Leaving the international arena of geostrategic politics for national and regional layers of interaction, the next two chapters on women's empowerment and civil society promotion delve deeper into the dialectics of globalization and the ways Arab regimes variously sought to co-opt, contain, and counter idioms of empowerment. Both chapters address more directly the question of how political aid projects are interpreted and implemented 'over there.'

# 3

## Patronizing Women

Western democracy brokers looking at the Middle East pay special attention to women. Many projects in the legal sector, dealing with elections, and encouraging civic involvement specifically addressed Arab women's rights and participation, and some women's empowerment projects cut across those categories. Like all political aid programs, activities for women consist mainly of research and instruction, on the one hand, and institution-building, on the other, or more generally with the production of specialized kinds of information. By the same token, women's empowerment is a sub-sector of socio-economic as well as political development assistance, noted for specialized thematic and institutional agendas grouped under two prevalent acronyms: WID (women in development) and GID (gender in development). WID and GID studies constituted a specialized field of academic and policy research beyond the recognizable transitology literature. Whereas until now our attention was mostly on national and international-level processes, the literature on gender empowerment leads us through anthropology, cultural studies, and political sociology to the participants'-eye view of interpersonal interactions, individual life experiences, and cross-cultural exchange.

From this perspective, we can consider how people interpret and instrumentalize the ideals of gender empowerment. Drawing on scholarship in women's studies, this chapter tackles the dual connotations of 'representing' Arab women by looking closely at the semantics and mechanisms of political aid. It asks: how did individuals and bureaucratic actors react to and act on aspirational and material enticements – how did they interpret discursive and institutional practices? This question is addressed in two parts. The first dissects the ways 'foreign' experts and 'local' interlocutors respectively adduce the significance of matters such as voting, Islamic law, media performances, and 'culture.' The second part, about the political sociology of international aid for various women's institutions, places recent initiatives in the historical context of feminine activism in national, pan-Arab, and international circles.

The chapter on law considered both an ever-present tension between law as a means of defending rights or as a tool of imperial governance, and a rich literature on articulations between and among legal regimes. In the gender empowerment sector, we find similar ambiguities between a view of international advocacy for emancipation and a theory of transnational governmentality. In terms of institutional pathways, too, this chapter echoes the political implications of fostering national institutions vs. funding adversarial non-governmental associations. On the other hand whereas international legal experts take legal pluralism, multiple jurisdictions, and differing interpretations of law for granted, recognize hybridizations, and mention *Shari'a* in narrowly delineated contexts, gender programming is relatively absolutist. It leaves little room for alternative readings and over-determines an ambiguous transliterated construct of sharia. In contrast with the relatively objective rubrics of electoral transparency, messages aimed at female voters or candidates seemed much more overtly ideological or subjective. Finally, therefore, this chapter anticipates the analysis of civil society promotion by placing women in the incredulous intellectual vanguard. My overall argument is that gender programming is paradoxical in the sense of merging aspirational messages of self-realization with a rescue paradigm, and political in the same ways as any infusion of resources into a competitive environment.

The word "patronizing" in the chapter title comes from a phrase bantered among bilingual development professionals about being "caught between the paternalism of Arab men and the patronizing of Western feminists." I first heard it in Cairo, years ago, from the prominent Sana'a University women's studies professor Raufa Hassan al-Sharqi, a successful fund-raiser and experienced consultant to donor-funded projects. It is a double entendre. International agencies extend funds, opportunities, and mentoring, but from a condescending position that assumes that Arab women need to be spoken 'for.' This chapter investigates how these two contradictory kinds of patronizing – substitute ways of 'representing' women – combine to hyper-politicize gender in ways that complicate the simplified empowerment paradigm. Speaking satirically in Arabic, Raufa Hassan also liked to render the English word 'gender' into a quadrilateral Arabic root (g-n-d-r) that can be modified, grammatically, to novel meanings. '*Yugandaru*' connotes 'they make things gendered,' or, perhaps, 'they genderize,' and (as *mustashraqun* are seekers of the Orient, or Orientalists), *mustagandarun* are the seekers of gender, or perhaps Genderists. Bilingual professionals couldn't help but make puns about patronizing and genderizing.[1]

Like the social science of democracy promotion more generally, the women's studies literature gives us two different ways of thinking about transnational regimes and the role of political aid projects. First, there is the normative content of liberal feminist internationalism – its altruism, its devotion to consciousness-raising, its emphasis on decency and principle, its ecumenical ethos of right and wrong that explicitly eschews cultural relativism in favor of purposeful culture change.[2] This position empathizes with the difficulties so many women face, and calls on privileged Westerners to utilize channels for advocacy available to us. On the idealism-realism spectrum, projects for women lean heavily toward normative ideals and away from militarism.

Moreover, there is objective evidence that principled ideas-driven international networks, conference declarations, institutional capacity-building programs and norm diffusion cross-fertilize reformist principles and a collective consciousness.[3] What is known as the 'Beijing apparatus' is alive and well south and east of the Mediterranean. One can see a two-way cross-national esprit de corps among many professional advocates for gender rights and equality, including Arab intellectuals, activists, and employees of women's institutions.

This is not only a matter of 'diffusion' and spread of 'Western' norms and values; women in Iraq, Egypt, Palestine, Yemen, and other countries have been agitators 'in their own right,' to use a hackneyed phrase, for a long time. Savvy elites have been meeting global counterparts since the 1920s, intensely

---

[1] Wit is often satirical, mocking power. For analysis of the political implications of popular humor, see James C. Scott, *Domination and the Arts of Resistance: Hidden Transcripts* (New Haven: Yale University Press, 1990); Wedeen, *Ambiguities of Domination*.

[2] See the interesting and sophisticated report, "Women as Full Participants in the Euro-Mediterranean Community of Democratic States," EuroMeSCo Report, April 2006: 9, 16–17.

[3] Martha Finnemore and Kathryn Sikkink give a nuanced argument: "Taking Stock: The Constructivist Research Program in International Relations and Comparative Politics," *Annual Review of Political Science* 4 (June 2001) 391–416; a foundational essay was John Gerard Ruggie, "What Makes the World Hang Together? Neo-utilitarianism and the Social Constructivist Challenge," *International Organization* 52 (1998) 855–88. A critique of this approach was offered by Laura K. Landolt, "(Mis)constructing the Third World? Constructivist Analysis of Norm Diffusion," *Third World Quarterly* 25:3 (2004) 579–591.

before and after the Beijing Conference in 1975, more regularly since the International Conference on Population and Development in Cairo in 1994, and even more frequently since the turn of the millennium. An impressive women's advocacy network is well connected to international women's circles.[4] The vivacity and accomplishments of this epistemic community are measured in the state and non-state agencies dedicated to women, the hectic conference calendar, a library of documentation, and considerably more discursive salience in Arabic than is commonly recognized in English.[5] Rhetorically, Arab summit declarations early in the twenty-first century from Beirut, Alexandria, Sana'a, and other locations, the formation of an official Arab Organization for Women, and Iraq's new constitution all acclaimed gender equality and full female participation in political and market systems. Substantive legal reforms or parliamentary quotas also signal some successes in individual countries. Thus, international solidarity networks working under UN auspices deserve credit for bolstering indigenous feminists' negotiations with governing bureaucracies.[6]

Furthermore, the threads of progressive, Socialist, or Third World conceptions of social and economic justice within the international women's movement falsify the commonplace knee-jerk nativist riposte that women's issues are an alien 'Western' construct. The Convention for the Elimination of All Forms of Discrimination Against Women (CEDAW) is the product of multicultural inputs, it can be argued, and the UN organization for women, UNIFEM, represents the aspirations of Arab, African, and Asian as well as Western women. This is all on the positive side, so to speak.

Nonetheless, quite a few feminist thinkers have critically deconstructed empowerment sermons, bureaucracies, and tokenism. In the context of the lopsided ubiquity of the verb 'to help' and of patron-client asymmetries embedded in the 'aid' industry, they have argued that their terms of reference seem to predispose expat WID and GAD consultants to homogenize audiences as passive recipients of knowledge and resources.[7] One

---

[4] Janet Afary, "The Human Rights of Middle Eastern and Muslim Women: A Project for the 21st Century," *Human Rights Quarterly*, 26:1 (2004) 106–125.

[5] Amal Sabbagh, "The Arab States: Enhancing Women's Political Participation," *Women in Parliament: Beyond the Numbers*, International IDEA, Stockholm, 2004: 52–71.

[6] Jaqui True and Michael Mintrom, "Transnational Networks and Policy Diffusion: The Case of Gender Mainstreaming," *International Studies Quarterly* 45:1 (2001) 27–57. Other scholars depict states bargaining with international conventions: see Clark, Friedman, and Hochstetler, "Sovereignty in the Balance."

[7] Georgina Weylen, "Analyzing Women in the Politics of the Third World," in Haleh Afshar, ed. *Women and Politics in the Third World* (London and New York: Routledge, 1996) 7–24.

scholar wrote that the Beijing/CEDAW apparatus functions as an international public sphere of two-way communication, while simultaneously, perhaps unwittingly, imposing a "discursive price of admission" that "effectively garbles the articulation of indigenous interests."[8] Furthermore, neo-liberal economic formulas for public sector lay-offs, cut-backs in social services, and charging fees at previously subsidized Women's Centers – patently injurious to already-insecure households – equated 'empowerment' with individual autonomy rather than with social movements.[9] Neo-liberal feminism called for independence from both families and welfare states so that women could be self-standing entrepreneurs in a free global market.[10] It is as if one earns money to rebel against patriarchy rather than to feed households. The exemplary woman who runs a successful marketing, lobbying, or electoral campaign is depicted as a pioneer, courageously 'standing up to' her heritage. She relies confidently on personal enterprise and private insurance rather than on family, mosque, or state welfare provisions. These storylines have been labeled global feminist narratives, and the CEDAW/UNIFEM establishment as a mode of "transnational feminist governmentality" that is produced, reproduced, and circulated from a center of gravity within the United Nations system.[11] We will encounter a similar notion in the chapter on civil society.

Critical feminist scholars find Orientalist and neo-liberal biases in the depiction of states and markets as solutions to problems said to be rooted in indigenous traditions. Anthropologists criticized sensationalized fascination with "cultural practices whose impact is felt directly on the body" like polygamy, veiling, clitoridectomy, family violence, and limitations on driving or travel, which are then generalized from statistically rare localized experiences to the whole Islamic world.[12] Voyeuristic, eroticizing exegeses rationalize a sort of in loco parentis on behalf of "dark women

---

[8] John Mowitt, "In the Wake of Eurocentrism: An Introduction," *Cultural Critique* 47 (2001) 3–15: 10–11.

[9] Lauren G. Leve, "'Failed Development' and Rural Revolution in Nepal: Rethinking SubalternConsciousness and Women's Empowerment," *Anthropological Quarterly* 80:1 (2007)127–172.

[10] Julia Elyachar, "Empowerment Money: The World Bank, Non-Governmental Organizations, and the Value of Culture in Egypt," *Public Culture* 14:3 (2002) 493–513.

[11] Frances S. Hasso, "Empowering Governmentalities Rather than Women: *The Arab Human Development Report 2005* and Western Development Logics," *International Journal of Middle East Studies* 41 (2009) 63–82.

[12] Laura U. Marks, "What Is That *and* between Arab Women and Video? The Case of Beirut," *Camera Obscura* 18:2 (2003) 40–69: 51, adding that in attributing many practices to culture, "Western activists are just not doing their homework" on the impact of education, health services, and international political economy.

trapped in hopelessly retrograde and brutal societies."[13] Post-colonial knowledge repeats stock phrases like "patriarchal culture" that are not investigated empirically so much as "known in advance" to characterize "native pathologies" with no Western analogies.[14] After the 9/11 attacks, many scholars drew attention to the complicated ways in which the Taliban's abuse of women generated an ethical imperative for the U.S. invasion articulated by First Lady Laura Bush.

Donor agency publications are important to people in dependent countries because they set the terms of reference for aid programs as well as research agendas. As mentioned earlier, bicultural scholars scrutinized the texts of *Arab Human Development Reports*. The *Reports* were collectively authored by large multinational teams of cosmopolitan intellectuals based in the Arab region who debated among themselves the balance between universal and indigenous concerns and a range of other national, regional, and ideological issues. In the 2005 edition dedicated to women, feminist scholars detected "dialects" of de-territorialized neo-liberal empowerment grounded in secular modernity and transnational governmentality that recommend "culture change" as a remedy for the "plight" of Muslim women constrained by "local" cultural practices, values, and beliefs.[15] These analyses amplified the earlier observations of a researcher at Bir Zeit University that WID and GAD documents consistently attributed women's status, roles, and prospects to religious, cultural and family values: thus female unemployment in Gaza and the West Bank reflected socio-religious attitudes, not military occupation or economic malaise; girls dropped out of school due to modesty codes, not family obligations or poverty; and discriminatory features of family law stemmed from the Quranic basis of Ottoman, Jordanian and Egyptian precedents, not from British or Israeli administrations or other factors.[16]

Either or both ways – we want to know how messages of empowerment were conveyed, interpreted, institutionalized, and internalized. What are the textual logics? What chords did they strike, for whom? What can we

---

[13] Ella Shohat, "Area Studies, Gender Studies, and the Cartographies of Knowledge," *Social Text* 20:3 (2002) 67–78: 77.

[14] Apollo Amoko, "The 'Missionary Position' and the Postcolonial Polity, Or, Sexual Difference in the Field of Kenyan Colonial Knowledge," *Callaloo* 24:1 (2001) 310–324: 316.

[15] See, in particular, Abu-Lughod, "Dialects of Women's Empowerment"; Hasso, "Empowering Governmentalities," 74–75.

[16] Lisa Taraki, "Society and Gender in Palestine: A Critique of International Policy Documents," Working Paper 2, Birzeit University: Women's Studies Programme, Ramallah, 1995: 4. Taraki diagnosed a "conceptual schizophrenia" between a stated gender-analytical framework and the portrayal of Palestinians as the "converse of the active-agent WID expert," 57.

discover about how some audiences construed key phrases and assumptions, and, in turn, how report writers signified those reactions? So, for instance: how did transitologists explain why women did or did not vote in the various electoral experiments analyzed in the previous chapter? What resources flowed to national institutions and/or non-governmental associations? Who heads the national machineries or prominent NGOs for women? What are the semantic and institutional practices? These two parts, both ethnographic, correspond broadly to the dual connotations of patronizing. The first explores why people might feel they are being spoken down to, whereas the second considers the benefits of patronage. Both parts complicate the clash-of-civilizations and battle-of-the-sexes plot-lines of the empowerment paradigm by recognizing the agency of individuals and institutions.

Arab, or even, say, Algerian, women are hardly a homogeneous interest group. Their responses and interests are more personal than collective. Many successful Middle Eastern women, including prominent writers and politicians and thousands trained and/or employed as gender specialists, write and speak passionately about cultural misogyny and religiously based oppression. Many take part in national and transnational women's forums. Hundreds of thousands seek out opportunities and legal protections through formal and informal institutions. So it is a gross overstatement to portray the quest for equality and/or empowerment a purely 'Western' or 'alien' agenda. Nonetheless, and on the other hand, in the context of cross-cultural communication the gender agenda can come across as a combination of naiveté, chauvinism, and tokenism. This chapter begins with several vignettes suggesting how people living in conditions of war or dictatorship question the meaning international experts attach to voting, religion, violence against women, or media portrayals of femininity and masculinity. Later we turn to more literal politics of 'representing' women though conference declarations, national machineries, parliamentary quotas, International Women's Day celebrations, and the 'state feminism' which in old days of Arab socialism promised that party-states would replace families as guarantors of women's welfare and granted perfunctory technocratic or legislative posts in return.[17] Eventually we

---

[17] For analysis of instances of "state feminism," see Maxine Molyneux, "The Law, the State, and Socialist Policies with Regard to Women: the Case of the People's Democratic Republic of Yemen 1967–1990," in ed. Deniz Kandioti, *Women, Islam, and the State* (London: Temple University Press, 1991); Mervat F. Hatem, "Economic and Political Liberation in Egypt and the Demise of State Feminism," *International Journal of Middle East Studies* 24 (1992) 231–251.

consider how First Ladies, princesses, politicians, and some counter-elites posed in haute couture as models of modern womanhood. This discussion begins where the previous chapter ended, with elections and the Iraq occupation, and ends by leading into the next chapter, on civil society promotion. As organized, the chapter opens with expressions of disbelief in simplified 'regimes of truth' and then backtracks historically to reveal some of the reasons for this disbelief.

## WHY SOME WOMEN MIGHT NOT VOTE

Earlier we established that elections do not necessarily transfer power or decide who will govern. So people who cast ballots might feel they are selecting political leaders, or pledging national allegiance, or expressing communal solidarity, or playing along with a charade, or something else. The women's political empowerment literature, however, usually assumes that female Arab voters are defying tradition to find a sense of political efficacy. Let us look into this last hypothesis. Women voted in all the elections mentioned in the previous chapter except Kuwait's. Egyptian suffragettes won the franchise two generations earlier. Beyond the Gulf monarchies, wherever Arab citizens could vote, adult women could vote and run for office. Yet in English and French, the trope persisted that for Muslim women to cast ballots was a courageous innovation, a cultural breakthrough with positive emancipatory signification – even if the election itself were fraudulent.

For instance, a detailed evaluation of the European Union's ambitious Euro-Mediterranean Democracy Initiative (known as MEDA) acknowledged that Egypt's ruling party "always wins a predictable majority of seats in parliament" through its media monopoly, arbitrary arrest of opposition candidates, restrictions on opposition parties, and permanent state of emergency.[18] Nonetheless, the EU considered programs comprised of "rallies, animated leaflets, and local community campaigns" to encourage Egyptian women to register to vote very important on principle. For the whole region, MEDA evaluators gave projects "in support of women's rights" what they called "high marks" for "relevance" because "most of the Mediterranean partner countries are Islamic societies with a deficit regarding women's rights."[19] This 'relevance' to a sweeping cultural generalization is not necessarily the 'relevance' to women who might ask what

---

[18] Nadim Karkutli and Dirk Buetzier, *Final Report: Evaluation of the MEDA Democracy Programme 1996–98* (Brussels, April 1999) 119.
[19] Karkutli and Buetzier, *Final Report*: 55.

is to be gained from casting a ballot for (or against) Mubarak or his ruling party.

If women voted in lower proportions than men, according to this way of framing things, it must be because of cultural inhibitions. For instance, the NDI/Carter Center report on the 1996 Palestinian elections detailed widespread doubts among people in the West Bank, Gaza, and East Jerusalem, noting that the elections were announced on barely three months' notice, dominated by the former guerrilla group Fatah, and watched by Israeli and Palestinian security forces. "Voters harbored real reservations regarding the nature and power of the body they would elect, and the future status of the Palestinian entity the Council would govern,"[20] the text acknowledged. There were genuine, well-founded (though ultimately unfulfilled) fears of campaign violence. Still, to explain why only twenty-seven women campaigned amidst some 650 male candidates, report writers resorted to primal rather than immediate factors: "the constituency-based majoritarian system that favored traditional elements of Palestinian society – the patriarchal family and the clan."[21] Tradition and patriarchy – rather than individual or networked skepticism, practical obstacles, or wariness of masculine violence – seem to define feminine behavior, then.

In the transcripts from the early 1990s into the new century, a notion that something transliterated as 'sharia' is responsible for Arab women's 'plight' seemed at once self-evident in English or French narratives yet nearly incoherent (if not downright offensive) in Arabic vernaculars. This point is related to the discussion in the chapter entitled Legal Jurisdictions of the concept of federalism sometimes rendered in Arabic as '*fadaraliyya*.' I argued there that although federal and *fadarali* refer to roughly the same thing, or category of systems, and have similar (though not identical) pronunciations, the connotations in Arabic of the foreign loan-word do not necessarily match the signification in English. This is even more true of the difference between the Arabic word *Shari'a*, meaning Islamic law, and English-language usage of the Anglicized word 'sharia.' Now *Shari'a* is a complicated concept with varying shades of meaning in different schools of Islamic law, and in different countries, and to pious Muslims, modern constitutional scholars and non-Muslims. Nonetheless I think it is safe to characterize it as a corpus of laws – not unlike the Napoleonic legal tradition, with its historical and modern variations – and that

---

[20] The National Democratic Institute for International Affairs and the Carter Center, *The January 20, 1996 Palestinian Elections* (Washington: NDI, 1997) 86.
[21] NDI and the Carter Center, *The January 20, 1996 Palestinian Elections*: 45.

the word *Shari'a* is related to the word for 'legitimate.' When English speakers use the term 'sharia' they usually mean something quite different. Its over-use, especially in the context of discussions of gender, compounds miscommunications. As in the discussion of federalism and the meaning of federalism, my purpose here is to call attention to the ways that messages are resignified.

Here is a close reading of a text that recounts conversations with Yemeni women and anticipates themes, exact phrases, and participant contretemps repeated more than a decade later in Iraq, and in other settings. An NDI report on the 1993 parliamentary elections attributed many problems to an amorphous, ominous, omnipotent factor labeled 'sharia,' which, as deployed repetitively in the text, carries sinister connotations quite unlike the signification of *Shari'a* in Yemeni Arabic. "Yemen's leaders interpret the sharia to formulate laws and define the legal rights of the citizen," it reads, unduly crediting a military dictatorship's familiarity with Islamic jurisprudence, over-estimating leaders' attention to the rule of law and ignoring the Socialist origins of South Yemeni statutes then still on the books. The next sentence reiterates: "The fact that Yemen's leadership is universally male means that women do not generally have a voice in influencing the way sharia is interpreted and hence do not participate in shaping their own legal rights."[22] Here, experts on elections seemed confused about the distinctions among executive, legislative, and judicial functions but certain that the problem lies with "sharia." The passage continues: an "increasingly restrictive interpretation of sharia ... may be the dominant factor limiting women from full participation...." Perhaps; but elsewhere, the report lauds "strides in women's participation" after unification in 1990. This apparent contradiction could have been resolved by asking voters about their differing personal experiences in the conservative North, the post-colonial South, and after unification.

NDI's team said focus groups were held to gain respondents' input on the design of further projects. Women were asked to express opinions on two questions: "Can there be democracy in an Islamic state?" and "Could or should sharia be interpreted in a more egalitarian manner...?" Why these were questions specifically for women on the occasion of a fiercely contested breakthrough election (where the main competitors were both secular formerly ruling parties) was not explained. Facilitators were

---

[22] National Democratic Institute for International Affairs, *Promoting Participation in Yemen's 1993 Elections* (Washington: NDI, 1994) 53.

disappointed that "only one women of the dozens interviewed directly criticized the negative effects of Islamic law on women" and that "Neither men nor women were prepared to discuss the sociological implications of Islam with respect to the role of women in society and politics." Note here the maddening lack of reportage on what respondents *did* say, only their failure to hold forth on the sociology of religion. The next line reads: "When a member of the delegation asked a Yemeni woman for her opinion on polygamy she turned to her friend and asked, 'Why is she pressing on with polygamy, what has it got to do with political participation?'" One of the few direct quotations from interviewees, this question seems to have been cited to illustrate Yemenis' inability to grasp something intuitively obvious to the report writers. Instead of making an explicit connection between monogamy and voting, the paragraph continues: "Several Yemeni women referred vaguely to 'enlightened interpretations' of the sharia. ... But efforts to ascertain what these enlightened interpretations could mean to specific issues in Yemen led to vague discussions."

Around that time, when I asked Yemeni women for their opinions about elections, a common response was "*la-tisadqi!*" or "don't you believe it!" I'm not sure if NDI's interpreters encountered this exclamation of disbelief, or translated it. The report writers clearly signified voting as positive and "sharia" as negative. They didn't seem to consider that perhaps some female raconteurs held Islamic law in higher esteem than their so-called leaders' promises to honor the will of the electorate; or that the whole matter of 'women's rights' was a partisan issue dividing the Socialist Party that formerly ruled the People's Democratic Republic of Yemen from conservatives in the North Yemeni establishment and their ultra-conservative Saudi patrons.[23] Ignoring these politics, NDI's report on the 1993 elections offered little insight into what women were thinking about the matter at hand, voting, and even less about personal experiences of citizens, candidates, parliamentarians, party members, or activists, or variations of opinion among Northern, Southern, Socialist, Islamist, urban, rural, literate, unschooled, young and old women on a range of matters including, but hardly limited to, marriage and Islamic law. Rather, the emphasis on what 'women' did *not* say homogenized their ignorance. In the end, returning redundantly to their own unexamined premises, "The delegation concluded that there is a strong relationship between the

---

[23] Recall that IRI's "1993 National Elections in the Republic of Yemen: Political Background Briefing" dismissed the appeal of the Yemeni Socialist Party, without mention of its progressive gender policies.

manner in which Islamic law is interpreted in Yemen and the extent of women's participation in civic and political life." Among its many recommendations was a "systematic and detailed survey" to "form the basis for properly focused civic education projects."

## INTERPRETING CULTURAL OPPRESSION

Themes of socio-religious oppression were reproduced in countless conferences, reports, and speeches and widely discussed. *Al-Ahram Weekly* ran distillations of the findings of the UN Fund for Women (UNIFEM)'s report called *Progress of Arab Women 2004*, whose overall theme was "knowledge poverty."[24] Its premises about backward cultural mindsets were echoed in public events such as the National Council for Women's three-day celebration of Egyptian Women's Day in 2007, where First Lady Suzanne Mubarak and other speakers quoted from the *Arab Human Development Report* on the need to eliminate the "cultural roots" of discrimination against women, to project positive female models in the media, and to rectify "a distorted self-image" that "perpetuates marginalization."[25] Rulers of Egypt, Tunisia, and other countries were quite happy to blame women's oppression on society rather than government. The idea that what was needed was culture change rather than regime change suited their governance purposes, while at the same time appealing to Western romantics.

These discourses were reproduced by national governments as well as international agencies, then. This did not imply widespread popular acceptance, however. A conservative group called the Egyptian Centre for Monitoring Women's Priorities set up shop to combat negative stereotypes of Islam, particularly in international development reports. Of the *Arab Human Development Report* its spokesperson wrote that the prevailing narrative of gendered suffering conveyed in the phrases "patriarchal society" and "prevailing male culture" and in insinuations that religion and the family tyrannize women amount to a convoluted raison d'être for interference.[26] She later took umbrage with a Carnegie

---

[24] Magda El-Ghitany, "Assessing Arab Women's Lot," *al-Ahram Weekly* No. 712, 14–20 October 2004. The "knowledge-based society" was the main theme of the second *Arab Human Development Report* in 2003, as discussed by Fatemah Farag, "Reclaiming the initiative," *al-Ahram Weekly* No. 661, 23–29 October 2003.

[25] Dina Ezzat, "It Takes Two Wings to Fly," *al-Ahram Weekly* No. 836, 15–21 March 2007.

[26] Amany Abulfadl Farag, "Questions of Identity," *al-Ahram Weekly* No. 830, 1–7 February 2007. Farag also notes that famed authors Nawwal al-Sa'adawi and Fatima Mernissi but not writers who publish primarily in Arabic are singled out for praise.

report's "prejudiced" and "discriminatory" portrait of Islamist women
as incompetent, victimized puppets suffering in ignorance under "gender
apartheid" and out of step with the Beijing+10 networks. The monolithic feminist paradigm offered, she said, is "not even a matter of consensus in the West" and "largely irrelevant to Arab women who are dying
in wars or of malnutrition."[27] From a different perspective, a veteran
democracy-and-development consultant critiqued the dual premises of
diatribes on the "women's rights trap": the pretext that powerful women
soften structural violence and the prescription to lobby narrowly for
compartmentalized gender rights rather than broadly for democracy
and justice.[28]

On another occasion, the featured speaker at a Women's Day event
organized by the Canadian International Development Research Centre
on Gender and Development Ten Years after Beijing provoked listeners
with the same question posed to Yemeni women more than a decade
earlier: "How can the Egyptian Constitution uphold gender equality
while at the same time referring to sharia as the principal source of
legislation in matters personal and domestic?" An *al-Ahram Weekly*
correspondent who said she anticipated another boring lecture from a
self-important foreign consultant instead found herself entertained by
rejoinders from the audience. It seems that a slide show of pictures of
veiled Arab women from the American press – presented as an exposé of
'negative' stereotypes – offended *hijab*-wearing attendees in ways that
surprised the speaker, who in turn did not take kindly to pointed objections. Capturing layers of signification, reiteration, and misunderstand-
ings, the column ended with a quote from a woman in the audience who
snickered at the speaker that "some people don't like to know about
opinions different from their own."[29] There is a pattern here of divergent
significations and cross-cultural miscommunication, chords that resonate
in international but not local circles.

Organizers of a symposium I attended in Amman in late 2009 were
disappointed by the low turnout among Jordanian women. Several well-
researched papers delivered in French or English offered historical

[27] Amany Abulfadl Farag, "Righteous Ideology," *al-Ahram Weekly* No. 866, 11–17 October
2007.
[28] Fatma Khafagy, "Empowerment: A Battle for Both Men and Women," *al-Ahram Weekly*
No. 780, 2–8 February 2006.
[29] Dena Rashed, "A Feminist Pickle," *al-Ahram Weekly* No. 733, 10–16 March 2005.

evidence or contemporary crime data to draw a bleak picture of the predicament of Arab womanhood. Yet in one of the few papers delivered in Arabic, an activist on behalf of battered women pointed out that family violence, whether at the hands of sexual partners or blood relatives, is a worldwide problem. The difference, she said, is that in some countries women and girls usually can find physical refuge and/or legal redress. Presenting testimonial evidence from Jordanian victims reluctant to go to the police for fear of practical problems such as loss of income, household breakup, or inept prosecution, and from male perpetrators insensible of their liability to criminal prosecution, she presented a solution not in terms of culture change but of social safety nets and stronger application of existing family and criminal statutes. The contrast between these presentations is that the Orientalist narrative treats misogyny as a cultural pathology, whereas the 'native' account analyzes individual personalities, family dynamics, institutional redress, and legal circumstances. Foreign experts called for cultural change and attitude adjustment. Local people wanted safety nets.

## VICTIMIZING IRAQI WOMEN

Did women who endured Saddam Hussein's brutal reign and the Anglo-American occupation believe that their suffering stemmed from Islam? Let us look at the interesting, detailed report on an opinion survey of 1,000 women in the three largest governorates conducted by the Iraq Center for Research and Strategic Studies in August 2004 for Women-to-Women International (WWI), an admirable non-profit advocacy agency dedicated to working with female victims of war. The text and bar-charts indicate that two-thirds of respondents blamed female unemployment on insecurity and the shortage of job openings. Only fifteen percent checked cultural concerns, and a tiny fraction pointed to male resistance. Most indicated that faith-based institutions offered more help meeting emergency needs for safety and welfare than political institutions. The report segued from this data to the following observations: "The degree to which women look to religious groups rather than to government to effect changes in society represents a disturbing trend. As women see a rise in religious influence they may be drawn in by promises made by fundamentalist religious institutions, which may later seek to limit their rights and freedoms." Especially when religious groups "usurp" services provision from the government, the text continues, women "may perceive no other choice but to follow and support those who they feel can deliver," turning "in desperation" to "religious groups with extreme viewpoints without realizing the long-term sacrifice of personal freedoms."[30]

These statements bear re-reading. "Usurp" is an attention-grabbing verb to characterize charitable provision of services a demolished state fails to administer, especially since elsewhere this report rightly deplored the disastrous fallout of military combat for Iraqi households. But what was "disturbing" is that women who trust Islamic welfare providers fail accurately to predict the self-defeating implications of their choice. Fortunately, the narrators were certain that the government (yet) to be elected under American auspices would deliver both social services and personal freedoms. Although its survey data did *not* show that parliamentary representation or secular family law were top priorities, the text acclaimed those who "speak for women" as secular, liberal, often internationally connected "women's groups" lobbying for these reforms. This convention, of conglomerating 'women' as a homogenous interest group, obscured the range of female political allegiances, from the Communist left to the Islamist right, while also ignoring geographic, communal, generational, class, and/or individual differences.

Consistent with WWI's eliminating-violence-against-women paradigm, this report was dedicated to fourteen Iraqi women murdered by other Iraqis between March and December 2004. They were two news reporters, two district council members, two translators, two women's activists, and a pharmacist whose body was "dumped on a highway in a traditional headscarf she never wore." The headscarf incident presumably signified that all these crimes were cultural or religious, rather than political or even criminal. Coded this way, the women's deaths are shocking. But because they seem sexualized, these incidents are also detached from thousands of other killings in a vicious civil war. The brief eulogies, meant to be humanizing and valorizing, are also slightly trivializing, as if victims were slain generically or biologically as women rather than individually for their personal positions or affiliations. If gender explained these homicides, it is unclear why hundreds of men were tortured and/or slaughtered during this period. Iraq was notably dangerous for reporters and interpreters: according to the Committee to Protect Journalists, 24 journalists were assassinated in 2004, and between 2003 and 2009, 128 males and

---

[30] Women for Women International, *Windows of Opportunity: The Pursuit of Gender Equality in Post-War Iraq*, Working Paper, Washington, January 2006. On political and legal battles for women's rights in Iraq, see 22–27.

11 females working for news agencies were assassinated. Several American soldiers and contractors published tributes to slain translators. Perhaps women were targeted for what they were writing, interpreting, or doing rather than for what they were wearing.

The story of the murder of an American named Fern Holland on March 9, 2005, initially followed an easy plot sequence. "The volunteers at the Zainab al-Hawra'a Centre for Women's Rights said the centre had never received any threats, but admitted some Iraqis opposed the idea of females enjoying more power in a country steeped in strict Muslim traditions," wrote one correspondent from the place Holland was working the day she died, adding that Holland had chosen to wear Western clothes.[31] If the American were gunned down for her feminism or for her attire, the villain evidently could be any man at all. Sleuthing for *The New York Times Magazine* turned up some other hypotheses. One suspect was the locally prominent owner of a house illegally built on the land of two poor widows that Holland had had bulldozed. Or perhaps the internet access, gymnasium, auditorium, and plush furnishings at the Women's Center stirred resentments among the unpaid officers at the under-equipped police station across the street, or on the part of the religious parties evicted from the government-owned facility to make way for the Women's Center. Holland had appeared on stage, surrounded by a massive security detail, with the CPA head and other officials who helicoptered in for the Heartland Conference at Babylon University in Hilla, while protesters massed outside.[32] Was this a cultural crime, or a political one? I don't know.

## SIGNIFYING MEDIA STEREOTYPES

Television, cinema, and the press can be a window on cultural values and perceptions. Consistent with a pillar of the Beijing Platform dedicated to combating sexist stereotypes in the media and education, feminist scholars and women's rights advocates took a particular interest in the portrayal of women in the Arabic language media. There's a library's worth of informative, insightful, scholarly articles, books, donor-financed reports, workshops, conferences, and press accounts about a large set of projects in

---

[31] The verb "admitted" suggests response to a reporter's prompt: Deborah Haynes, "Iraqi Women Shocked at Violent Shooting of American Female Crusader," *Agence France Presse*, March 12, 2004.

[32] Elizabeth Ruben, "Fern Holland's War," *The New York Times Magazine*, September 19, 2004.

which two paradoxical trajectories twist together. One vector is the construction of gender-analytic categories of knowledge, and around that body of information networks of advocacy and teaching that are gradually routinized in national and supra-national declarations and ultimately public consciousness. The other trajectory is dissonance about what constitutes a 'distorted' image and whose 'knowledge' counts.

The purposeful formation of an epistemic community for social change builds upon research, then training, then declarations of principle, and finally monitoring mechanisms. *Collectif 95 Maghreb Egalité* and others scrutinized plots and characters in North African film, television, and newspapers and "concluded that the media presented predominantly negative stereotypes of women." However, meetings and interviews with North African women showed that 'negative stereotypes' were signified differently by local audiences. In turn, foreign advisors interpreted these reactions in ways that fit a pre-existing paradigm. One survey of 250 women revealed that they were "generally unaware of the degree of stereotyping, even on television," according to consultants, and that "discriminatory perceptions had clearly been internalised." (Note again the emphasis on ignorance and false consciousness.) Therefore "it was decided that concrete efforts were needed to raise awareness." The British Council, working through the long-established, Cairo-based New Woman Research Centre, invited Egyptian intellectuals, activists, and artists to a weeklong workshop facilitated by an expert from India. "The process of forming a Women's Media Watch group to raise awareness by 'combating unacceptable images' proved more challenging than sponsors expected," however. Despite "a general feeling" among organizers that the workshop would lead to "agreement on a monitoring mechanism," it seems that "participants could not reconcile their differences over whether media images of women should be contested from a secular or a religious point of view and whether other forms of discrimination should also be included." Even in this interesting, empathetic, well-informed report, the foreigners wanted to put words in local women's mouths. By noting that one male editor "took a particularly aggressive stance against the whole project," but not quoting individual women's objections, the narration discredits heterodox viewpoints as inherently masculine and misogynist.[33]

---

[33] Naomi Sakr, "Women's Rights and the Arab Media," Centre for Media Freedom/ Middle East and North Africa, 2000 (a study funded by the Royal Danish Ministry of Foreign Affairs) 31–32. This is a 161-page collection of papers about careers in journalism, depictions of beauty, housewifely sit-com roles, and other matters.

These are matters of sociological interpretation and varied opinions. In the 1990s, Egyptian actresses starred or co-starred in Ramadan specials on the Companions of the Prophet, Egyptian soap operas, Oprah Winfrey-style talk shows, USAID-financed family planning messages, and other programs. In cinema, docudrama, and theater, female characters sometimes figuratively embodied national liberation. Ethnographers described variations and complications in how individuals related to these presentations of femininity and motherhood.[34] One anthropologist found in the anti-natalist campaign a strange message of impotence that might provoke castration anxieties in male audiences.[35] Moreover, amidst controversies about artistic expression and comportment stirred by puritanical readings of the Quran, around this time several prominent actresses and singers left stage and screen to don the veil, sometimes later returning to work wearing *hijab*.[36] Thus the network dedicated to combating media typecasting provoked a debate in Egypt about what Americans call 'political correctness.' One UN consultant wrote a cheeky report juxtaposing what she called "a framework which sets out to critique 'negative' images and to demand 'positive' media representations of women" with the simultaneous marketing of testosterone-laden Disney cartoons, sports championships, steamy soap operas, and macho movies.[37]

Research and meetings on gender roles gained momentum as the century turned, alongside the heated controversy within the Arab media about Danish cartoons of the Prophet and Euro-American depictions of Muslims and Islam. An extensive collection of research, programs, and 46 concrete recommendations was coordinated by the Anna Lindh Foundation for the Dialogue between Cultures for the 2006 Euro-Mediterranean Ministerial Conference on 'Equality of Opportunities.' It was a first-rate report in English with an extended bibliography in English and French about gender portrayals in the Arabic media.[38]

---

[34] For ethnographic analysis of ambivalent sociological reactions to teledramas, see Lila Abu-Lughod, *Dramas of Nationhood: The Politics of Television in Egypt* (Chicago: University of Chicago Press, 2005), especially 64–65 and 91–92.

[35] Kamran Asdar Ali, "Myths, Lies, and Impotence: Structural Adjustment and Male Voice in Egypt," *Comparative Studies of South Asia, Africa and the Middle East* 23:1–2 (2003) 321–334.

[36] Karin van Nieuwkerk, "From Repentance to Pious Performance," *ISIM Review* 20 (August 2007) 54–55.

[37] Margaret Gallagher, "Lipstick Imperialism and the New World Order: Women and Media at the Close of the Twentieth Century." Paper prepared for Division for the Advancement of Women Department for Policy Coordination and Sustainable Development. United Nations, December 1995.

[38] "Culture and Communication, Key Factors for Changing Mentalities and Societies," Study by the Anna Lindh Euro-Mediterranean Foundation for the Dialogue between

There were a host of separate programs around this theme. The NGO called Woman and Society, part of a CEDAW follow-up coalition, along with the UNICEF and al-Ahram Regional Institute for Journalism, held a seminar under the title Towards Just Media Coverage of Women's Issues. Papers were presented on the dearth of women quoted as authorities in news stories; depictions of rape victims as seductresses; gyrating dancers in advertisements; and a morality code laced in an ethos of feminine self-sacrifice. Expressing a widespread ambivalence, one Cairo-based feminist media critic wrote that she found the evidence persuasive; nonetheless, she expressed discomfiture at the "arrogance and elitism" of "chatter" about the "false consciousness" of female audiences.[39] Another reviewer, who also agreed that women often played marginal and/or stereotypical roles, likewise took exception to the tone of the presentation. She asked rhetorically: "So is demagogy the only alternative to misogynist stereotypes?"[40]

There were some interesting transmutations in this process. Foreign finance and co-production facilities opened new doors for independent female film and video production, and other forms of expression. While European and American backers savored harem settings and sexualized cruelty, Arab cinematographers, authors, and researchers certainly did exercise degrees of artistic freedom to begin to deconstruct clichés.[41] This is important. It underscores the value of some political aid and the reasons for 'constructivist' optimism. Nonetheless, many Arab (or bicultural) women producing knowledge about Arab women grappled with conflicted intersections of gendered domestic, state-bureaucratic, and international politics, and with problems of cross-cultural translation and signification.

## THE VOICE OF IRAQI WOMEN

Iraqi women were invited to countless trainings during the first couple of years after the overthrow of the old dictatorship to hear the CPA, its contractor Research Triangle Institute, consultants recruited by the British aid agency DFID, and a cadre of Iraqi-American and Anglo-Iraqi

Cultures for the 2006 Euro-Mediterranean Ministerial Conference on 'Equality of Opportunities,' 2006.

[39] Amina Elbendary, "The Word is Not Enough," *al-Ahram Weekly Online* No. 506, 2–8 November 2000; Amina Elbendary, "Women, Nation, TV," *al-Ahram Weekly Online* No. 612, 14–20 November 2002.

[40] Gihan Shahine, "Dinosaurs or Dolls?" *al-Ahram Weekly Online* No. 527, 29 March–4 April 2001.

[41] Marks, "What Is That *and* between Arab Women and Video?"

returnees talk about women's rights.[42] The largest gathering sponsored by USAID and the CPA was the Heartland of Iraq Women's Conference in October 2003, organized most visibly by Fern Holland and two prominent Iraqis recently returned from exile, Rend Rahim Franke and Safia Taleb al-Souhail. Some 150 women said to be "living in different parts of central Iraq" but "not necessarily representative of their communities" showed up to offer "a glimpse of what is on the minds of women in today's Iraq."[43]

The official text revealed more about what was on the minds of the organizers than the assorted views of Iraqi women, however. After recalling the misdeeds of Saddam Hussein, it presented a highly gendered wish-list for a parliamentary quota, regional Women's Centers, legal provisions for equal rights, reform of family law, and financial self-reliance via micro-credit loans. Some of these proposals seemingly had wider resonance among indigenous feminine constituencies than others. Themes that worked better in English than Arabic included statements calling for "deep cultural changes" and neo-liberal budgetary resolution that Women's Centers should be financially independent, not reliant on public sectors: here, cost-recovery accountancy was presented as a feminist 'right' to pay fees for services.

The twenty-page transcript in English reproduced a satellite address from Condoleezza Rice and a live appearance by Paul Bremer III. Focus groups reportedly debated "affirmative action." Note the turn of phrase, a slightly archaic, derogatory Americanism used mainly by opponents of the unratified Equal Rights Amendment to the U.S. constitution that would be meaningless in Arabic or the Iraqi context. The report mentions that Iraqi women debated Turkish-style secularist restrictions on wearing of the *hijab*. The Americans didn't seem to grasp these concerns. Seemingly the headscarf signified oppression to most outsiders but personal and religious liberty to some locals. Similarly, the terms *Shari'a*/sharia carried different meanings in native usage and as transliterated into English. Echoing earlier conversations in Yemen and elsewhere almost verbatim, Iraqis objected when foreigners told them that "Islam and sharia" are inconsistent with "democracy"; in turn, experts dismissed this viewpoint with the admonition that they "did not delve into what would happen in situations where

---

[42] On the complexities of interactions between women in Iraq and Iraqi women returning from exile, see Nadje al-Ali and Nicola Pratt, *What Kind of Liberation? Women and the Occupation of Iraq* (Berkeley: University of California Press, 2009).

[43] The American Islamic Congress (AIC) and the Iraq Foundation, "The Heartland of Iraq Women's Conference: preliminary report," University of Babylon, Hilla, Iraq, October 4–7, 2003: 4.

Islamic law might contradict principles of equal rights." Toward the end, the document conceded that participants explicitly *did* want the new government to provide health facilities and childcare.[44] Generally, however, although women were reportedly "not shy about voicing their opinions,"[45] those opinions were barely audible in the text. Even when locals' opinions were mentioned, they were overridden. A briefer account of the event testified that although "Opinions on female participation differed widely, some groups arguing for Sharia laws in Iraq, while others argued for quotas"; nevertheless, the conference "proposed a 30 per cent quota for women in all government institutions, including the establishment of a special division in each ministry dedicated to women's issues. Many also agreed that women should be involved in writing the constitution."[46] Clearly, even the self-selected audience had diverse and sometimes diametrically opposed viewpoints about proposals brought for their approval and issued on their collective behalf. Nonetheless, the official line is that 'women' want what those who 'speak for' them as a collective interest group demand.

Feminist scholars were already questioning how a collapsed state unable able to guarantee basic policing and utilities could possibly tender de jure individual rights to women.[47] The backdrop to these events included considerable mayhem, some of it sexualized violence, with Marines or mercenaries invading homes, frisking girls and grandmothers, and shooting or raping at least a few. The homo-erotic and dominatrix images of Abu Ghraib were not yet public, but the humiliation of Iraqi manhood was well under way.[48] How did different actors make meaning from the conqueror's slogan, gender equality, in this environment? At the very least there

---

[44] AIC, The Heartland of Iraq Women's Conference, 16 and 18, respectively.

[45] AIC, The Heartland of Iraq, 7. As Ruben told it, "Each group of women shouted down the speakers of the other groups," and one speaker was heckled for remarks on "separation of church and state" 72. See also Lucy Brown and David Romano. "Women in Post-Saddam Iraq: One Step Forward or Two Steps Back?" *NWSA Journal* 18:3 (2006) 51–70.

[46] Drude Dahlerup and Anja Taarup Nordlund, "Gender Quotas – A Key to Equality? A Case Study of Iraq and Afghanistan," *European Political Science* (summer 2004) 91–98.

[47] Denitz Kandiyoti, "Between the Hammer and the Anvil: Post-Conflict Reconstruction, Islam and Women's Rights," *Third World Quarterly* 28:3 (2007) 503–17, wrote "The invocation of women's rights for political expediency in the context of the 'war on terror' has tended to breed skepticism, if not outright resistance." 515.

[48] On complicated issues of bodily integrity, see Mary Ann Tetreault, "The Sexual Politics of Abu Ghraib: Hegemony, Spectacle, and the Global War on Terror." *NWSA Journal* 18:3 (Fall 2006) 33–50; and Rosalind P. Petchesky, "Rights of the Body and Perversions of War: Sexual Rights and Wrongs Ten Years Past Beijing," *International Social Science Journal* 57 (2005) 301–318.

was a disconnect between the optimistic zeal of diaspora speakers expecting to be voted or appointed to the high-level national positions they called for and life-long residents traumatized and/or jaded by brainwashing, faux elections, tokenistic state feminism, military brutality, sanctions-induced socio-economic decline, 'shock and awe' military bombardment, and a subsequent implosion of social order.[49] Ironically, the assault on culture seemed to fan the backlash of sectarian Islamism constituted as the alternative to either Saddam's or American versions of modernity.[50]

Many Iraqi women seemed dubious about economic autonomy and parliamentary quotas. At one educational session planned for 250 and attended by 80, an unemployed woman announced that women want jobs for their husbands and sons, too. The Baghdad manager of the national Women Advocacy Program wondered aloud whether the parliamentary quota wouldn't result in more "dummies sitting in the parliament."[51] A former political prisoner of the Iraqi police state, an exile-returnee, explained the empty chairs at the ribbon-cutting ceremony for another Women's Center in Diwanya in terms of the same "passive resistance" previously applied "against Saddam's despised General Union (or Federation) of Iraqi women."[52] In a subsequent column she observed that few Iraqi women share foreigners' anxieties that Islamic law will restrict women's rights. Token CPA appointments, she said, reduced "Iraqi women's historical struggle" to "bickering over a handful of nominal political posts" among an elite "holed up in guarded areas or the US-fortified Green Zone." With "women's rights" lowered to "an absurd discourse chewing on meaningless words" it is "no wonder" that American-backed women's groups, "suspected of being vehicles for foreign manipulation," are "despised and boycotted." Iraqi women, she

---

[49] Nadje Al-Ali & Nicola Pratt, "Women in Iraq: Beyond the Rhetoric," *Middle East Report* 239 (2006) 18–23, quote from a range of interviews.

[50] Nadje Al-Ali, "Reconstructing Gender: Iraqi women between Dictatorship, War, Sanctions, and Occupation," *Third World Quarterly* 26:4–5 (2005) 739–758.

[51] She is referring to women in the transitional assembly, according to Howard LaFranchi, "In Iraq, Security Trumps Women's Rights," *The Christian Science Monitor*, December 12, 2005.

[52] Haifa Zangana, "Why Iraqi Women Aren't Complaining?" republished from *The Guardian* at http://www.iran-bulletin.org/new/iraqiwomen.pdf. Eighteen elite Iraqi women invited to Beirut for a workshop named insecurity as their greatest concern and called for ending the occupation, creating jobs, freeing the press, and strengthening trade and agricultural unions: Woodrow Wilson Center for International Center for Scholars, "The Iraqi Elections: Women to the Ballot Box," December 22, 2004. For a broader analysis, see Nicola Pratt, "Gendering Political Reconstruction in Iraq," UEA Papers in European and International Studies, WP 3/2005.

concluded, know that the enemy is not Islam, nor their families, but the occupation itself.[53] As far as we know, this is one woman's individual opinion.

The progressive quota for parliamentary representation, wherein party slates were required to list one woman for every two men, was not the brainchild of neo-cons in the White House for whom 'quota' was a dirty word for 'affirmative action.' Nor was it a top concern expressed by most women living inside Iraq for whom '*qwota*' was a foreign loan-word, and who may or may not have shared high hopes for the nascent national legislature. Rather, the proposal entered Iraq via exile circles, especially in the United Kingdom, and was facilitated by transnational networks under the guidance of International IDEA, the main intellectual resource on the subject, and other think tanks. Inter alia, IDEA co-hosted a workshop in Cairo on Enhancing Women's Political Participation through Special Measures in the Arab Region with its partners, UNDP, UNIFEM, and Egypt's National Council for Women, and commissioned reform-oriented studies on electoral laws and systems, the functioning of political parties, and the role of women in politics.[54] With an NED grant, a scholar at Harvard's Kennedy School wrote an analysis of possible quota systems for Iraq that a high-profile democracy consultant handed the Iraqi Higher Women's Council to guide the constitutional proposals they submitted to the CPC and the Governing Council.[55] While Algeria, South Yemen, Saddam's Iraq, Syria, Tunisia, Arab League members Eritrea and Sudan, and, most recently, Morocco and Jordan had all experimented with mechanisms for token female representation in national legislatures, the whopping share of the elected Iraqi parliament was unprecedented for the region and unusual in the world. Leading women's lobbyists rejoiced in a hard-won victory.

On one level, this is exactly how internationalist constructivism should work: gender-sensitive, technically adept, policy-oriented research produces landmark advances to which people will become accustomed. The

---

[53] Haifaa Zangana, "Women of the New Iraq," *al-Ahram Weekly* No. 755, 11–17 August 2005.

[54] See Amal Sabbagh, "Overview of Women's Political Representation in the Arab Region: Opportunities and Challenges," *The Arab Quota Report: Selected Case Studies*, Quota Report Series, compiled from workshop held on 5–6 December 2004 in Cairo, Egypt, International Institute for Democracy and Electoral Assistance, Stockholm, 2007.

[55] Pippa Norris, "Increasing Women's Representation in Iraq: What Strategies Would Work Best?" report prepared at the Kennedy School of Government for the NED, February 16, 2004, Cambridge, MA. See Diamond, *Squandered Victory*: 131.

achievement of a transnational epistemic knowledge network in helping to position Iraqi women as lawmakers stood out amidst electoral and judicial undertakings that defied cosmopolitan conventions. Nonetheless, as described in the previous chapter, in the events neither women nor men could campaign openly for fear of assassination; the names of new legislators were only published months after both rounds of elections; and the new parliament failed to establish its governing authority. Moreover, contrary to the Western expectation that female parliamentarians would constitute an inherently secular neo-liberal constituency, most women elected under the party-list system were neo-Islamist conservatives with a Shi'a orientation. By 2006, female parliamentarians, officials, and activists expressed ambivalence about tokenistic gains amidst socio-economic deterioration.[56] Women remained noticeably under-represented in party leaderships, the constitution-writing and review committees, positions outside the Ministry of Women's Affairs, and backroom haggling to form a government.[57] The moral victory of a parliamentary quota was devalued further in 2010 when stalemated elections were followed by protracted negotiations resulting in a conspicuously male government. Thus, instituting a quota for the representation of Iraqi women was a symbolic achievement, but not necessarily a very substantive one.

## NATIONAL MACHINERIES

So far, this chapter has focused mainly on how authors of some illustrative reports signified selected political expressions and reinterpreted counterpart's reactions to confirm pre-determined conclusions. The emphasis has been on discursive practices and problems of translation – not from English to Arabic, necessarily, so much as from philosophical ideals into societies wracked by military and structural violence. Now we turn our attention toward policy praxis. How were the motifs analyzed here interjected into specific national political and bureaucratic configurations? What were the institutional practices and mechanisms for their implementation? What happened next? What about the political representation of women?

To patronize is also to provide financial or logistical support for specific projects, pathways, or clients. Accordingly, foreign sponsorship of women's

---

[56] Huda Ahmed elicited strong but varied opinions reported in "Women in the Shadows of Democracy" *Middle East Report* 239 (2006) 24–26.
[57] Al-Ali and Pratt, *Women in Iraq*, Chapter Three, detail these developments.

agencies was no less politicized than other kinds of political aid and civil society financing. In the institutional landscapes of Cairo, Amman, or Baghdad there are historically independent women's movements, government-organized agencies for women, donor-oriented women's organizations, and hybrids of mixed parentage. This section of the chapter focuses on Arab women's rendezvous in UN conferences and the national politics surrounding representation of women. It shows a strong Westphalian bias toward national machineries linked through interstate bodies, conferences, and declarations. These followed an archetypal international regime-building template: national representatives to transnational conferences co-sign normative declarations, construct and license parallel institutions, and track progress toward stated norms.[58] In a curious dialectic, this discursive and bureaucratic project co-enabled ruling Iraqi, Egyptian, South Yemeni, and Tunisian party-states to present themselves as women's rights champions. Constructivism works, but in paradoxical and political ways different from the GAD paradigm's assumption of male recalcitrance.

Inherently inter-governmental, United Nations organizations have a dirigist boilerplate for internationally coordinated parallel national bureaucracies. According to its web page in 2006, UNIFEM's Western Asia's mission was based on the belief that "the best way to help Arab women is to strengthen the organizations they create and control." Even before the 1975 Conference on Women in Mexico City established UNIFEM, the plan was to set up "national machineries," defined as "any organizational structure established with particular responsibility for the advancement of women and the elimination of discrimination of women at the central national level."[59] Conferences in Nairobi in 1985 and Beijing in 1995 charged these national machineries with integrating gender into public policy and coding gender-disaggregated data. Whereas earlier conferences had celebrated 1970s-style anti-colonial and/or socialist concerns with national self-determination, non-violence, labor solidarity, communal rights, and basic human needs, Beijing's platform

---

[58] For an optimistic view, see Martha A. Chen, "Engendering World Conferences: The International Women's Movement and the UN," in Thomas G. Weiss and Leon Gordenker, eds, *NGOs, the UN, and Global Governance* (Boulder: Lynne Rienner, 1996).

[59] Mervat Tallawy, "International Organizations, National Machinery, Islam, and Foreign Policy," in ed. Mahnaz Afkhami and Erika Friedl, *Muslim Women and the Politics of Participation: Implementing the Beijing Platform* (Syracuse: Syracuse University Press, 1997) 128–140: 29.

emphasized individual rights and opportunities in a globalized neo-liberal world order.[60] Multilateral and bilateral donors were increasingly inclined to support national institutes or even ministries of women's affairs "regardless of whether such a demand is a national priority, internally generated or not," according to a writer who observed that such institutions don't exist in Canada or the United States.[61]

Under any circumstances the establishment of institutes or ministries is a politicized bureaucratic process. Demand for some national women's machineries was internally generated, but often in politically complicated ways. Several Arab governments were party to this multilateral regime-building enterprise from its beginnings after World War II.[62] There were Arab delegations to the Mexico City conference in 1975, and more at each subsequent gathering. In Syria, Iraq, Tunisia, and what was then South Yemen, national women's organs were formed under ruling party umbrellas. National women's councils, federations, ministries, and departments appeared in Egypt, Jordan, both Yemens, the Occupied Territories, Algeria, Lebanon, Kuwait, Qatar, Bahrain, and Sudan. Later, with European support, UNIFEM projects in Jordan, Lebanon, occupied Palestine, Syria, and Yemen offered technical and financial assistance to groups activated for the Beijing conference.[63] These policies fused nationalist feminism with feminist internationalism.

This fusion of international efforts with governmental co-optation of women's movements was especially pronounced in Egypt. There, one scholar explained, donor support contributed to transforming empowerment into a set of activities that gave the illusion of wide-scale activism, but actually re-enforced existing power structures.[64] Thus, anti-colonial and post-colonial Egyptian feminist participation was gradually amalgamated to the governance strategy of a ruling party that replaced existing

---

[60] Mervat F. Hatem, "In the Eye of the Storm: Islamic Societies and Muslim Women in Globalization Discourses," *Comparative Studies of South Asia, Africa, and the Middle East* 26:1 (2006) 22–35.

[61] Nahla Abdo, "Imperialism, the State, and NGOs: Middle Eastern Contexts and Contestations," *Comparative Studies of South Asia, Africa, and the Middle East*, 30: 2(2010) 238–249: 240.

[62] Waltz, "Universal Human Rights."

[63] Noeleen Heyzer and Ilana Landsberg-Lewis, "UNIFEM and Women's Climb to Equality," in ed. Afkhami and Friedl (1997) 153–161. See also Sakr, "Women's Rights and the Arab Media," 18.

[64] Mariz Tadros, "Between the Elusive and the Illusionary: Donors' Empowerment Agendas in the Middle East in Perspective." *Comparative Studies of South Asia, Africa, and the Middle East* 30:2 (2010) 224–237: 231–233.

women's charities and political groups with national corporatist structures (parallel to the peasant's unions, professional syndicates and youth
federations created or consolidated concomitantly, as discussed in the
next chapter). Subsequently, the Egyptian Women's Organization and
the National Council for Women flourished under the UN Decade for
Women (1975–85) and the leadership of media-savvy First Ladies Jihan
Sadat and then Suzanne Mubarak. Mrs. Mubarak and appointees to the
National Council for Women commandeered neo-liberal conceptions of
individual women's rights, collective representation of women's concerns,
and diatribes about culture change in the fanfare for International Women's
Day.[65] And Egypt led the creation, under Arab League auspices, of the Arab
Women's Organization run by a Supreme Council of First Ladies promi-
nently featuring Suha Arafat, wife of Palestinian leader Yasser Arafat,
Queen Rania of Jordan, Suzanne Mubarak, wife of Egyptian President
Hosni Mubarak, and Leila Ben Ali, wife of Tunisian President Zine El
Abidine Ben Ali.[66] They met in November 2001 under the Arab League
logo. A human rights activist wrote that "Raising the flying colours of
'women's rights' and organising a huge number of meetings and conferences" headed by female members of ruling families, Arab governments
"have used and blunted international pressures for reform by making concessions in domains that do not reflect directly on the political system and its
balance of forces."[67]

In a great advertising campaign, Marrakesh in June 2003 hosted the
Global Summit of Women for nearly 700 people from 80 countries. The
web site credited corporate sponsors Royal Dutch Shell, IBM, Hudson
Highland Group, FedEx, Cisco Systems, and *Les Eaux Minerales
D'Oulmes*. The summit was attended by women from countries not usu-
ally involved in democracy summits (Bahrain, Oman, Iraq, Kuwait, even
Saudi Arabia), along with the more commonly represented countries

---

[65] For context, see Dina Ezzat, "Bridging the Gender Gap?" *al-Ahram Weekly* No. 669,
December 2003, about Suzanne Mubarak's release of reports co-produced by the National
Council for Women (NCW) with the World Bank and UNICEF, respectively; and
Seheir Kansouh-Habib, "The Woman Beyond the Machinery," interview with Farkhonda
Hassan, secretary-general of the NCW on the occasion of its 7th Annual Conference,
*al-Ahram Weekly Online* No. 835, 8–14 March 2007.

[66] Reem Laila, "Women in Action," interview with Wadouda Badran, head of the Arab
Women Organization, *al-Ahram Weekly* No. 693, 3–9 June 2004: the AWO, ratified in
2001 by 13 of the 22 Arab League member-states, has an executive council comprised of
state agencies for women as well as a Supreme Council of First Ladies.

[67] Bahey Eldin Hassan, "Democratize or Disintegrate," *al-Ahram Weekly* No. 862, 13–19
September 2007.

FIGURE 6. From L to R, Suha Arafat, wife of Palestinian leader Yasser Arafat, Queen Rania of Jordan, Suzanne Mubarak, wife of Egyptian President Hosni Mubarak, and Leila Ben Ali, wife of Tunisian President Zine El Abidine Ben Ali, attend the extraordinary Arab Women's Summit in Cairo November 2001 to mark the Year of the Arab Woman. The photographer's caption continues: "Representatives of the 22 member states of the Arab League took part in the opening session of the conference." Photo: Marwan Naamani/AFP/Getty Images. Used with permission.

(Egypt, Jordan, Lebanon, Morocco, and Algeria). Around the same time, the Kingdom of Morocco elevated its gender empowerment index by allocating a fraction of seats in the national parliament to females. Neighboring Tunisia, presenting itself as the most liberated enclave in the Arab region, also tried to rally women via a Ministry of Women and the Family, the National Observatory for Women, the National Council for Women and the Family, and the Centre for Research, Documentation, and Information on Women; and a number of ostensibly non-governmental organizations closely affiliated with the country's ruling elite.

Combining an externally oriented state feminism along the lines of Morocco and Tunisia and a "first lady" strategy, Jordan publicized its National Council for Women, headed by Princess Basma, a polished spokesperson for various Jordanian governmental and non-governmental organizations at international forums. Since its inception, the National

Council (JNCW) had enjoyed financial support from USAID's Democratic Initiatives, the *Ebert* and *Adenauer* Foundations, UN Beijing preparation funds, and other sources. The Princess Basma Women's Resource Center worked on projects related to elections, and the Princess herself presided over the founding meeting of the Arab Media Women's Centre in Amman. NDI partnered with the JNCW to train female candidates for the 2003 parliamentary elections, and with the Arab Women's Media Center to prepare journalists to cover the election story and to engage women in election-related activities. The German aid agency GTZ, and JNCW, seconded to the Queen Zein Al Sharaf Institute for Development a two-year training program in gender-sensitive organizational development that brought in European professional consultants and trainers. By addressing Jordanian and international gatherings, publishing reports, offering personal donations, and co-opting other female notables, princesses and RONGOs set the parameters for gender communication in Jordan while representing the voice of Jordanian womanhood abroad. Queen Rania, the stylish and articulate English-speaking spouse of King Abdullah, later performed this role brilliantly.

Iraq had been a prototype for state feminism, sending delegates to the First Eastern Women's Congress in Damascus in 1930 and the Second Eastern Women's Congress in Tehran in 1932, and hosting the Arab Women's Conference in Baghdad in 1934. After the 1958 coup against the pro-British monarchy, the new government banned the Iraqi Communist Party's League for the Defense of Women's Rights, and instead licensed a rival Organization of Republican Women. When the Ba'ath took power it promised full citizenship rights, and created the General Federation of Iraqi Women (GFIW) as part of what a pair of scholars termed the "fascist apparatus of the party-state."[68] A scholar who heard "love songs" sung to Saddam at the 1980 GFIW meetings inferred that the dictatorship sought to win women's loyalty in order to weaken provincial authorities, but not to empower women enough to alienate religious and tribal elites. All 19 of the Ba'ath party's women candidates for parliament that year won. Women's centers, day-care, literacy training, and other services were useful, according to this researcher. But there was also resistance "expressed by absenteeism in places of work and what

---

[68] Jacqueline S. Ismael and Shereen T. Ismael, "Gender and State in Iraq," in ed. Suad Joseph, *Gender and Citizenship in the Middle East* (Syracuse, N.Y.: Syracuse University Press, 2000) 194.

appeared to me to be work sabotage, wastefulness, and/or inefficiency."[69] People who saw things this way would not have been impressed by the CPA's concessions of parliamentary seats or furnishing of women's centers.

## THE POLITICS OF NON-GOVERNMENTAL FUNDING

This chapter now segues into the next, because political aid projects co-existed with state feminism – sometimes. Within the context of UN-sponsored transnational conferences and democracy broker portfolios, non-governmentalism became a major trend. Notwithstanding the statist bias of bilateral and multilateral agencies, donors also targeted women's and other NGOs. Two vectors present themselves. First, agencies from Ford to the *Ebert Stiftung* to the Canadian International Development Agency prioritized feminist organizations in their NGO funds disbursements. Second, there is a process of NGO accreditation under the Beijing machinery, eligibility for which rests, in turn, on consultative status with the UN's Economic and Social Council (UNESCO) and, more generally, much paperwork and red tape.

These two processes were linked by donor capacity-building programs intended to prepare organizations to meet the administrative, programmatic, and accounting mandates of UNESCO, the Bank, USAID, the EU, and so forth. In the late twentieth and early twenty-first centuries, in other words, various resources became available to women's agencies meeting the superstructural criteria of international organizations and conforming to their professional practices. The availability of dollars, euros, and junkets stimulated a new generation of private women's agencies, and competition among them for 'brand certification.' Even as large numbers of organizations won one or two small grants, the major winners naturally came from an elite bevy of tough, smart, educated, intercontinental professionals. Two renowned Arab authors, Fatima Mernissi and Nawwal as-Sa'adawi, who lived their very public lives at the convex interface of Arabism and globalism, exemplified the paradoxes of feminist marketing.

As in other sectors, qualifying think tanks to bid for contracts was an explicit aim of gender programming. On a big-ticket scale, the World Bank announced in 2005 a $800,000 grant to the Tunis-based Center of Arab

---

[69] Suad Joseph, "Elite Strategies for State-Building: Women, Family, Religion, and State in Iraq and Lebanon," in ed. Deniz Kandiyoti, *Women, Islam, and the State* (Philadelphia: Temple University Press, 1991) 186.

Women for Training and Research (CAWTAR), partner to previous externally financed projects, to administer grants to other research and advocacy institutions. A job like this reproduces expert knowledge consistent
with the World Bank's sophisticated methodological standards and its
goal of integrating women into global markets as business owners, workers, and borrowers. Scores of programs, from three-day workshops to
masters' programs such as the one at Sana'a University in Women's
Studies and Social Analysis financed by the Netherlands Embassy, trained
women to gather and format gendered data.

Building national and cross-border inter-organizational networks was
fundamental to the UNIFEM strategy. For example, a $50,000 Advocacy
for Women's Legal Rights project supported the *Association Democratique
des Femmes du Maroc* (ADFM), the professional advocacy organization
run by Fatima Mernissi. According to UNIFEM's webpage in 2001,
its "initial catalytic funding enabled the association to build and broaden
its resource base (UN and bi-lateral)." The association "stands at the
forefront of the national women's movement" and took the lead in a
"civil society network" to advocate reform of family law. ADFM had
already secured grants from the EU for legal counseling and voter education
and was a member of the NED-organized World Movement for Democracy.
While her husband was president, Hillary Clinton met in Rabat with
members of ADFM and others in this network that basked in the ensuing
publicity. With money from the *Ebert Stiftung*, ADFM took the lead in
the *Collectif 95 Maghreb Egalité* program, submitted proposals to the
World Women's Conference in Beijing, and also produced a sophisticated
Parallel Report of Moroccan NGOs on the Application of CEDAW.
The *Collectif* also documented "honor crimes," studied media stereotypes,
compiled a feminist dictionary of Quranic terms, and joined the 15
Moroccan and hundreds of other UNESCO/Beijing accredited NGOs
at the special session of the General Assembly entitled Women 2000:
Gender equality, Development and Peace for the twenty-first century. Such
networks constituted an important public phenomenon in Morocco and
elsewhere.

Among Cairo's gender advocacy think tanks, the Arab Women's
Solidarity Association (AWSA) enjoyed particularly high international
visibility. Founded in 1982 by the much-translated author Nawal al-
Sa'adawi after her release from political detention, and given UNESCO
consultative status in 1985, AWSA garnered global recognition and funding for its campaigns against honor killings and female circumcision.
Subject to imprisonment, a fraudulent lawsuit to annul her marriage, the

banning of some of her writings, and administrative harassment of AWSA, al-Sa'adawi was also a wealthy, forceful, complicated, and controversial figure who (inter alia) mounted a short-lived presidential campaign in 2005 and joined the Tahrir protests in 2011. AWSA's conferences tackled national issues from patriarchy to right-wing attacks on feminist activism, but also took aim at the structural and sexualized violence of American and Israeli occupations of Iraq and Palestine.[70] Her international fame for rebelling against Arab and Islamic cultural norms led some Egyptian and Arab progressives to argue that Western Orientalists selected her as 'the' voice of Egyptian and Arab feminism.[71] Al-Sa'adawi's career and AWSA's transnational conferences traverse the heuristic lines we draw between or among national, transnational, and global politics.

For all their stardom, Mernissi and al-Sa'adawi were by no means the only prominent female public intellectuals or activists in North Africa. I mentioned Raufa Hassan, head of the well-funded and controversial Women's Studies Center at Sana'a University, earlier. The 2011 Yemeni Nobel Peace Prize laureate Tawakkul Karman, honored as an emblematic local leader of the Arab uprisings, headed a successful NGO called Journalists Without Chains that had raised funds from a range of international donors. Another prominent Yemeni woman, Amal Basha, volunteered for the initially left-leaning group called No Peace Without Justice, and served on the board of the Foundation for the Future, discussed in the next chapter. There were many others in Yemen alone, many of whom were to play prominent roles in Yemen's uprising against the Salih dictatorship and the National Dialogue Conference of 2013. Scores of Mediterranean women's advocacy organizations and think tanks, some of them with unique profiles and niches, attending trainings or won grants or contracts for projects dealing with legal aid, family violence, electoral campaigns, voter education, gender analysis, media watchdogs, entrepreneurial advocacy, and so on.[72] Let us not disparage these efforts as Western imperial agendas. Nonetheless, the most internationally networked individuals and organizations did not reflect the full, wide

---

[70] Nawal Sadawi, "The Seventh International AWSA Conference Rationale and the Way Forward," *Meridians: Feminism, Race, Transnationalism* 6:2 (2006) 22–32.

[71] Hatem, "Economic and Political Liberation in Egypt," 247; Amal Amireh, "Framing Nawal El Saadawi: Arab Feminism in a Transnational World," *Signs* 26:1 (2000) 215–249.

[72] Reem Laila, "Towards Gender Equality," *al-Ahram Weekly* No. 693, 3–9 June 2004, reviewed a survey of donor-funded gender programs in Egypt.

spectrum of women's or feminist orientations.[73] More foreign capital was invested in businesswomen's organizations than in labor organizations with far larger memberships. In view of the popular followings of these organizations, the refusal of the EU and other donors to deal with Islamist organizations showed an obvious ideological bias.[74] As discussed further in the next chapter, donors' operational and documentary requirements, as well as cocktail hour liaisons, tended to favor NGOs headed by bi- or trilingual professionals or public personalities over voluntary or membership-based organizations.

As in other fields, international patronage for Palestinian women's organizations was notably divisive. Along the lines of the First Lady model, the NGO called *Miftah* headed by the prominent peace-process negotiator Hannan Ashrawi enjoyed special access to international backing in the 1990s. Overall, research in the Territories revealed that the twin ideological commitments to the Oslo Accords and neo-liberal economics seemed to attract dollars and euros, whereas sympathizers with either Islamists or revolutionary nationalists missed the gravy train.[75] The preferred structure of 'women's groups' was a charismatic executive director assisted by a salaried staff with nominal input from a board of directors and hardly any grassroots involvement. One apt turn of phrase held that "NGO-ization" transformed social causes into 'projects' with a plan, a timetable, and a limited budget, 'owned' for purposes of accountability to funders: NGO dependence on "modern communication methods such as the internet, PowerPoint, and conferences – globalized tools, not local ones" is "not a bad thing" in itself, wrote an academic scholar and participant observer, except that projects "aim" at a "target group" that is not a natural, existing social group, much less a constituency with a voice in project design, but an imaginary audience for the project itself. This make-believe dysphonic woman is an object, not an agent, of her own enablement.[76]

---

[73] On generational, political, and ideological variations among Egyptians feminists, see Mariz Tadros "A Movement for All Seasons," *al-Ahram Weekly* No. 419, 4–10 March 1999; Lina Mahmoud "Sixty Years on," *al-Ahram Weekly* No. 734, 17–23 March 2005.

[74] Federica Bicchi, "Want Funding? Don't Mention Islam: EU Democracy Promotion in the Mediterranean," *CFSP Forum* 4: 3 (2006) 10–12.

[75] Manal Jamal, *After the Peace Process: Foreign Donor Assistance and the Political Economy of Marginalization in Palestine and El Salvador* (PhD diss., McGill University, Montreal, 2006).

[76] Islah Jad, "The NGO-ization of Arab Women's Movements," *IDS Bulletin* 35:4 (2004) 24–42: 38, citing research by her graduate students.

Research in Iraq yielded similar findings about NGO professionalization and the ways some norm entrepreneurs forged successful careers. A fascinating comparison of two different American programs in Iraq featuring workshops, seminars, and conferences for women concluded that participating NGOs became professionalized, depoliticized, and detached from the larger Iraqi women's movement and social justice causes.[77] Other researchers pointed to deliberate, creative utilization of normative and material capital for personal gain or political causes.[78] These observations of detached professionalization combined with active agency applied to almost every country. Across the region, funding priorities favored women who internalized and reproduced certain gender-analytic rhetorics. Iraqi women under both the old regime and the occupation resignified and instrumentalized these logics of representation.

## A CLASH OF IDEOLOGIES IN IRAQ

Iraq provided the most poignant example of the patronizing politicization of feminist claims and the paradoxes of institutionalized idealism. This story turns on contradictory trajectories. UNIFEM and other UN-affiliated organizations operated during and beyond the sanctions era, working, as usual, through national institutions. As reported on its web site, UNIFEM took part in the UNICEF-organized workshop, Monitoring and Implementation of CEDAW, in early 2001, well before the Anglo-American invasion, to "strengthen the capacity" of the National Committee for the Advancement of Iraqi Women and 'NGOs' (whatever that meant, in that context) in their monitoring of Iraq's implementation of the Convention for the Elimination of Discrimination. Accordingly, UNIFEM, with UNDP and Iraq's Ministry of Labor and Social Affairs, initiated the project Support to the National Committee for the Advancement of Iraqi Women.[79] This National Committee, in turn, delivered to the United Nations a plea to lift the crippling penalties that was, at the same time, a thinly veiled anthem to Saddam Hussein. Here, the criminal regime formally appealed to the UN, in the name of women's

---

[77] Nadeen El-Kassem, "The Pitfalls of a 'Democracy Promotion' Project for Women of Iraq," *International Journal of Lifelong Education* 27:2 (2008) 129–151, compared the U.S.-based Independent Women's Forum and Iraqi Women's Will.

[78] Al-Ali and Pratt, *Women in Iraq*, 146–148.

[79] Retrospectively, see Saeid N. Nashat, "A Look into the Women's Movement in Iraq," *Farzaneh* 6:11, 2003: 54–65.

advancement, for the repeal of trade sanctions and the ending of air raids enforced by the United States.

Multilateral organizations are uniquely positioned to weather revolutionary or state-collapse situations. True to United Nations tradition, UNIFEM accelerated its activities in post-war Iraq, documenting gender violence, convening seminars, publicizing rules of war and conventions against torture, and fostering an Iraqi women journalist's network and a Voice of Women Arabic-language radio station. Working with International IDEA, UNIFEM and its partners advanced Iraq's gender quota for parliamentary elections. Once the manager of the sanctions-and-weapons regime, yet also on some level complicit in the Ba'ath party's corporatist feminism, the UN now seemed from certain vantage points aligned with the occupation.

Yet there were frictions between American neo-conservatives and the Beijing platform. UNIFEM openly defied the occupation in at least some of its programs. Moreover, at least one of MEPI's main Women's Pillar projects in Iraq went to an organization dedicated to American-style religiously based 'family values' and openly hostile to the spirit of Beijing and CEDAW. The Independent Women's Forum (IWF) was awarded $10 million from USAID under MEPI for programs to prepare women for elections, investment activity, and other forms of competition in public life. A five-day conference in Amman, Jordan, in April 2005 for 1,300 Iraqi women featuring two Congressional delegations and a long list of expert speakers was co-sponsored by the Iraqi Women's Educational Institute, an organization formed by IWF, the American Islamic Congress, and the conservative Washington-headquartered Foundation for the Defense of Democracies. Contrary to UNIFEM and most European programming, IWF, founded by leading Republican women including the Vice President's wife Lynne Cheney, castigated the CEDAW treaty on its web site on August 16, 2002, as a violation of U.S. sovereignty by UN monitors, a form of socialism, an assault on motherhood, and "bitter gender politics." Pointing out that the United States has not ratified the relevant UN documents, the Heritage Foundation condemned the Beijing+10 initiatives as excessively sexualized, dismissive of family values, and antithetical to the real interests of women.[80] Ironically, some of these objections, grounded in

---

[80] Jennifer A. Marshall, Melissa G. Pardue, and Grace V. Smith, "Beyond the Words at Beijing+10: How U.N. Policy Falls Short of Women's Best Interests," The Heritage Foundation Backgrounder #1829, February 28, 2005. Like so many Arabs, they contended that the family shields women against violence, whereas the Beijing language treats the family as a site of abuse.

evangelical Protestantism, resemble the attitudes of Islamist atavists, female as well as male, in Iraq and other Arab countries. Global governance regimes are not synonymous with American foreign policy.

## THE PARADOXES OF INSTITUTIONALIZED IDEALISM

Other feminist scholars have dismantled the discourses and some institutional practices of women's rights framed as civilizational inspirations and antipathies. I have tried to bring these critical perspectives to bear on the study of democracy promotion and to consider how these messages are interpreted and repurposed on the ground. First, we looked at dialogues between experts delivering a consistent message about the false consciousness of people with different opinions about law, elections, the sources of their oppression, or what they wanted from government. Presented with dogmatic cultural determinism, some got annoyed; others snickered or heckled good-naturedly; quite a number penned intellectual rebuttals.

To say that Iraqi or Tunisian women are not passive recipients but rather active agents is in itself patronizing. It bears saying anyway. This discussion traced participation in transnational organizing throughout the twentieth century, including legacies of state feminism in Arab socialist republics. The historical accounts made it clear that Westerners who imagined themselves to be introducing the idea of gender emancipation in post-colonial Arab societies had not read much of the history of colonialism, agency, and tokenism. Against this backdrop we looked at down-to-earth competition over material and figurative capital. In recent years, ruling cliques, First Ladies, opposition activists, prominent public personalities, norm entrepreneurs, businesswomen, college professors, professional gender specialists, and think-tank researchers variously seized new opportunities to advance specific, varying causes and interests. We have seen, too, an expanding transnational gender regime that fosters professionalized national machineries, supports prominent NGOs, and gets some governments to sign declarations of equality. Yet at the same time we heard many activist feminist intellectuals, including, or especially, bilingual professionals, express complicated views about how these institutional networks stand in relation to popular movements and grassroots concerns.

I devoted a separate chapter to projects for women because gender-related projects are so prevalent in the Middle East, and in order to bring critical feminist scholarship to bear on serious study of political aid. The investigation of empowerment projects, which cut across the judicial, legislative, and civil society sectors, has been instructive in several ways. First, in terms of the familiar sentimentalism vs. realpolitik debate, projects for women seem to demonstrate chivalry over military strategy. On the other hand, the United States has not been a leader in advancing gender quotas, the CEDAW convention, or national machineries. Instead, the UN-centered UNIFEM/Beijing complex is an example of a far-flung regime that expands what many scholars call neo-liberal globalization, a trajectory that transcends American, or even OECD, influence because it is effectively a post-national, global governance regime.

Therefore, looking at gender empowerment projects directed our attention to intersections of nationalism and globalization where transnational regimes are forged, and where, as we have seen, there is quite a lot of cross-cultural dialogue. Thinking about how meanings are constructed, we saw conflicting regimes of truth if not a totally free marketplace of ideas. The mostly bilingual professionals cited here might feel 'caught between' dynamically interposed official agencies purporting to 'represent' them; but they also expressed meanings that transcended transcripts of domination. The dialects of empowerment and even some of the critical deconstructions of knowledge-as-power assume the gullibility of target audiences. This assumption does not stand up to empirical scrutiny, even, as here, of its own transcripts.

Instead, many professional women dismissed sweeping cultural-religious stereotypes as ignorant of actual national political struggles and real sites of violence. Harping on sharia (rather than, say, existing or proposed national family law) is especially counter-productive. Other naïve assumptions were that the police are there to protect girls from their fathers; or that the state apparatus is more trustworthy than the mosque; or that everywoman identifies with the Princess. Moreover, too many foreigners present a negative image of victimization and indoctrination to women quite self-confident in their careers, communities, and activism.

Finally, then, although the motifs are culturally laden, the politics of state feminism, transnational women's organizations, and resource completion are just that: politics, in the old-fashioned sense of competition for power in public spheres. Project pathways and institutional arrangements matter. The positioning of women's or human rights' institutions in or beyond central executive bureaucracies, for instance, have very specific political implications, here fortifying the executive authority of national regimes and there threatening that authority. Human rights institutions or machineries for women could draw feminist energies away from social justice movements toward national or transnational governance projects, or provide some space for counter-hegemonic activism, or all of the above. The next chapter takes this investigation further by examining the especially disputatious circuits of NGO finance, which in turn requires thinking about the boundaries of 'national' and 'government.' It does not isolate women's activities from other civil society initiatives. Many of the authors cited are female. It illustrates further the common struggles of campaigners navigating transnational spheres of non-governmentalized political advocacy. It shows why it is important to recognize that aid for political transitions consists of discrete, funded project activities undertaken via specific institutional partnerships, draws attention to the transnational complexity of those arrangements, and reiterates the political argument that the intelligentsia creatively translated and utilized the logics and practices of this aid.

# 4

This book opened with a vignette. Police were investigating aggressively what foreign democracy brokers were doing in Egypt, how funds were being channeled to Egyptian advocacy groups, and whether these operations were lawful. The Minister of International Cooperation, Fayza Aboulnaga, alleged there was an "unauthorized" transfer in 2011 of nearly $48 million to local offices of American or international agencies and $6 million to twelve Egyptian organizations, and questioned whether they were properly accredited under the infamously restrictive Law 84 of 2002. By March 2012, Aboulnaga said the amount of American aid piped to NGOs in Egypt during the previous ten months reached $150 million.[1]

This case, as it unfolded, demonstrated how political aid, especially through non-governmental conduits, could be deeply disputatious inside non-democratic polities and in the international arena. It was especially so during the extraordinary circumstances of social upheaval and regime transition in 2011. But fights over NGO registration had been going on in Egypt and other countries with similar legal and regulatory systems for a couple of decades. In 2011, the White House's show of support for a post-Mubarak "transition to democracy" ran afoul of previous negotiations. After Mubarak's resignation on February 11, the Obama–Clinton State Department decided to fast-track $65 million in budgeted official aid to four American groups and selected liberal Egyptian NGOs. This allocation reversed an earlier concession to Mubarak that permitted his ministers

---

[1] Fayza Aboulnaga, "Why Egypt Moved against Unregistered NGOs," *Washington Post*, March 9, 2012.

to vet grantees. The new policy skirting the Ministry of International Cooperation's aid distribution pipelines drew kleptocrats' ire.

Meanwhile, even as Mubarak and then the SCAF attributed mass popular uprising to outside troublemaking, American journalists published stories about how U.S. government-funded projects had "nurtured young democrats" with training on organization, social networking, and new media.[2] These stories intensified Egyptian anxieties about foreign snooping and domination. Next, as also mentioned in my Introduction, seven Egyptians hired by the Washington-based International Republican Institute to conduct elections-related training workshops resigned in protest against policies they said were designed to help liberal secular parties compete against the Muslim Brotherhood.[3] These developments and the rumors they fed set the stage for the December 29 raids on American, German, and Egyptian think tanks that the Anglophone press called "non-governmental pro-democracy groups"; temporary suspension of American arms transfers to Egypt; a multi-million dollar bail payment followed by the departure of most of the foreign nationals charged; and protracted court proceedings for forty-some Egyptian and foreign employees of NDI, IRI, Freedom House, and the *Konrad Adenauer Stiftung*. We will return to this convoluted argument at the end of the chapter, after a close look at many earlier spats over NGO licensing, NGO funding, and NGO laws in Egypt and elsewhere.

For another preview of conflicts over this issue, consider the ruckus over the funding practices of the Foundation for the Future years earlier. The Foundation was an NGO funding conduit proposed under the Broader Middle East and North Africa Initiative unveiled by the Bush administration at the 2004 Sea Island Summit of the G-8. Several regional allies including Egypt accepted invitations to join the Sea Island Summit. Yet even friendly governments that signed onto an annual multilateral conference called the Forum for the Future and initiatives relating to women and entrepreneurial business ventures balked specifically at the Foundation's 'non-governmental' designation. Egypt's delegation to the second annual

---

[2] For instance, Charles J. Hanley, "U.S. Training Quietly Nurtured Young Arab Democrats," *Washington Post*, March 12, 2011; Ron Nixon, "U.S. Groups Helped Nurture Arab Uprisings," *New York Times*, April 14, 2011.

[3] The evidence for these assertions was corroborated by Desmond Butler, "U.S. Democracy Aid Went to Favored Groups in Egypt," *The Guardian*, June 12, 2012, citing interviews and providing links to the October resignation letter and WikiLeak cables that tend to substantiate the contention that American democracy brokers hoped to support liberal groups especially against the Muslim Brotherhood.

Forum for the Future in Manama was adamant that only 'officially licensed' organizations could be eligible to apply for Foundation grants or to participate in the Forum's parallel NGO meetings.[4] Finally, at the third Forum in 2006 at a Jordanian Dead Sea resort, compromise language excluded applications from "terrorist organizations, illegal entities, their surrogates, and associations advocating or resorting to violence."[5] All official parties seemed satisfied with this omnibus exclusion of extra- and anti-systemic entities. Meanwhile, FFF, as the Foundation of the Future inevitably came to be known, appointed a prominent regional board of directors, issued instructions on how to apply, opened offices in Amman, and began holding its own annual regional conferences. This storyline also continues later in this chapter.

Both these anecdotes were examples of deep-seated authoritarian 'push-back' or 'backlash' against civil society promotion. Either episode could be cited from one perspective as proof of the American quest for full spectrum dominance in the MENA region, and from another as evidence of the Egyptian regime's authoritarian obsessions. They were but two among seemingly endless arguments over what is or is not 'governmental.' Likewise both raised conceptual issues and authoritarian hackles over how 'non-governmental' agencies operate inside and/or beyond sovereign institutional domains. Furthermore, both episodes and many somewhat lower profile court cases put rights defenders, advocates for social justice, and other civic actors on the hot seat.

The main tension in this chapter comes from the interaction between civil society promotion and the dictatorial pushback against it. As in the chapter Patronizing Women, I try to present the story from the vantage point of participants, professionals, and activist intellectuals working in the interstices between two different regimes of co-optation. Whereas in previous chapters we considered both 'positive' and critical scholarly perspectives on legal, electoral, and women's regimes, in this chapter I begin with the intellectual critique of civil society promotion and the

---

[4] Bahey Eldin Hassan, "Broader Middle East Initiative: Arab Governments Strike Back," *Arab Reform Bulletin* 4:2 (2006); Sherine Bahaa, "Waiting for Plan B," *al-Ahram Weekly* No. 769, 17–23 November 2005; Robin Wright, "U.S. Goals Are Thwarted at Pro-Democracy Forum: Demand by Egypt Derails Middle East Initiative," *Washington Post*, November 13, 2005; NED, "The Backlash against Democracy Assistance," report prepared for Senator Richard J. Lugar, Chairman, Committee on Foreign Relations, United States Senate, June 8, 2006 ("the Lugar report").
[5] Foundation for the Future "Charter Principles," at http://www.foundationforfuture.org/documents/principles.html.

construct of the NGO, which many scholars associate with neo-liberal globalizations' assault on national sovereignty. The counter-argument emerges from detailed investigation of authoritarian regulation and re-regulation and the limits of donor influence in this contentious field. The investigation bores into the workings of Egyptian corporatism, the long, ultimately futile campaign to reform Arab NGO laws, and strange permutations in occupied Iraq and counter-terrorism policies. Following up on distinctions in the chapters on law and gender between backing public sector institutions (especially in the executive branch of central governments) and supporting independent non-profit agencies (especially but not only adversarial advocacy organizations), the chapter focuses attention on the pathways and professional practices of political aid. In particular it extends the discussion of rival legal jurisdictions by looking at legislation and court cases.

## NGOS, GONGOS, AND DONGOS

In everyday English usage, the term 'NGO' connotes a non-governmental, non-profit, cause-driven association motivated by altruistic intent rather than pecuniary or political gain. NGOs are the good guys. However, scholars who scrutinized the habits of North–South NGO funding already warned us not to think that 'non-governmental' is synonymous with 'democratic.'[6] Many scholars and activists have critically interrogated prototypes of NGOs or CSOs as units of civic engagement: this construction, they argue, constitutes a potentially potent classificatory scheme that excludes mass or spontaneous mobilization. One perceptive critic of development aid argued that civil society promotion amounts to the professionalization and institutionalization of certain patterns of knowledge.[7]

The construct of the NGO, originally meant to distinguish independent advocacy from inter-governmental transactions, is problematic.[8] The

---

[6] William F. Fisher, "Doing Good? The Politics and Antipolitics of NGO Practices," *Annual Review of Anthropology* 26 (1997) 439–464, on Northern funding of Southern NGOs. For a self-critical perspective from Europe, see Elisabeth Johansson-Nogues, "Civil Society in Euro-Mediterranean Relations: What Success of EU's Normative Promotion?" EUI Working Papers, RSCAS, 2006/40 (2006) 17.

[7] Escobar, *Encountering Development*.

[8] As observed in "Sins of the Secular Missionaries," *The Economist*, January 29, 2000, the NGO tag was coined by the UN to distinguish non-state actors from its member states. The catch-all category enabled donors to favor business associations over grass-roots groups or labor unions, according to Jude Howell and Jenny Pearce, "Civil Society: Technical Instrument or Social Force for Change?" in ed. David Lewis and Tina Wallace, *New*

governmental/non-governmental binary is a convenient dummy variable defining civic energies aphophatically for what they are not. Inside the industry there are a range of rhyming variations distinguishing parastatal qua-NGOs, government-organized GONGOs, royally-organized RONGOs, donor-oriented DONGOs, World Bank initiated BINGOs, and even entrepreneurial B-Y-O (bring-your-own) "bringos."[9] But they all call themselves NGOs, even in Arabic, where in lieu of translation the identical acronym is often rendered in text in Latin alphabet letters or in speech as pronounced in English. Overall, the ubiquitous neologism of the NGO is an imprecise linguistic expression that is left, as we will see, for various governments and donor agencies to define bureaucratically and ideologically. In practice, an NGO is something registered as such with national governments, the United Nations, or donor agencies. In comparing and contrasting criteria for inclusion and patronage, this chapter illustrates the politics and paradoxes of 'NGOization.' Many observers deduced that political aid stimulated a proliferation of professional, rather than grassroots, NGOs.

Calling Freedom House or NDI or International IDEA non-governmental, with the possible additional implication of apolitical, is not quite accurate. Most Western-based democracy brokers are 'NGOs' by fiat: that is, they were created and/or funded by governments to be 'NGOs.' During the Cold War, American, British, Canadian, and other NATO legislatures each endowed national 'non-governmental' political foundations to foment liberalization and combat communism abroad through unofficial channels.[10] NED's conservative champions envisioned a role now forbidden by Congress to the Central Intelligence Agency (CIA), of bolstering pro-American opposition parties, unions, and media in countries allied with the Soviet Union or led by left-leaning parties.[11]

---

*Roles and Relevance: Development NGOs and the Challenge of Change* (Bloomfield, CT: Kumarian Press, 2000) 76–87.

[9] See also Sheila Carapico, "Mission: Democracy," *Middle East Report* 209, 28:4 (1998) 17–20, 40; and Carapico, "NGOs, INGOs, GO-NGOs, and DO-NGOs: Making Sense of Non-Governmental Organizations," *Middle East Report* 214, 30:1 (2000) 12–15.

[10] Bill Brock, "The Democracy Program: A Strong Foundation" *Commonsense* 6:1 (1983) 89–90. For a more comprehensive analysis, see Michael Pinto-Duschinsky, "Foreign Political Aid: The German Political Foundations and their U.S. Counterparts," *International Affairs* 67:1 (1991) 33–66. See also Thomas Carothers, "The NED at 10," *Foreign Policy* 95 (1994) 123–129.

[11] Joshua Muravchik, *Exporting Democracy: Fulfilling America's Destiny* (Washington: The American Enterprise Institute, 1991) 204–206, applauded the NED as a civilian institutional complement to military occupation, crisis intervention, and covert operations. This is why leftists in Latin America call NED a CIA front.

Shortly thereafter, the German *Stiftungen* that had pioneered overseas political aid (only to find their efforts to destabilize foreign governments the subject of domestic controversy) won West German federal budgetary support on grounds that they would pursue the national interest by 'indirect' means.[12] Such "semi-private bodies" could engage in political advocacy "at two removes," wrote a prominent European expert: first through the European Commission, then in turn back to the national political foundations.[13] Even the relatively few, mostly American organizations with private endowments, notably the Ford Foundation, the Soros Foundation's Open Society Institute, and the Carter Center at Emory University, helped extend U.S. foreign policy beyond formal governmental agencies.[14] Overall, the transnational democracy establishment is a publically funded endeavor. IRI, NDI, the *Stiftungen*, and kindred agencies are GONGOs or DONGOs as well as NGOs.

Overseas franchises of Northern NGOs, the proliferation of NGOs inside countries in the global South, new extra-governmental funding capillaries, and the booming NGO conference hospitality industry have been cited by critical scholars as symptoms of intensified globalization. Although its inception was in the Cold War era of geo-strategic politics, civil society promotion came of age in the neo-liberal era as a tool for dismantling centralized Soviet-style 'command' economies. Specifically they aimed at privatizing nationalized industries and opening markets to multinational companies. The construct of the NGO itself, then, and the free-market ideas NGOs were expected to produce and circulate, sold capitalist reasoning as freedom.[15] As we will see in the case of Egypt, NGO funding conduits were also a way of reducing government spending on welfare services.

---

[12] Michael Pinto-Duschinsky, "The Rise of 'Political Aid,'" in eds. Larry Diamond et al., *Consolidating the Third Wave Democracies* (Baltimore and London: The Johns Hopkins University Press, 1997) 297–98.
[13] Richard Youngs, "Democracy Promotion: The Case of European Union Strategy," Brussels, Center for European Policy Studies Working Document No. 167, October 2001, 12.
[14] Irene L. Gendzier, "Play It Again Sam: The Practice and Apology of Development," ed. Christopher Simpson, *Universities and Empire: Money and Politics in the Social Sciences during the Cold War* (New York: The New Press, 1998) 57–95.
[15] This reasoning associated free trade with the freeing of ideas and people, wrote Rebecca Saunders in "Uncanny Presence: The Foreigner at the Gate of Globalization," *Comparative Studies of South Asia, Africa, and the Middle East* 21: 1–2 (2001) 88–98: 93–94.

The literature on globalization yields some insights into the practices of political aid in the Middle East. Some contemporary scholars viewed the "outsourcing" of functions through unofficial non-inter-state channels as a quintessential part of a "neo-liberal mode of transnational governmentality" that replicates expert knowledge to establish graduated layers of rule different from the Westphalian conventions of sovereignty.[16] We already saw this concept at work in other sectors. By similar logic, civil society assistance sought to achieve consensual compliance by penetrating and coopting civil society, "and *from therein* [to] exercise control over popular mobilization and mass movements."[17] The ethnography and sociology of globalization do not lead us to believe this hegemony is magically attained, however. Instead, from-the-ground perspectives recognize ruptures, mutations, and contradictions.

These are non-linear trajectories of cause and effect. A prominent sociologist defined neo-liberal globalization as a twofold process comprised of (a) the promulgation of supra-national connections above, beyond or between countries; and (b) their penetration deep inside sub-national territorial and institutional domains. She invited us to investigate sovereign litigations of 'denationalization' at both levels so as to discover how governments produce new regulations, legislation, court decisions, and executive orders.[18] I find both the dual connotations of denationalization and the recommendation discerningly to investigate sovereign push-back very helpful. The disputes analyzed in this chapter were (so to speak) domain disputes and conflicts over extra-governmental, denationalized frontiers.

Contemporary social scientists inspired by the ideas of the French philosopher Michel Foucault on imprisonment, discipline, and 'gentler ways' of punishment have applied the notion of governmentality at two scales. First there is the national scale where colonial powers helped create states capable of governing and post-colonial governments consolidated their authority. A landmark study of colonial Egypt showed that

---

[16] James Ferguson and Akhil Gupta, "Spatializing States: Toward an Ethnography of Neoliberal Governmentality," *American Ethnologist* 29:4 (2002) 981–1002; Aihwa Ong, *Neo-Liberalism as Exception: Mutations in Citizenship and Sovereignty* (Durham and London: Duke University Press, 2006). Along with Sassen, these theorists focus on economic, financial, and labor transactions, mentioning civil society promotion as a possible further example.

[17] Robinson, "Globalization, the World System, and 'Democracy Promotion' in U.S. Foreign Policy" 643, emphasis in original.

[18] Sassen, *A Sociology of Globalization.*

administrative measures to organize, categorize, and contain social life, educate the native population to self-discipline, and, importantly, to "represent" Egypt in European exhibitions collectively functioned (at least in one historical era) to bring the population under control.[19] Another, comparative study analyzed how national 'legibility projects' collected, standardized, aggregated, and catalogued data to produce a "god's eye view" that would enable governments to remake society in their own image – only to see those grand schemes fall apart.[20] These analytical tools help us to understand Egyptian NGO legislation, for instance. The rather newer notion of transnational governmentality yields parallel insights into how supra-national regimes register, standardize, and potentially regulate civic engagement. Yet transnational modes of domination might not secure permanent civic hegemony defined in narrowly bureaucratic terms. Therefore we need to ask about both regimes whether local agents recirculate or repurpose prevailing transcripts. How does all this look to civic activists in the middle?[21] Let us start with scrutiny of Egyptian corporatist authoritarianism. It nationalized all forms of civic activism (including women's advocacy, as we saw in the last chapter) in the service of a state governance program, and sought in particular to cartelize 'foreign aid.'

## NATIONALIZED VOLUNTARISM IN EGYPT

Extra-governmental funding conduits such as FFF and NED challenged the Egyptian bureaucracy's ways of concentrating, co-opting, and containing civic energies as well as controlling foreign patronage. Bureaucratic devices were well entrenched in Egypt, where there was a long history of efforts to nationalize even 'apolitical' humanitarian rescue by harnessing it to the executive power of the state apparatus. All forms of voluntarism and activism had long since been amalgamated to the central executive. Here is a case in point. On October 12, 1992, 500 Caireens perished and 1,000 others were injured during an earthquake. While official national rescue

---

[19] Timothy Mitchell, *Colonizing Egypt* (Cairo: American University in Cairo Press, 1988).

[20] Scott, *Seeing Like a State:* 58, adding, the "grand plan of the ensemble has no necessary relationship to the order of life as experienced by its residents."

[21] Peter A. Tamas, "Spoken Moments of a Pernicious Discourse? Querying Foucauldian Critics' Representations of Development Professionals," *Third World Quarterly* 28:5 (2007) 901–916, argues that scholars influenced by Foucault can contend either that official knowledge reproduces its own discourses or that local agents play with and resist the constraints of those forms of domination.

teams slowly mobilized, domestic and foreign charities and the Egyptian physicians' and engineers' syndicates rushed emergency personnel to the epicenter of damage in a rundown quarter of the old city. They were blocked by a police cordon, and somebody saw police escorting the Norwegian ambassador's wife from the scene. Three days later, Military Order No. 4 of 1992 banned independent relief efforts, directing that all local and international donations be channeled through the Egyptian Red Crescent, chaired by First Lady Suzanne Mubarak and overseen by the Ministry of Social Affairs. This decree mandated seven years in prison for anyone caught collecting domestic or foreign funds without permission.[22]

Order Number 4 thickened an existing regulatory morass. A permanent State of Emergency already prohibited public gatherings and allowed indiscriminate arrest. Highly obstructive laws, notably the *Qanun Jama'iyat*, the infamous Law 32 of 1964 governing "associations" (or "societies"), were already on the books. Usually rendered in English as an NGO law (although the "non-governmental" part is not in the Arabic), Law 32 and subsequent iterations, decrees, and policies authorized the Ministry of Social Affairs (MoSA) to supervise voluntary activities via mandatory registration, auditing, reporting, and security criteria. In addition, pyramidal federations (the Arabic singular is *Ittihad*, as in the word for federalism) for women's groups, charities, labor unions, professional syndicates, agricultural cooperatives, sports leagues, community development associations, civil companies, and so forth co-opted civic energies into organizations headed by regime cronies who doled out public rents as patronage. Universities, research centers, libraries, legal institutes, art galleries, religious endowments, and the media were expropriated and appended to highly centralized bureaucracies. To escape suffocation, public intellectuals met or registered abroad, organized as non-profit companies, and/or applied overseas for support. Thus we see nationalization vs. denationalization of activism.

Conventional inter-state development assistance draining through national ministries, authorities, entities, and enterprises reinforced this corporatist pipeline. For a long time, all aid from the Soviet Union, the United States, the World Bank, and other donors followed a standard dirigisme. It enlarged state sectors. In the post-socialist, neo-liberal

---

[22] Quoted by Ezzat El-Saadani, "Where Does Charity Begin?" *al-Ahram Weekly*, 17–23 December, 1992. See also Jallau Halawi, "Cold Comfort for Camp Dwellers," *Al-Ahram Weekly*, 17–23 December, 1992, 2; Ibrahim Nafie, "PM Defends Relief Efforts," *al-Ahram Weekly* 5–11 November 1992.

era the World Bank and the OECD urged de-nationalization, non-governmentalization, privatization, decentralization, and divestiture from the public sector. But they also hewed to the paradigm of 'state capacity-building': official ODA still tended to engorge central agencies such as ministries of privatization or international cooperation. Nonetheless, especially in somewhat socialized indebted economies, the neo-liberal 'Washington consensus' recommended trimming national budgets by divesting public-sector social services to non-profit entities known by donors as PVOs (for private voluntary organizations), CDAs (community development associations), or 'welfare' NGOs.

Plumbing matters: Heretofore, ODA for social services was routinely funneled through MoSA to the Federation of Community Development Associations or other parastatal agencies. By the early 1990s, the CDA Federation had received grants from the Canadian, Netherlands, and American bilateral development programs, among others, via MoSA. Some aid was administered through non-profit international PVO contractors like CARE, Save the Children, and Catholic Relief Services. Often the stated objective was to improve the "capacity" of the Federation. The goal of a two-stage, multi-million dollar Local Development project funded by USAID, for instance, was to "strengthen the capabilities and the efficiency of local government to coordinate and stimulate the potential of local PVOs."[23]

An incipient tension was surfacing. Urging the debt-strapped Egyptian bureaucracy to jettison obligations to deliver social services, donors pushed privatization, cost-recovery, and user-fees.[24] These were neo-liberal recipes for 'rolling back the state.' Yet conventional aid still augmented governmental supervisory capacities; centrally administered decentralization initiatives seemed to help Cairo burrow ever more deeply into rural and community life. As European experts later observed in a far-reaching report, the terms of structural adjustment "required that the Egyptian government reduce social spending, and suggested that social assistance be shifted to NGOs – even though their room for maneuver was subsequently reduced because their work was deemed to impinge upon the prerogatives of the state." Thus the government was able to reclaim a

---

[23] Sara Loza et al., *Final Report Assessment of PVO Activity under the Local Development II Project*, submitted by the Social Planning, Analysis, and Administration Consultants (SPAAC) to USAID/Cairo, April 30, 1991.

[24] Timothy Mitchell. *Rule of Experts: Egypt, Techno-Politics, Modernity* (Berkeley: University of California Press, 2002) 227–229.

portion of foreign public financial assistance earmarked for NGOs while formally conforming to donors' "good governance" criteria.[25]

Freelance Egyptian organizations felt squeezed between dual exigencies. To bypass MoSA apparatchiks, and later the increasingly powerful aid-driven Ministry of International Cooperation, development agencies coached existing or new PVOs to qualify as independent project partners. This meant presenting, usually in English (or perhaps French) a suitably 'developmental' mission statement, three years of audited accounts, a legally responsible board of directors, and a credentialed staff. For many non-profits, it was an attractive offer, but not an unmitigated blessing. The Coptic Evangelical Organization for Social Services (CEOSS, founded in the 1950s with the help of Presbyterian missionaries) was the first to qualify to bid directly for USAID contracts. The Upper Egyptian Christian Association, the Egyptian Junior Medical Doctor's Association, and the Alexandria Businessman's Association followed suit. Soon a somewhat more heterogeneous array of some 75 groups, all legally registered either under Law 32 or as "civil companies" (connoting 'non-profit') were upgrading their managerial and accounting procedures to meet USAID's procedural and financial requirements. One prominent Egyptian development consultant said USAID's quarter-million dollar program with CEOSS (through the American contractor, Catholic Relief Services) imposed "hard-nosed business" practices and required charities to concern themselves "with logistical procedures rather than program results" and become "responsible to officialdom rather than to the rural poor."[26] Meanwhile, the Arab Women's Solidarity Association, the Egyptian Organization for Human Rights, the Egyptian Society of Human Rights Supporters' Cultural Club, the Arab Association for Arts, Culture, and Information, and the Arab Office of Youth and Environment filed for NGO registration with the United Nations. This became a UN-NGO nexus.

More connections to Egyptian NGOs, PVOs, CDAs, and so on were forged. USAID set up a multi-million dollar NGO Support Center to manage its socio-economic development projects. The World Bank,

---

[25] Euro-Mediterranean Human Rights Network, *Freedom of Association in The Euro-Mediterranean Region*, Copenhagen, 2007: 28, adding that these circumstances cleared some space for human rights groups to establish themselves.

[26] Iman Bibars, "The Rising Interest in Private Voluntary Organizations and their New Role in Development: A Study of the Impact of the New Role of PVOs on their Performance as Grass Roots Organizations and their Relationship with Large Aid Donors," paper presented at Princeton University, May 1988, 10–15.

other donors, and the Egyptian executive bureaucracy jointly established a Social Fund for Development as an Egyptian non-governmental agency. Its mission was to offset the deleterious effects of fiscal retrenchment on vulnerable communities and thereby reduce the likelihood of the "IMF riots" that swept Egypt and the global South in the late 1970s. A revolving credit facility, the Social Fund was a rather technical accounting exercise in public finance outside the state budget. Revenue-neutral welfare services and micro-credits managed by non-profit non-governmental brokers were supposed to bolster essential social facilities and income-generating activities without adding to government spending. Simultaneously, by putting purchasing power in the hands of consumers, it would provide an economic stimulus: this is known as "demand creation." An incredulous Egyptian development consultant asked rhetorically at the time whether Social Fund loans to businessmen's associations were about "poverty alleviation" or "creating artificial demand for something which is not a need, while real needs still have to be addressed."[27]

The two regimes seemed mostly, but not always, adversarial. The Ministry of Social Affairs positioned itself as the Social Fund's concierge. Sometimes, since the Fund had registered as an Egyptian non-profit, MoSA claimed extensive jurisdiction down to multi-stage approval of each sub-project. But when the Social Fund approved financing for Regional CDA Federations, the Ministry asserted that the Fund was a foreign donor obligated to transfer money to the Federations through MoSA channels. The Ministry froze the Federation's funds, so the Federation sued the Ministry for breach of procedure. As lawsuits wended through Egyptian courts, the Social Fund and other umbrella funding entities adjusted their procedures. Subsequently, a scholarly inquiry highlighted the ways in which the Fund helped to formalize and literally to map the informal economy of Cairo's lower-class neighborhoods, concluding that "Foucault's conundrum of governmentality" can reside in either nation-states or global institutions such as the World Bank.[28]

The examples of earthquake relief, Military Order 4, the Social Fund, the CDA Federation, and Law 32 indicated scuffles over control of resources for humanitarian or social development projects earmarked for what donors call 'welfare NGOs.' Civil society promotion via 'advocacy NGOs'

---

[27] Sawsan El-Messiri, "Will it Trickle Down," *Al-Ahram Weekly* 17–23 September 1992.
[28] Julia Elyachar, "Mappings of Power: The State, NGOs, and International Organizations in the Informal Economy of Cairo," *Comparative Studies in Society and History*, 45:3 (2003) 571–605.

was even more intently controversial. In the name of democratic advocacy it differed from welfare-oriented conventional aid in two important ways. First, as already analyzed with respect to projects for women, and unlike economic initiatives with material consequences, the content of political aid was almost entirely informational and ideological. Ergo, its practitioners and counterparts were constituted as professional lobbies generating semantic, informational or instructive products. The second contrast is that even though conventional ODA snaked through parastatal and quasi-non-governmental sub-contracting channels, it remained primarily intergovernmental (bilateral or multilateral), administered by mutual consent. By contrast, political aid for NGOs that evaded conceptual and administrative border patrols goaded special pushback from police states.

## KNOWLEDGE PRODUCTION

If political aid delivers information, persuasion, and symbiotic meanings, then organizations specialized in democratic transitions overseas resembled think tanks.[29] Think tanks are "idea brokers," professional research agencies with a policy mission that "monitor the latest political developments, pursue short-term research projects, organize seminars and conferences, publish occasional books or reports," and apply for funds to keep their operations afloat.[30] Democracy brokers and political institutes self-identify as think tanks based on the work they do. The turn-of-the-century web sites of the French Socialist Party's *Fondation Jean Jaures* and the *Friedrich Ebert Stiftung* of Germany's Green Party associated themselves with "a wider family of social-democratic foundations, named '*fondation*' here, 'think tank' there, or '*institut*' elsewhere"; the Christian Democrats' *Konrad Adenauer Stiftung* considered itself a cross between a think tank and a political aid agency. Accordingly, research has shown that projects in the Middle East bolstered certain categories of research and instruction, or counterparts specialized in the production of those categories of information and ideas.[31]

---

[29] Peter R. Weilemann, "Experiences of a Multidimensional Think-Tank: The Konrad-Adenauer-Stiftung," in ed. James G. McGann and R. Kent Weaver, *Think Tanks and Civil Societies: Catalysts for Ideas and Action* (New Brunswick and London: Transaction Publishers, 2000) 169–186.

[30] James C. Smith, *The Idea Brokers: Think Tanks and the Rise of the New Policy Elite* (New York: The Free Press, 1991) xv. Incidentally, his original "idea broker," American Enterprise Institute founder William J. Baroody, was the son of a Lebanese immigrant.

[31] Martha A. Chen, "Building Research Capacity in the Nongovernmental Organization Sector," ed. Merilee S. Grindle, *Getting Good Government: Capacity Building in the*

Applied transitology borrowed the logic of civil society funding from the Keynesian economic stimulus paradigm that underlies much conventional development assistance: financial and institutional resources would kindle 'demand' from extra-governmental lobbies, public action committees, watch-dog groups, businesswomen's associations, investigative journalists, and advocates for the poor.[32] This 'demand' template called for grants, training, and conference interactions to generate empirical evidence and ideological rationales for liberal democracy.[33] Accordingly, projects encouraged publications and training by professional research centers, media institutes, offices of gender analysis, human rights monitors, opinion survey companies, educational foundations, law academies, legal counseling centers, and such.[34] More than in other world regions, research showed, think tanks were the proximate beneficiaries of civil society promotion in the Middle East.[35] They were considered "useful organizational vehicles" for influencing public opinion "through the sponsorship of specific research agendas and policy dialogues."[36] According to investigation in Egypt and Palestine, the main impact of civil society programs was neither on the "macro" level of national reform nor the "micro" level of grassroots sentiments, but rather at the "meso" level of elite advocacy.[37] Further research in Palestine suggested a paradox of "heteronomy," whereby the success of NGOs in the donor circuit was inversely related to grassroots concerns, and disproportionate resources were funneled

*Public Sectors of Developing Countries* (Cambridge, MA: Harvard Institute for International Development, 1997) 229–253.

[32] Rasha Saad, "Potential Partners across the Barricades," *al-Ahram Weekly No.* 476, 6–12 April 2000, on a three-day conference on NGO-government relations jointly organized by UNESCO, the al-Ahram Centre for Political and Strategic Studies, the French Centre of Legal, Economic and Social Studies and Documentation (CEDEJ), and the Tunis-based Institute of Research for Development. See also Amy Hawthorne, "Middle Eastern Democracy: Is Civil Society the Answer?" Carnegie Papers Middle East Series Democracy and Rule of Law, Project Number 44, Washington, March 2004.

[33] Diane Stone, "Think Tanks, Global Lesson-Drawing, and Networking Social Policy Ideas," *Global Social Policy* 1:3 (2001) 338–360: 340.

[34] James M. Scott, "Transnationalizing Democracy Promotion: The Role of Western Political Foundations and Think-Tanks," *Democratization* 6:3 (1999) 146–170.

[35] Erik C. Johnson, "Policy Making Beyond the Politics of Conflict: Civil Society Think Tanks in the Middle East and North Africa," in ed. McGann and Weaver ( 2000) 337–365.

[36] Oliver Schlumberger, "Arab Political Economy and the European Union's Mediterranean Policy: What Prospects for Development?" *New Political Economy* 5:2 (2000) 253–255.

[37] See Imco Brouwer, "U.S. Civil-Society Assistance to the Arab World: The Cases of Egypt and Palestine," European University Institute Working Paper RSC No. 2000/5, Badia Fiesolana, San Domenico, Italy; Sheila Carapico, "Foreign Aid for Promoting Democracy in the Arab World," *Middle East Journal* 56:3 (2002) 379–395.

through highly professionalized "multiplicator" NGOs relaying messages from donors and filtering bottom-up communications.[38]

According to knowledgeable observers and participants, then, civil society advancement reproduced oratorical modalities of knowledge. Protégées commented on striking similarities in the priorities of donors "allocating supply" and NGOs "articulating demand."[39] A consultant to the European Union in Palestine wrote that "development brokers" using multimedia technologies implant "ready-made acronyms" and "disembodied English expressions" with some symbolic power but limited practical relevance.[40] One campaigner described the emergence of cosmopolitan NGO spaces where English is the lingua franca, humanitarian norms are shared, and metropolitan office practices prevail.[41] Others heard in transnational conferences echoes of key motifs, sociological assumptions, rhetorical tags, and methodologies.[42] After a while, foreign consultants found little difference between "hybrid" Palestinian and Lebanese professional research consulting institutions and European counterparts.[43] The term "Creolization" implied institutional as well as linguistic cross-breeding.[44] Progressive intellectuals formerly in the nationalist vanguard of the first *Intifada* found themselves recast as "missionaries preaching the importance of advocacy, workshops and training programs," their energies diverted from grassroots to "deterritorialized" activism.[45] The "project logic" itself as well as the

---

[38] Challand, *Palestinian Civil Society*, covers both "advocacy" and "welfare" NGOs, noting donor preferences for the former.

[39] Sari Hanafi, "Donors, International NGOs, and Palestine NGOs: Funding Issues and Globalized Elite Formation," in ed. Sarah Ben Nefissa and Nabil Abd al-Fattah, *NGOs and Governance in the Arab World* (Cairo: AUC Press, 2005) 337–360: 353.

[40] Khalil Nakhleh, "A Critical Look at Foreign Funding to Palestine: Where Is It Heading," in Nader Izzat Said, ed., *Funding Palestinian Development* (Ramallah: Birzeit University Planning for Development Series No. 2, September 1998) 25–31: 26, 28–29.

[41] Rema Hammami, "NGOs: The Professionalization of Politics," *Race and Class* 37:2 (1995) 51–63.

[42] Timothy Brennan, "Cosmo-Theory," *The South Atlantic Quarterly* 100:3 (2001) 659–691.

[43] Ulrich Vogt, "The Existing Relations between Arab and European NGOs," in "The Role of NGOs in the Development of Civil Society: Europe and the Arab Countries," proceedings of a Bruno Kreisky Forum-Arab Thought Forum seminar in Amman, Jordan, on December 6–7, 1997, Amman and Vienna, 1997: 103.

[44] Pierre-Jean Roca, "Insiders and Outsiders: NGOs in International Relations," in eds. Ben Nefissa and Abd al-Fattah (2005) 39–54: 44.

[45] Sari Hanafi and Linda Tabar, "The Intifada and the Aid Industry: The Impact of the New Liberal Agenda on the Palestinian NGOs," *Comparative Studies of South Asia, Africa and the Middle East* 23:1–2 (2003) 205–214.

"NGOization" of street-level movements transform a social cause into an accounting unit while fostering both a culture of dependency and fancy-hotel modes of consumption.[46] This is how it looked to practitioners on the ground.

Inside Arab sovereignties, ownership of the means of production and distribution of political knowledge had been nationalized by the mid-to-late twentieth century. Formerly independent academies, libraries, and research institutes and their private endowments were placed under ministries of *Awqaf*, education, information, social affairs, and so forth.[47] New national science centers and university-affiliated think tanks were tasked to manufacture and circulate official mottoes, propaganda, and patriotic information. Thus scholarship, publishing, and mass media were heavily controlled. Nine of Morocco's top ten top research centers, for instance, were affiliated with public universities or owned by the government.[48]

Democracy assistance began to reshape research agendas and institutional landscapes at resource-starved think tanks. At Cairo University's Center for Political Research, foreign money covered all the studies of Egyptian civil society, women, and human rights in the 1990s; roughly half of all regional and international studies; and all the work of the Center of Developing Countries. The relatively autonomous public sector al-Ahram Center for Strategic Studies, a division of the state-owned publishing house, received foreign funds for some public opinion surveys. Several private liberal think tanks including the Egyptian Center for Economic Studies and the Group for Democratic Development recovered most of their costs from USAID, Ford, the Adenauer and Ebert *Stiftungen*, NED, NDI, IRI, the European Human Rights Commission, and the Royal Netherlands Embassy.[49] Overall, and over

---

[46] Islah Jad, "NGOs: Between Buzzwords and Social Movements," *Development in Practice*, 17: 4–5 (2007) 622–629.

[47] Stephen Sheehi, "Arabic Literary-Scientific Journals: Precedence for Globalization and the Creation of Modernity," *Comparative Studies of South Asia, Africa and the Middle East* 25:2 (2005) 438–448; Nawaf Salam, "Civil Society in the Arab World: The Historical and Political Dimensions," Islamic Legal Studies Program, Harvard University, Occasional Publications 3, October 2002.

[48] Driss Khrouz, Ali Hajji, and Muhamed Boussetta, "The Development Research Environment in Morocco: Situation and Prospects," in ed. Eglal Rached and Dina Craissati, *Research for Development in the Middle East and North Africa* (Ottawa: International Development Research Center, 2000) 175–176: 181.

[49] Karima Korayem, "The Research Environment in Egypt," in ed. Rached and Craissati (2000) 145–146. Donors are listed in order of spending.

time, the compilation and processing of political information was being partially detached from state public sectors and patriotic ideological spheres.

Donors commissioned scores of surveys, studies, and reports on NGO/CSO landscapes. This was partly a search for suitable sub-contractors and partly a mapping project reflected in the publication of NGO directories. NGO and PVO directories were produced for Egypt, Palestine, Yemen, Jordan, and other countries. The genre is distinctive. A United Nations directory for the West Bank, issued by the Office of the Special Coordinator in the Occupied Territories, for instance, provided, in English and Arabic, alphabetically organized in the Latin alphabet, the name, address, phone and fax numbers, officers, background, and activities of each of 400 NGOs in 10 cities and towns. Most also self-identified in English by Roman-alphabet acronyms. Directories were organized more or less like telephone books, with entries clustered by geographic location but not distinguishing among, for instance, the local offices of NDI, the Catholic charity CARITAS founded in Latin America, professional organizations, political party affiliates, development contractors, non-profit law offices, or business networks. The key criterion for inclusion is an office address: physical premises. Low-budget, spontaneous, or informal associations would not appear on the map or in the directory. Ultimately, directories seemed to be but were not 'really' reliable maps of civil society.

The next step after cataloguing NGOs and what were later called CSOs was to license some for UN observer status or to bid on contracts or qualify for grants. Procedural bureaucratization comes as no surprise: applicants needed to demonstrate adherence to organizational routines. The Middle East Policy Initiative printed a 40-page instruction manual for grant applicants. It began with 12 pages on why and how NGOs should engage in "strategic planning" based on a clear "mission statement" and well-kept "financial accounts." Seven pages outlined MEPI's four pillars – democracy, economic growth, education, and women's empowerment – and what is meant by a "reform program." Then three questions were posed, roughly as follow: Does your organization work in one of MEPI's four pillar areas? Does your organization promote reform? Do you qualify for funds from the U.S. Government (by meeting standards of accounting, bylaws, and anti-terrorism pledges)? NGOs, universities, and other institutions that passed these tests could submit proposals for workshops or other programs to bolster civil society organizations, programs for youth, NGO webs, women's participation in public life, good governance, the rule of law, or public awareness.[50] Like FFF, MEPI issued a "transparency directive" requiring display of its logo on bumper stickers, posters, websites, pamphlets, or other materials produced under its grants.[51]

Donors' thematic and administrative requirements invite us to think in terms of transnational governmentality. The Anna Lindh Foundation for the Dialogue between Cultures' objectives of improving mutual perceptions, youth and artist exchanges, and coexistence and themes of cultural diversity seemed more imaginative and perhaps broadminded than MEPI's. But its call for proposals consonant with "strategic fields" and the lengthy application form with its rubrics of "target groups" and "long-term multiplier effects" as well as financial, managerial, and technical "proficiency requirements" paralleled the parameters of FFF, MEPI, and other transnational CSO grant-making agencies.[52] Overall, NGO organizers needed to mimic certain categories and methodologies of knowledge production. For the most part, with only a couple of exceptions that would later stir controversy, no mass, youth, labor, or faith-based congregations were eligible.

Leading donors also fostered formal national or transnational NGO federations known as 'networks,' beyond and above the level of sovereignty. Perhaps they took their cues from the 'constructivist' literature on international networks. The Anna Lindh Foundation established national networks of partner organizations – NGOs, non-profit companies, and some other categories. Membership conferred opportunities to apply for funds and participate in meetings. USAID published an "NGO connect" guidebook for its civil society division defining "networks" as "civil society groups, organizations and sometimes, individuals that come together voluntarily to pursue shared purposes of social development or democratic governance." True to the genre, the manual emphasized the necessity of planning, organization, and expertise. "Successful networks are not created overnight," it cautioned, advising that "[n]ew networks should consider the level of social capital existing among members and the extent to which the environment can be considered 'enabling' for the network's aims

---

[50] MEPI, "Guidebook for Applicants" http://www.medregion.mepi.state.gov/uploads/images/ vxi1jzmXnk6nQQ4O4DV3hQ/Microsoft_Word_-_Guidebook-Applicants-Eng_Dec1707 .pdf

[51] Foundation for the Future Visibility Guidelines, http://www.foundationforfuture.org/? q=en/node/289/menu_id=214.

[52] Anna Lindh Foundation Euromed, "Guidelines for Grant Applicants Responding to ALF Call for Short Term Project Proposals, ref. no ALF/CFP/2009/ST1, Deadline for Submission of Proposals 30 April 2009."

and prospective activities." Finally, "Even the most collaborative network will fail if it does not have a sound technical program strategy and the expertise to achieve its desired social impacts."[53] This is a highly managerial model of democratic change.

Many partners felt that human and material assets were siphoned away from ground-level activism toward paperwork, specialized routines, and organizational meetings. To craft successful grant proposals, native English-speaking exchange student interns were recruited. Professionally produced audits and reports were essential to success. A report to a German foundation gave the example of the Democracy and Workers Rights Center, which in one year produced fourteen audited reports, twenty-five quarterly reports, and twenty-five annual reports for its external donors, each with its own format. Documentation obligations were so "onerous" that DWRC hired four new administrators and spent more than $70,000 a year "servicing donors."[54] Other organizations in the Territories and across the region spent time and energy entertaining civil society tourist 'missions' from abroad that visited with amazing frequency. (Methodologically, this observation urged me to turn away from requesting personal interviews and toward analyzing published transcripts and public performances.)

Mapping projects, licensing criteria, and ceremonial certifications signify transnational governmentality, here a kind of domination exercised through the denationalization and non-governmentalization of civic involvement. Thematic agendas, declaratory principles, registration procedures, NGO directories, and control of purse-strings impose self-discipline. Many scholarly critics interpreted this as a way of regimenting or foreclosing proletarian and subaltern movements. Latin American and African specialists labeled operational NGOs helping to privatize welfare services "subcontractors" in the "relief and reconstruction complex"[55] or "modern-day secular missionaries."[56] Alongside this, and sidelining poverty-alleviating welfare and service entitlements, think tanks were

---

[53] Darcy Ashman, "Supporting Civil Society Networks in International Development Programs," Academy for Educational Development Center for Civil Society and Governance, Washington, D.C., December 2005: 7, 11, 12.

[54] Iain Guest, "Defending Human Rights in the Occupied Palestinian Territory – Challenges and Opportunities," Friedrich Ebert Foundation, February 2007: 57.

[55] Walden Bello, "The Rise of the Relief and Reconstruction Complex," Transnational Institute, *Focus on the Global South* (2006) 26.

[56] Firoze Manji and Carl O'Coill, "The Missionary Position: NGOs and Development in Africa," *International Affairs* 78:3 (2002) 567–583.

enlisted to rationalize neo-liberal economic policies and cloister intellectual counter-elites into non-confrontational, white-collar activities outside the body politic.[57] One observer concluded that "The idealized space where the weak are supposed to be fighting their battles for freedom and justice has been hijacked by segments of the (petite) bourgeoisie who have found their niche in the growing sector of NGOs."[58] Concurrently, the separation of welfare from advocacy seemed to disfavor social justice activism.

This is a cogent theoretical analysis, I find. As a grand strategy for domination, however, it ran up against antidisestablishmentarian counter-reactions from client states. It ultimately failed to forestall mass upheaval in Egypt, Tunisia, and Yemen. The next section explains how dictators reasserted what they claimed as sovereign rights to police domestic civic spheres. After that we will consider donors' efforts to analyze and offset the backlash; and then, activists' reactions.

## THE BACKLASH

What practicing transitologists call the 'pushback' or 'backlash' against civil society promotion occurs when governments in countries where democracy brokers are keenly involved press criminal charges for slander or tax evasion to gag media and advocacy outlets or to put them out of business by cutting the strings of external finance.[59] This acerbic reflux was by no means a peculiarly Arab malady. Russia and some other former Soviet states were considered prime examples. Still, among the large group of stalled democratizers thwarting the work of democracy brokers, Egypt stood out for its status as a favored confidant, ally, and client frequently praised as a 'moderate' Arab state faithful to the war on terrorism, peace

---

[57] Sangeeta Kamat, "NGOs and the New Democracy: The False Saviors of International Development," *Harvard International Review* XXV:1 (2003) 65–69: 66; see also James Petras, "NGOs: In the Service of Imperialism," *Journal of Contemporary Asia* 29:4 (1999): 429–440; James Petras, "Imperialism and NGOs in Latin America," *Monthly Review* 49:7 (1997) 10–27; William I. Robinson, "Globalization, The World System, and 'Democracy Promotion' in U.S. Foreign Policy," *Theory and Society* 25:5 (1996) 615–665; Omar G. Encarnación, "Beyond Civil Society: Promoting Democracy after September 11," *Orbis* (Spring 2003) 705–720.

[58] Maha Abdel Rahman, "The Politics of 'UnCivil' Society in Egypt," *Review of African Political Economy* 91 (2002) 21–36.

[59] Arch Puddington, "The Pushback against Democracy," *Journal of Democracy* 18:2 (2007) 125–137. These methods replaced cruder methods of repression, he argues.

with Israel, and open markets.[60] The same might be said of Jordan, Tunisia, Morocco, Algeria, and Yemen.

Already tetchy internal struggles in these countries, the Palestinian Territories, and eventually Iraq over associational rights, licensing procedures, and fundraising were complicated by foreign involvement. It wasn't only groups and concerns linked to Western and UN agencies that were at risk of harassment. To the contrary, stronger, larger Islamist and labor movements faced ruthless repression precisely because their populist followings were more threatening to social order. However, some prominent secular dissidents' access to international audiences and resources sparked particular angst amongst incumbents determined to corner the market for Western assistance. "Liberalized autocracies" or "institutional semi-authoritarian" governments that staged elections and adopted pro-business policies without relinquishing centralized executive control perturbed democracy experts, who considered concessions to the liberal opposition a smart survival strategy for governments such as Egypt's.[61]

Here's one well-recognized absurdity. On the one hand, G-7 powers succored and armed the same authorities that denied associational freedoms. For all the fuss about foreign funding of NGOs, especially for advocacy work, political aid was but a fraction of all economic, much less military, blandishments to friendly dictatorships in Egypt, Yemen, Jordan, Morocco, Algeria, and Tunisia. Donor agency negotiators were not unconscious of this conundrum: a World Bank report on meetings with heads of Moroccan NGOs during a period of neo-liberal austerity "revealed a fair amount of anger against both the government and the Bank," who were seen as "close partners whose interactions are totally non-transparent to society at large" but jointly associated in the public mind with increased household and national indebtedness.[62]

Beyond familiar modalities of repression including censorship, surveillance, intimidation, arbitrary arrest, and riot squads, national security states devised more subtle ways to stifle civic, humanitarian, and developmental initiatives. Sometimes specifically in response to the influx of

---

[60] James G. McGann, "Pushback against NGOs in Egypt," *International Journal of Not-for-Profit Law* 10:4 (2008).

[61] Daniel Brumberg, "Democratization in the Arab World? The Trap of Liberalized Autocracy," *Journal of Democracy* 13:4 (2002) 56–68; Marina Ottoway and Martha Brill Olcott, *The Challenge of Semi-Authoritarianism* (Washington: Carnegie Endowment for International Peace Democracy and Rule of Law Project No. 7, December 1999).

[62] The World Bank, Morocco: Country Assistance Evaluation (Washington, May 14, 2001), Report 22212, Box 3.1: 12.

project funds for advocacy, governments deployed on several fronts. First, client bureaucrats tried to recapture rents by founding their own human rights and women's groups, dubbed GONGOs. Tunisia infamously staffed faux NGOs with security operatives to penetrate civil society gatherings and compete with autonomous groups for funds and seats at international forums; a *Washington Post* columnist called this a masterful "Putinesque, postmodern political charade, supporting a whole panoply of phony political parties, phony human rights groups, phony elections."[63] Jordan's queens and princesses manufactured RONGOs to serve as partners for internationally sponsored projects in fields ranging from environmental preservation to family law. While prominent individual Palestinian politicians were starting up their own institutions, the PA patronized three NGO umbrella organizations and began regulating associations and their external financial resources through ministries of interior and social welfare.[64] Yemeni human rights defenders confronted one or both of two familiar scenarios: either their founders' conferences were overwhelmed by known operatives of the ruling party and its security apparatus, or another organization with a similar name and objectives quickly assembled to vie for members and foreign favor.

A slight variation on this subterfuge, executed with special finesse by the relatively accommodating Jordanian and Moroccan monarchies, was to hail donor initiatives and offer patronage. In pledging funds to the Foundation for the Future, Qatar and Jordan bought into the G-8's democracy-human rights-civil society programs. The Qatari royal family set up ostensible NGOs, notably the Arab Centre for Democracy, a fully-fledged grant-making democracy foundation on the Western model, headed by the emir's wife Sheikha Mouza bint Nasser al Misnad. In offering space for FFF headquarters and numerous transnational conferences, Amman positioned its leaders at the podium, often to deliver keynote addresses. Casablanca, Rabat, Sana'a, and Amman also lent their names to international declarations on associational, civic, and press freedoms. Jordan and Morocco tolerated secular middle-class organizations of liberal intellectuals who countered Islamist forces, cultivated positive

---

[63] Anne Applebaum, "A Good Place to Have Aided Democracy," *Washington Post*, February 13, 2007.
[64] See Brouwer, "U.S. Civil-Society Assistance to the Arab World"; Benoît Challand, "The Evolution of Western Aid for Palestinian Civil Society: Bypassing Local Knowledge and Resources," *Middle Eastern Studies* 44:3 (2008) 397–417; and Denis J. Sullivan, "NGOs in Palestine: Agents of Development and Foundation of Civil Society," *Journal of Palestine Studies* 25:3 (1996) 93–100.

relationships with Western counterparts, and respected the 'red lines' of censorship and comportment.[65]

Nonetheless, in another tactic, Jordan too revised legal parameters for NGO fund-raising and other activities. In the late 1990s, Amman enforced a 1971 law making the National Planning Council the intermediary for all foreign disbursements, and then passed another Social Institutions and Associations Law detailing complex procedures for ministerial authorization of financial transfers from abroad.[66] One scholar discerned that proctoring civic energies in surveillable, state-delineated spaces subject to the government's "panopticon gaze" was a major feature of Jordan's purported liberalization.[67] For several years running, Parliament entertained proposed legislation authorizing the Prime Minister to vet all foreign transfers, make licensure contingent on as many as 50 founding members' signatures, and require prior Ministry of Interior permission for any public gathering.[68]

Nearby in the Palestinian territories, where national 'governmentality' was hardly a foregone conclusion, these politics were even thornier. Contrary to pressures to denationalize functions in Egypt, Yemen, and Tunisia, under the Oslo Accords donor agencies were engaged in a truncated kind of state-building. The United Nations, the EU, individual European states, Japan, Canada, Gulf monarchies, Oxfam, Christian charities, and others reallocated resources from grassroots welfare providers to PA bureaucracies, while USAID and the World Bank devised ways to work with what was still not a sovereign nation-state. Consultants from organizations ranging from Australian Legal Resources International to Transparency International met reform-oriented Palestinian intellectuals and other officials. The PA wrestled vigorously over NGO funds estimated at about $100 million in the late 1990s, especially the World Bank's $15 million NGO facility.[69]

---

[65] Andrew R. Smith and Fadoua Loudiy, "Testing the Red Lines: On the Liberalization of Speech in Morocco," *Human Rights Quarterly* 27 (2005) 1069–1119.

[66] Asma Khadr, "International Aspects of the Arab Human Rights Movement," paper presented to An Interdisciplinary Discussion Held in Cairo in March 1998, Harvard Law School and the Center for the Study of Developing Countries at Cairo University, Cambridge, MA, Harvard Law School Human Rights Program, 2000.

[67] Quintan Wiktorowicz, "Civil Society as Social Control: State Power in Jordan," *Comparative Politics* 33:1 (2000) 43–61:49.

[68] Steven Heydemann, *Upgrading Arab Authoritarianism*; Kareem Elbayar, "NGO Laws in Selected Arab States," *International Journal of Not-for-Profit Law* 7: 4 (2005) 3–27: 14–15.

[69] Hammami, "Palestinian NGOs Since Oslo," 18.

International experts once considered Palestinian Law 1 of 2000 an "ideal," relatively lenient Arab NGO law.[70] Yet one way the nascent national authority attempted to constitute itself as a state was by regulating autonomous associations. Internal wrangling for control of civil society became more internally tempestuous after the decisive Fatah-Hamas split in 2006 when the Fatah-led executive in the West Bank amalgamated historically active local Zakat committees to the PA's provincial authorities. That year, the Palestinian legislature proposed banning NGOs from engaging in "political activity" and establishing a commission to oversee charities and non-profits. Two years later, the office of the presidency issued a decree requiring all associations to re-register, and the Ministry of Interior threatened to close down more than 100 societies. Disputes ensued over regulation of both secular and religious associations. During this period, the *Friedrich Naumann Stiftung* of the German Liberal Party organized several local meetings under the Arab Laws Reform initiative. One was a conference entitled Promoting Government-Civil Society Dialogue and Reforming Laws about the challenges of fund-raising and operating under conditions of both occupation and authoritarianism.

As usual, Egypt took the lead in re-legislating new mechanisms of control. Law 153 of 1999 extended the Ministry of Social Affair's writ to foreign associations; outlawed political and syndical activities by NGOs; and closed loopholes in Law 32 that had enabled some organizations to register as non-profit civil companies and thus bid for international contracts while evading ministry regulations. Amidst MoSA declarations that the law would "empower" associations and "entitle" non-profit civil companies to comply, Law 153 passed quickly despite hunger strikes, demonstrations outside Parliament, and petitions from a NGO Forum for the Promotion of the Non-Governmental Sector in Egypt, only to be overturned by the Supreme Constitutional Court on procedural grounds.[71] While pursuing another, similar law (enacted two years later), the government resorted to "sensationalist scare tactics" alleging "foreign infiltration" and "colonial proxies."[72]

---

[70] Elbayar, "NGO Laws in Selected Arab States," 23.

[71] Gamal Essam El-Din, "...While NGOs Step up the Fight," *al-Ahram Weekly* No. 431, 27 May–2 June 1999; Egyptian Organization for Human Rights, "By Direct Order ... Assassination of Civil Society in Egypt: EOHR's Criticisms against Law 153 of 1999 on Associations and Civil Institutions," Cairo: 22 June 1999; Mariz Tadros, "NGO Law under Fresh Fire," *al-Ahram Weekly* No. 479, 27 April–3 May 2000; Mariz Tadros, "Legal shortcomings," *al-Ahram Weekly* No. 485, 8–14 June 2000.

[72] Hussein Abdel-Razeq, "Human Rights and the Numbers Game," *al-Ahram Weekly* No. 413, 21–28 January 1999.

Scholars and practitioners reflected on the contradictory trajectories that fed this furor. One ethnographer saw a campaign launched by 19 associations and joined by dozens of others as a significant, if flawed, challenge to systemic governmental subjugation of the public civic sphere. Citing Gramsci's hypothesis that civil society can be either – or both – the terrain for consolidation of the ruling apparatus or (and) the site of its contestation, this ethnographer explained how the NGO lobby defied legal and technocratic strangulation. Yet its inability to garner consensus around claims for liberty to obtain out-of-country support so crucial to most of the original nineteen's operations – and adoption instead of non-confrontational UN and government slogans about NGO contributions to national socio-economic development goals – fatally flawed the initiative. Ultimately, she argued, although the government re-asserted its custodial prerogatives, transnational linkages bolstered counter-hegemonic projects defying tyranny.[73] This is a persuasive argument for the positive effects of transnational civil society programs.

Other observers reached dissimilar conclusions, however. One blamed the campaign's failure on leading organizations' heavy reliance on external subsidies, widely viewed in Egyptian society as illegitimate, selling-out, self-enriching activity.[74] After encouraging objectors to enrage the Cairo government, another scholar indicated, donors abandoned their grantees in order to preserve bilateral diplomatic, economic, and military relations with the Mubarak regime.[75] Both sides in this academic debate offered compelling arguments; antithetical conclusions were both supported by convincing evidence and cogent analysis.

The backlash continued. In addition to cloning and re-legislation, another already familiar line of attack was to take the staff of NGOs privy to dollars and euros to court, and indeed to prison. After the secretary-general of the Egyptian Organization for Human Rights was brought up on charges related to a $25,000 grant from Britain under Law 32, the Ibn Khaldun Center for Development Studies, one of Cairo's best-known think tanks, got into trouble for a Ford Foundation-funded

---

[73] Nicola Pratt, "Bringing Politics Back In: Examining the Link Between Globalization and Democratization," *Review of International Political Economy* 11:2 (2004) 311–336. She deconstructs the simplistic discourses deployed against "foreign funding" in Pratt, "Human Rights NGOs and the 'Foreign Funding Debate' in Egypt," in eds. Chase and Hamzawy (2005) 114–126.

[74] Vickie Langohr, "Too Much Civil Society, Too Little Politics: Egypt and Liberalizing Arab Regimes," *Comparative Politics*, 199: 36 (2004) 181–204.

[75] Hicks, "Transnational Human Rights Networks."

workshop on ethnic minorities focused on Egypt's Coptic community, and another project financed by the European Union that the government said was "harmful to Egypt's reputation." Observers questioned whether program content or the source of funds irked the government so much.[76] Even some human rights groups closed ranks with the government against foreign involvement in domestic affairs. Ibn Khaldun's head, Saad Eddine Ibrahim, an Egyptian-American sociology professor at AUC, was tried before the Supreme State Security Court along with colleagues at his Center and the Hoda Association for the Support of Women Voters. The charges were violating Military Order No. 4 of 1992, issued right after the earthquake, which carried the heaviest penalty; and penal crimes of bribery, publishing false information damaging to Egypt's reputation, and defrauding the European Union. The EU denied being hoodwinked. Convictions were followed by acquittals in retrials. Ibrahim eventually served three years of a seven-year sentence under the Military Order before his release in 2003. This travesty made him a hero in international human rights circles, all the more after the Ibn Khaldun Center was harangued again by ruling party members petitioning to close it down in 2004.[77]

These were battles over symbolic capital, monetary resources, and ownership of national narratives about rights and justice. They were also boundary disputes about claims of trespassing. When, whether on their own or in consultation with international agencies, governments created national machineries for women or national human rights councils, they staked rhetorical and institutional claims to feminism and legalism in an ongoing quest for absolute executive jurisdiction. So, for instance, ruling party or family elites could 'represent' women. Adversarial rights monitoring by professionals trained and/or financed from abroad contradicted those claims. They did so in front of domestic and international audiences, perhaps eroding crony structures. Ruling kleptocrats cloned parastatal GONGOs to recapture not only small change for advocacy projects but also public patriotic narratives; and brought charges of defaming the state or slandering the President against human rights defenders documenting serious abuses. In the highly publicized cases of the imprisonment of Saad Eddine Ibrahim and the Sudanese accountant at the Ibn Khaldun Center,

---

[76] Mariz Tadros and Jailan Halawi, "Prominent NGO Figure Arrested," *al-Ahram Weekly* No. 489, 6–12 July 2000; Nicola Pratt, "Egypt Harasses Human Rights Activists," *Middle East Report Online*, August 17, 2000.

[77] Saad Eddine Ibrahim, "Egypt's Unchecked Repression," *Washington Post*, August 21, 2007.

for instance, opinion was divided as to whether international pressure
failed to keep them from prison or helped eventually to secure his release.

## THE CAMPAIGN TO REFORM ARAB NGO LAWS

Civil society programming penetrated national territorial and institutional
boundaries. In addition it also activated spheres geographically outside
and metaphorically above sovereign civic realms. This is the other connotation of denationalization. I want to call special attention to this supra-
national zone of sponsored activism, including the human rights and
women's conferences mentioned in earlier chapters. Intercontinental meetings in five-star facilities with trilingual interpreters speaking into head-
phones from glassed-in cubicles signaled globalization, extra-territoriality,
and de-nationalization. In some ways, the workshops and web sites constituted portals of counter-elite expression outside the bounds of national
censorship, an opportunity to rail against restraints on association, and to
bring abuses into the international limelight. These meetings were rather
more upscale than the usual academic conference. They were civil, informative multicultural conversations in zones of harmonization in one way.
In another they constituted schizophrenic spaces. They could be seen as
air-conditioned hot air; imperial co-optation of bilingual secular counter-
elites; or spaces for extra-systemic freedom of association.

All along, there was a strong transnational Arab-regional dimension to
democracy promotion in the Middle East, in the tier between domestic and
global. Considerable material and symbolic capital was invested in NGO
networks of the caliber invited to the Forum for the Future and dozens of
other high-end summits. These extra-territorial Arab and Mediterranean
consortia, pretty much outside the Arab League's purview, went unnoticed
in national case studies of domestic civil society or bilateral aid programs.
But they were a salient component of political aid. The Ibn Khaldun
Center's founder counted among the non-governmental federations
"inspired or induced" by the world-wide UN conferences in the nineties
the Arab Democracy Network, the Arab Organization of Human Rights,
the Arab Network for the Protection of Human Rights Activists, and the
Cairo-based Arab NGOs Network.[78] In a complex co-sponsorship, the
Ford Foundation in Cairo and UNDP jointly backed affiliations of international, Arab, and national organizations with IFEX, the International

---

[78] See Saad Eddine Ibrahim, "Arab Social-Science Research in the 1990s and Beyond: Issues,
Trends, and Priorities," in ed. Rached and Craissati (2000) 111–140.

Freedom of Information Exchange that raised both public and corporate money for its projects. MEPI, the World Bank, the OECD, UNDP and others fostered an Arab Center for the Rule of Law and Integrity head-quartered in Beirut, with a branch in Amman and associates in ten other Arab countries. In 2010, something called the Network of Think Tanks for Developing Countries was hosted by the Egyptian Cabinet's Information and Decision Support Center with support from the Japan Foundation, the Swedish Institute of Alexandria, UNDP, and other agencies.

These were interlocking webs. Their proliferation beyond and inside national domains was consistent with a theory of transnational non-governmental governmentality in an era of neo-liberal globalization, which is often thought to erode the conceptual boundaries of states. Practitioners knew this. At a World Bank meeting for NGO delegations under the Mediterranean Development Forum sessions, one contributor remarked on the "the rising influence of the donor-civil-society nexus."[79] A self-identified pro-market civil society think tank, *Maroc 2020*, associated with a Bank-sponsored Global Development Network, hosted a *Club de Madrid* study of ways to strengthen rights of association financed by the European Commission's Initiative for Democracy and Human Rights and the United Nations Fund for Democracy. These examples of quasi-non-inter-governmental matrices were symptomatic of globalization, and intensified transnationalism in the Mediterranean, closely allied with the neo-liberal Washington consensus. These trajectories are not self-actualizing, however; the counter-offensive was fierce.

The single most sustained MENA conference initiative, a decade-long crusade to modify Arab laws of association, seemed to relocate advocacy from national to transnational arenas. Ultimately it was an example of the limited effects of transnational advocacy. Picking up on the work of Egyptian dissidents, UN Human Rights Commissioner Mary Robinson opened an Arab conference in 1999 on human rights in Cairo with care-fully worded remarks on associational freedom. Meanwhile, a series of workshops co-sponsored by the World Bank and the European Union through the *Naumann Stiftung* led to the Amman Declaration on Rights of Free Association, formation of a Network of Lawyers Reforming NGO Laws, and an Arab Initiative for Freedom of Associations. Founded by legal practitioners from Jordan, Lebanon, Egypt, Palestine, and Syria, this experiment was later joined by Tunisians, Yemenis, Algerians, and

---

[79] Guilain Denoeux, "The Politics of Morocco's 'Fight Against Corruption,'" *Middle East Policy* VII: 2 (2002) 165–189.

Moroccans. With sustenance from the *"Bunian"* (an Arabic term for "network") program implemented by Naumann and co-funded by the European Commission, it held at least two World Bank-sponsored workshops in Amman under the auspices of the Jordanian Ministers of Social Affairs and Justice. The International Center for Not-For-Profit Law offered legal advice.[80] Soon another meeting yielded the Casablanca Declaration on freedom of association. This project could be hegemonic in the imperial sense yet counter-hegemonic with respect to the banalities of domestic repression.

In the early twenty-first century the Amman-based European-Arab-UN *Bunian*, a self-conscious network stretching from Copenhagen to Casablanca via web sites, publications, and conferences, stepped up the drive. With assistance from the Danish International Development Agency, the then-nascent Euro-Mediterranean Human Rights Network conducted a feasibility study and recommended the establishment of a Euro-Mediterranean Human Rights Foundation to Support Human Rights Defenders, with a precise mandate to improve organizational expertise in drafting proposals for legislative and regulatory reform. Another roundtable on cultural dimensions of associational liberties during the Euromed Civil Forum in Marrakesh was led by the *Fondation René Seydoux pour le monde méditerranéen*, based in Aix-en-Provence. (Meanwhile a newly created interstate Arab League Civil Society Commission scheduled a symposium called Laws' Reform between Aspiration and Reality in Cairo in cooperation with the *Naumann Stiftung* and the Arab Center for the Rule of Law and Integrity in Beirut, where the Secretary General of the Arab League gave the keynote address.)

The crusade for regulatory reform continued on various fronts. The EU proposed to provide 20 million euros to mobilize NGOs working among the poorest and most vulnerable strata of society, on the condition that Egypt adopt "new and appropriate NGO legislation" freeing humanitarian associations from interference and permitting them to receive direct

---

[80] According to ICNL's website in April 2001, co-sponsors were the Charles Stewart Mott Foundation, the Hitachi Foundation, USAID, the World Bank, the NED, the Inter-American Development Bank, the Asia Foundation, Asian Development Bank, the Rockefeller Brothers Fund, UNDP, the Soros Foundations/Open Society Institute, the Ford Foundation, the Nonprofit Sector Research Fund of the Aspen Institute, the Charities Aid Foundation, the Aga Khan Foundation, CIDA, the Center for Democracy, the Commonwealth Foundation, UNHCR, GTZ, the Council of Europe, the Fiduciary Foundation, and anonymous donors.

foreign aid.[81] Trying another tack, the *Club de Madrid*, self-identified as an independent non-governmental organization of seventy former heads of state, embarked on a dialogue on freedom of association across MENA in conjunction with the Madrid-based think tank, *Fundación para las Relaciones Internacionales y el Diálogo Exterior*, that goes by the acronym FRIDE; the European Initiative for Democracy and Human Rights; and the United Nations Democracy Fund. FRIDE and the Euro-Mediterranean Human Rights Network published excellent research reports on conditions for NGOs in the region.

The cause was further taken up by the International Center for Not-for-Profit Law (ICNL), then with offices in Washington, Central Europe, and the former USSR. Like other democracy brokers, ICNL self-consciously promised to work with local partners to support indigenous law-reform efforts rather than supplanting or directing their work. In addition to commissioning studies and offering research fellowships, ICNL organized a forum on Strengthening Civil Society in the Arab Region in Beirut, followed by a two-day Civil Society Dialogue Preparatory Meeting to the Forum for the Future in Amman called Assessing the Arab Legal Environment: A Map for Development. Together, representatives of at least 40 Arab civic organizations designed a presentation to G-8 and Arab leaders on creating an enabling legal environment.

## MAPPING THE BACKLASH

So many accounts of harassment of its overseas grantees filtered back to Washington that the Senate Foreign Relations Committee asked the NED for a report. Known as the Lugar Report, it painted counter-moves in Eurasia as a panic response to democracy brokers' positive interventions in the Orange Revolution in the Ukraine, the Serbian uprising, and other 'Color Revolutions.' It also cited the recent expansion of offices of NED's affiliates in the MENA region as an indication of successes. The report offered extensive testimonials from NED, its affiliates, Britain's Westminster Foundation for Democracy, and other institutes. It cited ICNL's list of eight constraints that dictatorships impose on democracy promoters – restrictions on freedoms to associate; impediments to legal registration; restraints on foreign and domestic financing; use of discretionary power; curbs on political activities; arbitrary interference in NGO internal affairs; establishment of 'parallel' or ersatz NGOs; and

---

[81] Pace, Stavridis and Xenakis, "Parliaments and Civil Society Cooperation," 82–83.

harassment, prosecution, or deportation of civil rights advocates. Another volume from NED's World Movement for Democracy identified legal barriers to entry, operational activities, speech and advocacy, contact and communication, and funds; and named corresponding rights to association, freedom from government interference, to free expression, communication and cooperation, to seek and secure resources, and to state protection of these rights.[82] The rights to cooperation and to seek and secure resources were just beginning to be recognized in international law circles, thanks in part to ICNL's efforts.

Many autocrats lashed back. Tunisia ranked in the Lugar Report with Zimbabwe, Uzbekistan, Kazakhstan, and Venezuela in establishing NGO "fronts"; a box titled "Tunisia: a Far Cry From Civil Society" began thus: "In Tunisia, state-sponsored GONGOs monitor the activities of independent NGOs while GONGO representatives attend conferences and other civil society events to collect intelligence for government agencies monitoring independent NGOs."[83] In the inaugural issue of ICNL's *Global Trends in NGO Law*, Bahrain, Jordan, and Yemen were cited for revising NGO laws to tighten central oversight, and criticized, along with Egypt, for restricting foreign funding and using government support as a management device. Curbs on trans-border exchanges of knowledge and expertise were labeled a kind of "intellectual protectionism."[84] This is a great phrase, further illustrated by Mubarak's insistence on appointing national delegates to the Anna Lindh Foundation, meetings on the Istanbul Action Plan on Women's Rights, and other transnational institutions and conferences.[85]

The Egyptian government fought back during the years 2005 and 2006, rocked by a presidential election campaign and demonstrations of solidarity with the Palestinian *Intifada*, both matters of alarm to Cairo.[86] Officials goaded mosque preachers to rail against $1 million in American embassy grants for NGOs' elections-related projects, it was reported; yet

---

[82] NED, *Defending Civil Society: A Report of the World Movement for Democracy*, co-authored by International Center for Not-for-Profit Law and World Movement for Democracy Secretariat at the National Endowment for Democracy, Washington, February 2008 ("the Lugar report").

[83] NED, *Defending Civil Society*, 27.

[84] *Global Trends in NGO Laws* 1:1 (2009).

[85] Johansson-Nogues, "Civil Society in Euro-Mediterranean Relations," 15; Kausch, "Defenders in Retreat," 16.

[86] Mohamed Agati, "Undermining Standards of Good Governance: Egypt's NGO Law and Its Impact on the Transparency and Accountability of CSOs," *The International Journal of Not-for-Profit Law* 9:2 (2007).

plainclothes security agents at an Egyptian Democracy Support Network elections workshop supported by the Transatlantic Democracy Network backed off when they recognized European and American diplomats at the gathering.[87] In another example of slander and intimidation that presaged the furor in 2011/2012, a training session on how to cover elections, conducted by the U.S.-based International Centre for Journalists with USAID financing, was smeared with allegations that ICJ was a 'CIA front' with ties to Israel.[88]

This conflict seemed interminable. Egypt revised its Law of Associations, again, tightening restrictions even more. Law 84 of 2002, replacing Law 153 of 1999 and Law 32 of 1964, gave MoSA even more latitude to police, disband, or sue associations on grounds such as "threatening national unity" or "violating public order or morals." It imposed cumbersome, intrusive procedures for permits, and criminal penalties for technical or political violations. Like earlier laws, Law 84 mandated re-registration and criminalization of activities by unregistered groups, and regulated the scope of civic engagement. Associations could be dissolved for unauthorized domestic or foreign fund-raising or for foreign affiliations. The New Woman Association, the Arab NGO Network, and the Egyptian Organization for Human Rights exclaimed that these provisions put Egypt behind Jordan and even Tunisia in terms of forbearance for autonomous organizing.[89] Yet even over public protests the measure passed. One scholar described the "judicialization of politics" whereby human rights monitors utilizing foreign monies won small victories in thousands of public interest litigations but endured trial and imprisonment of internationally prominent leaders.[90]

There were further arrests and provocations during and after negotiations over the Foundation for the Future: the New Woman Foundation was prohibited from campaigning for female nominees to the 2005 Parliamentary elections, the Egyptian Association Against Torture was refused licensure by an Administrative Judiciary Court on the grounds that its mission was too political, and a member of Parliament challenged the $1 million in grants for elections monitoring and related activities as "a

[87] NED, *Defending Civil Society*, 30, 36–37.
[88] Mustafa El-Menshawy, "'Baseless' Accusations," *al-Ahram Weekly* No. 756, 18–24 August 2005.
[89] Mariz Tadros, "Governing the Non-Governmental," *al-Ahram Weekly* No. 588, 30 May 5 June 2002.
[90] Moustafa, "Got Rights?"

blatant breach of diplomatic norms that could open the door wide for more American meddling in Egyptian affairs."[91]

International democracy brokers and rights' monitors rightly denounced Law 84 and the ensuing crackdown. A working paper for FRIDE and the *Club de Madrid* program dubbed Egypt "the vanguard of authoritarian upgrading," where democratization is "not in progress but in retreat."[92] Enumerating cases in which MoSA withheld licenses, foiled permits for foreign grants, and froze NGO accounts or security agents interfered, Human Rights Watch noted heightened incentives for donors to evade government scrutiny of politically sensitive projects.[93] Wrangling continued over amendments to Law 84 proposed in 2006, 2007, and 2008 that would ease the most ludicrous obstacles to registration and the detested ban on campaigning, thus clearing some more space for purely domestic activities, especially welfare services, but expressly limiting external grants except through the newly renamed Ministry of Social Solidarity, and curtail possibilities for affiliation with international bodies.[94]

These dynamics seemed dialectical. Domestic repression banished organizers to offshore portals and international councils, where they continued domestic struggles in the transnational/pan-Arab arena. Yet these venues had their own discursive price of admission and conditions of patronage. Oppressive internal restrictions legitimated outside interference, which prompted greater repression, which impelled the intensification of transnational schemes, which generated yet more intense backlash. In an age of globalization, dictatorship helped create the circumstances for its own negation in the form of extra-territorial activism. Simultaneously, donors' civil society programming seemingly intensified counter-reactions in the form of upgraded predatory curbs on organizational freedoms. The outcome, then, was a synthetic transitory space for elite activism that at least partly eluded both national and global forms of authority, but was itself a zone of highly antagonistic politics. At the end of this chapter we

---

[91] Quoted by Gamal Essam el-Din, "USAID Grants Attacked," *al-Ahram Weekly* No. 736, 31 March-6 April 2005.

[92] Kristina Kausch, "Defenders in Retreat: Freedom of Association and Civil Society in Egypt," FRIDE, Madrid, 2009.

[93] "Egypt: Margins of Repression: State Limits on Nongovernmental Organization Activism," Human Rights Watch, New York, 2005.

[94] Amira El-Noshokaty, "Civil Matters: The Call for Amendments to the Current NGO Law Is an Ongoing Struggle," *al-Ahram Weekly* No. 839, 5–11 April 2007; Dina Guirguis, "Egypt: NGO Bill Imperils Civil Society Funding," *Carnegie Arab Reform Bulletin*, February 2008.

will listen to more commentary from bilingual intellectuals about their experiences in that space, which echo some of the wisecracks from women cited in the previous chapter.

By this time, political aid for non-governmental activities was deeply disputatious, recognizably paradoxical, and incredibly stressful. Yet there are three further turns of irony to consider before closing this chapter. First, Americans instituted in Iraq NGO restrictions on a par with the prevailing repressive standard for the region. Second, the U.S. Department of Homeland Security cracked down on transnational Muslim charities as "terrorist fronts." Finally, even though activists almost universally concluded that civil society promotion was intended to forestall possibilities for subaltern mobilization or other unruly forms of contentious politics, in 2011 the Egyptian government accused foreign organizations of inciting street protests.

## DUBBING IRAQI CIVIL SOCIETY

The Occupying Authority did not respect freedom of association in Iraq by the standards espoused by ICNL and the Lugar Report. For all the international denunciation of abominable Laws of Association, in a strange instance of reverse osmosis, the occupiers imitated this legal framework in Iraq. The detailed ICNL survey of Arab NGO laws in 2005 added the Coalition Provisional Authority's Order Number 45 of June 2004 to its list of highly restrictive legislation in Arab countries. Registration with the CPA was compulsory and cumbersome, licenses could be revoked without judicial review, any organization deemed a "threat to the public order, safety, stability, or security of Iraq" was banned, and associations were required to be "non-political."[95] In conjunction with de-Ba'athification decrees, this order imposed ideological and partisan criteria on registration and restricted enrollment to groups sympathetic to the new state-building process.

The irony was not lost on professional democracy brokers (or even some amateurs). The International Human Rights Network, an organization based in Oldcastle, Ireland, held a meeting in Amman for Iraqi NGOs to meet NGO representatives from other Arab countries. IHRN's report reflected critically but quite delicately on the "distinct, but complementary,

---

[95] Elbayar, "NGO Laws in Selected Arab States," compared the new law for Iraq to similarly restrictive legislation in Algeria, Egypt, Jordan, Lebanon, Libya, Morocco, Palestine, Saudi Arabia, and Yemen.

roles of human rights NGOs and government in a democracy." Measures to strengthen Iraq's newly elected central government should not extend to making NGOs beholden to the administration, it cautioned. With a nod to "valid administrative reasons" to coordinate the influx of foreign aid, it nonetheless warned of fundamental problems that arise when ministries act as "gate-keepers" for civil society handouts. When external donors let the Ministry of Human Rights they helped create host a seminar on Mapping Human Rights Activities for Iraq they tacitly recognized ministerial authority to do that mapping. The Oldcastle report demurely recommended that "consideration be given to identifying or developing non-governmental channels for support to Iraqi human rights." It advised donors to avoid the perception that human rights is a "foreign agenda" or a "tool of the occupation," offering suggestions for non-governmental finance, a Donor Code of Conduct, and transparency of funding.[96]

At that workshop in Amman, paid for by Britain's DFID, a rare opportunity for Iraqis to compare notes with other Arab human rights defenders, the discussion turned again to the conflicting ways governments and international agencies each control and license NGO activities. The Oldcastle consultants for IHRN clearly recognized that laws instituted by the CPA reproduced some notoriously high-handed regulations from Arab governments in the name of state building. Presumably they were attuned to the use of the word "mapping." They described earnest deliberate efforts to include rural, non-elite organizations. Nonetheless, somehow IHRN could not help but duplicate some of the registration procedures such as a nine-page registration form delineating the organizational and rhetorical conditions of inclusion.

Initially some expected that USAID, its corporate contractors Chemonics and Research Triangle Institute, the American parastatal foundations, and others had brought to Iraq an expert venture in political engineering that would empower policy champions to generate demand for a simplified template of market democracy.[97] Yet an unusually humorous book about the American venture in Iraq, written by two young American backpackers hired by the CPA to handle its NGO Assistance Office, told a different kind of story. INGOs including Oxfam, *Médecins Sans Frontières* and the NGO Coordination Committee in Iraq evaded

---

[96] IHRN "Human Rights NGO Capacity Building-Iraq: Next Steps Report," International Human Rights Network, Oldcastle, Ireland, February 2005, passages cited 7 and 10.

[97] Herbert Docena, "Silent Battalions of 'Democracy'" *Middle East Report* 232 (2004) 14–21.

registration with the CPA under Order 45 on the grounds that the decree violated Geneva Convention obligations on the occupying power to facilitate humanitarian missions and made Iraq an extraordinarily hostile environment in which to work. Many Iraqi and foreign groups did line up to fill out the forms to register with the CPA as NGOs and qualify for access to American coffers, of course.[98] Unfortunately, the sub-contractor approach soon seemed to backfire as Iraqi partners, staff, and interpreters were targeted for collaboration with the occupation.[99]

Visiting transitologists discerned how donor priorities shaped what they defined as civil society and the legal parameters within which it operated. An Australian–Iraqi Forum representative who surveyed 4,000 Iraqi NGOs then certified by Iraq's Ministry of Planning found that the most common activities were women's micro-enterprises, cultural violence against women, and raising awareness about democracy.[100] Americans led the exposés of the horrific crimes under Saddam Hussein, but there was only very limited reporting on present-day abuses.[101] Rights to national self-determination, personal security, and protection from arbitrary detention were violated by occupying forces. Moreover, Order 45 and other decrees remained in effect after formal Iraqi independence, unless and until new laws were passed by a nearly paralyzed Parliament. The new government opted to retain the system of mandatory registration that effectively outlawed spontaneous associative activity.[102] A roundtable entitled Towards an Enabling Legal Framework for a Strong Civil Society in Iraq organized in the Iraqi Kurdish city of Irbil by UN and EU agencies invited Lebanese, Moroccan, Jordanian, and Canadian experts to discuss newly proposed amendments with the NGO Coordination Committee in Iraq. Yet Iraqis seemed only rarely to attend other regional conferences for Arab NGO networks. Overall, neither civic monitoring of government actions

---

[98] Ray Lemoine and Jeff Neumann, *Baghdad by Bus* (Penguin, 2006). A major challenge in their jobs, therefore, was to screen for bogus NGOs.

[99] Kevin Begos, "Faded Dreams of Contracted Democracy," *Middle East Report* 234 (2005) 24–27.

[100] Salma Al-Khudairi, NGO Capacity Building Project-Iraq, Australian-Iraqi Forum, May 2005.

[101] The UN hesitated to monitor the unfolding human rights disaster, according to a report from Monitoring of Human Rights in Iraq Network, "First Periodical Report of Monitoring Net of Human Rights in Iraq," MHRI, First Report, 20 August 2005, Baghdad, translated from the Arabic, which focuses on war crimes during the American assault on Fallujah.

[102] Hoshyar Salam Malo, "The Future of Civil Society in Iraq: A Comparison of Draft Civil Society Laws Submitted to the Iraqi Council of Representatives," *International Journal of Not-for-Profit Law* 10:4 (2008).

nor convening with Arab jurists seemed high on American agencies' to-do list in Iraq.

## NGO NETWORKS AND THE WAR ON TERROR

In a risibly tragic reverse-feedback loop, moreover, U.S. and UK security directives in turn emboldened Arab allies to enact sweeping 'counterterrorism' measures. This is not just my contention. The American Civil Liberties Union issued a 155-page report on violations of both U.S. standards of religious freedom and international legal safeguards in its prosecutions of Muslim and Arab charities. Grounds for the freezing and seizing of assets, publicly announced investigations, law enforcement raids, and intrusive surveillance were derived from the International Emergency Economic Powers Act, the Antiterrorism and Effective Death Penalty Act of 1996, the USA Patriot Act of 2001, and the Intelligence Reform and Terrorism Prevention Act of 2004. The most famous case began in December 2001 with closure of the Texas-based Holy Land Foundation on grounds of donations to Palestinian Zakat committees alleged to be in league with Hamas or persons connected to Hamas. It ended seven years later with convictions on 108 criminal counts of material support for terrorism, money laundering, conspiracy, and tax fraud.[103]

NATO and Arab reactions to the millennial events of September 2001 confounded the already conflicted relationship between Arab civil society and international democracy brokers. Whereas heretofore there had been legal proceedings, surveillance, slander, asset seizures, and other problems inside the Middle East, now Western governments resorted to comparable measures to embargo private donations to groups that President Bush said might be terrorist proxies. Immediately after the al-Qa'ida attacks on the United States, many Northern agencies suspended disbursements to most or all Arab non-profits for fear they might be indirectly implicated in terrorism.[104] The long-implicit anti-Islamist ideological filter in NGO funding became explicit.[105] Moreover, under new guidelines, American grantees and contractors were required to sign a two-page affidavit

---

[103] ACLU, *Blocking Faith, Freezing Charity: Chilling Muslim Charitable Giving in the "War on Terrorism Financing"* New York, June 2009.
[104] Angela Grunert, "Loss of Guiding Values and Support: September 11 and the Isolation of Human Rights Organizations in Egypt," *Mediterranean Politics* 8:2–3 (2003) 133–152.
[105] Bicchi, "Want Funding? Don't Mention Islam," 10–12.

testifying that no person or entity connected directly or indirectly to broadly defined "international terrorism" would benefit.[106] These directives, aimed at Hamas, Lebanon's Hizbollah, al-Qa'ida and its affiliates, and sometimes the Muslim Brotherhood or other Islamist opposition parties, were consistent with the security hurdles imposed by repressive Middle Eastern security establishments, and also with the language for NGO eligibility negotiated at the Dead Sea meeting of the Forum for the Future.

The guilt-by-association policy brought apprehension and dismay to the dense professional NGO community of Gaza and the West Bank.[107] The Palestinian umbrella group called PNGO protested the Certification Regarding Terrorist Financing pledge as both impractical and ideologically offensive, since it seemed to require that signatories distance themselves from the nationalist movement in all its manifestations (even to exclude, for instance, members of extended families). When rumors surfaced that a well-funded human rights think tank misspent several million dollars, tales of personal enrichment, crooked audits, and other misuses of foreign grants began circulating amidst accusations that USAID, the Ford Foundation, and other agencies applied stringent rules to smaller organizations while indulging a few high-profile favorites.[108] New donor restrictions after Hamas' narrow victory in the divisive 2006 elections caused further consternation. After the last-minute retraction of a grant from the *Konrad Adenauer Stiftung* for a conference on refugees at al-Quds University, one educator surmised that the aim of outreach projects was to

---

[106] Bettina Huber, "Governance, Civil Society, and Security in the Euro-Mediterranean Partnership, Lessons for a More Effective Partnership," EuroMeSCo Paper 39, Lisbon, December 2004.

[107] For an account and analysis of both detective work and protests, see Christian Erickson, "Counter-Terror Panoptics: Surveillance Programs and Human Rights NGO Opposition in Comparative Context," paper presented at the annual meeting of the International Studies Association 48th Annual Convention, Chicago, February 28, 2007.

[108] Iain Guest, "Funding Scandal Shakes Confidence in Palestinian Civil Society," The Advocacy Project, April 2003.These controversies cut the other way, too. A pro-Israeli group called NGO Monitor established to track how "politicized NGOs distort Israeli history" invited Congress to pressure the privately endowed Ford Foundation to cut off funding for Palestinian, international, and even Israeli associations seen as furthering anti-Zionist agendas. Edwin Black, "Funding Hate: Ford Foundation Draws Scrutiny as terrorism Rules Begin to Bite. Does Funding Trickle Down to Terrorists?" *New York Sun*, October 21, 2003; and "Ford Foundation: 2007 Review of Funding for Political NGOs Active in the Israeli-Palestinian Conflict," *NGO Monitor*, January 28, 2008; "EU Funded NGOs Promote Palestinian Positions on Jerusalem," *NGO Monitor*, May 19, 2009.

promote "docile democracy" or even the "demobilisation, de-radicalisation and de-politicisation of their 'partners.'"[109] In Beirut, sit-ins, demonstrations, and petition campaigns in solidarity with the Palestinians called for a boycott of the U.S. embassy and USAID. Beyond the furor among recipients and non-recipients, a scholarly study of foreign funding for civil society groups in Lebanon and Jordan suggested that Western donors' ideological discrimination in favor of liberal secular groups who were contractually forbidden to contact religious conservatives exacerbated sectarianism and tensions within civil society, closing off potential dialogic projects and ultimately enabling governments to pit different elements of the opposition against one another.[110]

Likewise, in the post-9/11 environment, several Arab governments enacted new anti-terrorism legislation and policies giving state security apparatchiks new latitude.[111] Increased American and NATO security cooperation was explicitly aimed to toughen the intelligence-gathering and coercive capabilities of armed forces in Egypt, Yemen, Jordan, and other countries. It was widely felt that donors shrugged off strong-arm tactics aimed at curtailing protests against economic austerity as well as Islamist militancy: a European consultant called this the "joint stability trap."[112] Arab police and prosecutors used the pretext of anti-terrorism to increase surveillance, prosecution, and harassment of the nationalist, secular, liberal, and progressive opposition as well as Islamist parties and groups.

## DID CIVIL SOCIETY PROMOTION FOMENT REBELLION?

Not only were the democracy-promotion projects marginal within the political landscape in Egypt, meaning that the overwhelming majority of activists avoided them like the plague because they knew it would be a kiss of death for their

---

[109] Sari Hanafi, "The Politics of Funding," *al-Ahram Weekly* No. 828, 18–24 January 2007, adding that "In their concern for the rights of women, animals, and the disabled, ... international donors ignore the Wall, checkpoints, and confiscations."

[110] Francesco Cavatorta and Azzam Elananza, "Show Me the Money! Opposition, Western Funding, and Civil Society in Jordan and Lebanon," in ed. Holger Albrecht, *Contentious Politics in the Middle East: Political Opposition under Authoritarianism* (Gainesville, FL: University Press of Florida, 2010) 75–93.

[111] Moataz El Fegiery, "Arab States: How Criticizing the Government Becomes Illegal," Cairo Institute for Human Rights Studies, July 15, 2007, translated by Kevin Burnham.

[112] Huber, "Governance, Civil Society, and Security in the Euro-Mediterranean Partnership." On the 'partner vetting system' see also Walter Pincus, "Foreign Aid Groups Face Terror Screens," *Washington Post*, August 23, 2007.

credibility, but also the circle of democracy activists itself was marginal in this revolution.[113]

Social scientists, not to mention ruling elites, are often taken by surprise by the rapidity with which an apparently deferential, quiescent, and loyal subordinate group is catapulted into mass defiance.[114]

For over a decade before 2011, bilingual Arab intellectuals and other local project partners echoed widespread public skepticism about the parlances and mechanisms of civil society promotion. Mindful of colonial histories, invasions, and military backing for national security states, they took a critical view of definitions of terrorism as anti-systemic rather than structural violence, calls for technocratic 'reform' over real elections, and purely ceremonial inclusion in international civil society forums.[115] The fixation with NGOs, international funding of NGOs, liberalization of NGO laws, and non-governmental representation at international conferences seemed to misconstrue bases of social solidarity in Afghanistan, Palestine, and elsewhere, wrote one observer.[116] To most, it appeared that democracy 'promotion' was designed to foreclose prospects for unruly or take-to-the-streets revolutionary upheavals by entrusting democratization to paid Western consultants and their slick promotional advertisements. Figure 7, an *al-Jazeera* political cartoon depicting Uncle Sam (indicated by a red-white-and-blue hat) attempting to lasso a raging bull labeled "the January 25th revolution" conveys something about the futility of efforts to capture a mass movement.

Bilingual public intellectuals invited to international conferences spoke frequently about the paradoxes of civil society sponsorship and the patron-

---

[113] Lila Abu-Lughod and Rabab El-Mahdi, "Beyond the 'Woman Question' in the Egyptian Revolution" *Feminist Studies* 37:3 (2011) 683–691.

[114] Scott, *Domination and the Arts of Resistance*, 224.

[115] Sami E. Baroudi, "Arab Intellectuals and the Bush Administration's Campaign for Democracy: The Case of the Greater Middle East Initiative," *Middle East Journal* 61:3 (2007) 390–418; the International Crisis Group, "The Broader Middle East and North Africa Initiative: Imperiled at Birth," ICG Middle East and North Africa Briefs, Brussels/Amman, 7 June 2004. Shahida El-Baz, "Globalisation and the Challenge of Democracy in Arab North Africa," *Africa Development* XXX:4 (2005) 1–33, especially pages 14–18 and 25–27. Examples of editorial opinion from Europe and Egypt included Gilbert Achcar, "Fantasy of a Region That Doesn't Exist – Greater Middle East: The U.S. plan," *Le Monde Diplomatique*, April 2004; Galal Amin, "Colonial Echoes," *al-Ahram Weekly* No. 684, 1–7 April 2004; and more substantively, Ignacio Álvarez-Ossorio Alvariño, "The European Strategy for the Middle East," Jean Monnet/Robert Schuman Paper Series 4:19, December 2004.

[116] Olivier Roy, "The Predicament of 'Civil Society' in Central Asia and Greater Middle East," *International Affairs* 81:5 (2005) 1001–1012.

FIGURE 7. Political cartoon depicting Uncle Sam attempting to lasso a raging bull labeled "January 25th Revolution." Cartoon: Fuad Muheyash/Al-Jazeera. Used with permission.

client relationship between Middle Eastern invitees and Atlantic backers. A Cairo seminar called International Aspects of the Arab Human Rights Movement dwelt on what one discussant called "risks" of accepting invitations to international conferences that come "with strings attached" and might end up bolstering neither indigenous human rights movements nor human rights protection.[117] A prominent Egyptian said resources and themes originating in the North for programs in the South reflected vertical power imbalances that define and constrain even human rights discourses.[118] Aid "depends on personal relations and knowledge of complex procedures within foreign funding agencies" rather than qualitative criteria, agreed a well-respected Yemeni intellectual.[119] The bottom line, wrote another conferee, was that the most common form of corruption "is when organizations design projects in line with donor priorities."[120]

[117] Hani Shukrallah, "International Aspects of the Arab Human Rights Movement," Harvard Law School Human Rights Program, 2000.
[118] Mustapha K. al-Sayyid, "International Aspects of the Arab Human Rights Movement," Harvard Law School Human Rights Program, 2000.
[119] Mohammed A. Al Motawakkel, "International Aspects of the Arab Human Rights Movement," Harvard Law School Human Rights Program, 2000.
[120] Khadr, "International Aspects of the Arab Human Rights Movement."

Overall, innuendoes of embezzlement, corruption, illegality, and "fronts for foreign companies" permeated the discussion.[121]

These viewpoints were very widely aired. Another roundtable on NGOs and Governance in the Arab World organized by UNESCO's Management of Social Transformations Program began with a concept paper by a Tunisian researcher critiquing the World Bank's definition of good governance.[122] When NGOs from poor countries mobilize resources to participate in summits and parallel meetings, a colleague wrote later, "They lend their support to the powers that invited them."[123] Speakers at a Beirut seminar on Civil Society from the Arab Perspective: Experiences and Challenges in Iraq and the Region criticized the American military's role in civil society "promotion" and observed that international organization's high-level collaboration with undemocratic governments betrayed low-key partnerships with local pro-democracy movements.[124]

In January 2010, the Foundation for the Future invited about 90 experts to a workshop at the King Hussein Convention Center on the Dead Sea funded by the European Commission, "under the patronage," as the web account put it, of His Excellency the Jordanian Minister of Political Affairs, to present papers analyzing past research on CSOs in Egypt, Palestine, Iraq, the three Maghreb countries, Jordan, and the GCC. One paper presented a typology of the many scores of donor-funded studies of Egyptian CSOs – academic publications, empirical comparative studies, conference publications, occasional papers and reports issued by civil society organizations, CSO directories, donor publications, evaluations, issue-based publications on topics such as human rights or child welfare, training materials, web-based sources, materials on NGO laws and regulations – and identified gaps in the voluminous literature, notably a conspicuous absence of analyses of aid effectiveness and research designed by Egyptians for Egyptians rather than "imposed by donors."[125] The heads of the 100-person research team at the Cairo-based Arab Network for NGOs

---

[121] Mariz Tadros, "The Egyptian Controversy," *al-Ahram Weekly* No. 476, 6–12 April 2000.
[122] Sarah Ben Néfissa, "ONG, gouvernance et développement dans le monde arabe," UNESCO Management of Social Transformations, Discussion Paper No. 46, Cairo, April 3, 2001.
[123] Roca, "Insiders and Outsiders," 48–49.
[124] Zeina Halabi, "Arab Civil Society: Assessing Interpretations and Determining Challenges," commissioned by Henrich Böll Foundation, Middle East Office and Arab NGO Network for Development, September 2004.
[125] Mahi Khallaf, "Civil Society in Egypt: A Literature Review," paper presented to the Foundation for the Future Regional Conference on Research on Civil Society Organizations: Status and Prospects, Jordan, January 26–28, 2010.

and at Amman's *al-Urdan al-Jadid*, two of the best-funded think tanks in
the region, highlighted their organizations' extensive reports and NGO
surveys, which the Egyptian concluded were part of a larger effort to define
civil society as a private-sector responsibility in order to offset the potentially destabilizing effects of globalization.[126] The presentations on
Palestine and Iraq, respectively, each reflected woefully on definitions of
CSOs that sideline Islamic and communal bases of popular solidarity in
favor of what the Iraqi author called the American "neo-liberal model."[127]
A European academic researcher familiar with the NGO scenes in Egypt
and Palestine drew attention to "a whole disciplining apparatus" to promote "a very managerial understanding of 'civil society'" and a "blossom-
ing" of conferences, "teaching modules for NGO activists, introductory
courses to the Logi-Frame analysis, cycle management for civil society,"
and tutorials in fundraising, and concluded that "most international
donors have overlooked the peripheries" and instead systematically draw
on a tiny group of privileged urban NGOs "to infer or instill a strategic
mapping of civil society action."[128]

Speaking from intercontinental portals to Western democracy brokers
and 'makers,' well-networked bilingual public intellectuals and rights
advocates reflected self-consciously on the detachment of serene, super-
clean, high-end conference suites from the gritty, alienated, intermittently
restive 'street' outside. The rarified rubrics of 'civil society' seemed more
and more insensible to episodic informally organized subaltern forms of
civic activism. NGO portals felt utterly detached from the anti-war demonstrations, work stoppages, sit-ins, and dissident artistic performances
spreading across Yemen, Egypt, Jordan, Morocco, and the region.
Moreover, substrata of popular expression were not rendered legible by
the mountain of directories, strategic maps, civil society surveys, and so
forth. If anything, the definition of civil society as formal NGOs participating in ceremonial networks discounted the possibility of grassroots
collective action; intensive highly professionalized data collection, political

---

[126] Amani Kandil, "A critical review of the Literature about the Arab Civil Society," and
Hani Al-Hourani, "Civil Society in Jordan: A Literature Review," Foundation for the
Future Regional Conference, 2010: passage cited, Kandil, "A critical review," 39–40.

[127] Jamal Hilal, "Civil Society in Palestine," and Hayder Saeed, "Civil Society in Iraq,"
Foundation for the Future Regional Conference 2010.

[128] Benoît Challand, "Comments on Palestinian CSOs: How to Trace Down the Impact of
External Aid?" Foundation for the Future Regional Conference, 2010. A logi-frame or
log-frame is a tabular format widely used in development planning circles to specify linear
connections between problems and solutions as proposed by donor agencies.

intelligence, and codification schemes yielded few clues to community mobilization.

Full-time civic organizers, lawyers, academics, artists and others knew about bilateral and multilateral backing for repressive dictatorships that adopted neo-liberal policies, the endlessly fruitless so-called 'peace process,' and counter-terrorism strategies. Feminists, labor organizers, rights defenders, most other civic agitators, and social entrepreneurs believed that transnational democracy brokers eschewed mass politics. Few, if any, of the reports, conversations, and conferences cited here hinted at collective actions, public displays of dissent, or anything remotely resembling resistance. UNESCO's Management of Social Transformations rubric, mentioned earlier, expressed this bias perfectly: transformations are social and manageable, not political or economic and unruly. The political scientist who joined the American project in Iraq only to find it a "squandered" opportunity advised Western democracies in 2008 to design programs for the Arab world to facilitate a "soft landing" from authoritarianism.[129] A bicultural observer from Carnegie's office in Doha observed in the spring of 2011 that – in stark contrast to post-Communist situations such as Ukraine and Serbia – democracy aid to Egypt, Jordan, Morocco, Algeria, and Yemen had heretofore emphatically not emphasized that democracy entails alternation in executive power or supported groups agitating for regime change; instead, Arabs were advised to wait patiently for long-term reforms.[130] Egyptian protesters pointed ruefully to "made in America" logos on the tear-gas canisters lobbed against protesters in the days, weeks and months after January 25, 2011 and noticed when a new shipment of stronger gas arrived. Pundits observed that the Obama White House and the Clinton State Department clung to Ben Ali and Mubarak until the very end.

Nonetheless, Egyptian rumor-mills and the Anglophone press circulated tales of American instigation of the uprisings. One narrative credited a private citizen, Gene Sharp, the Boston-based author of a widely translated compilation of 198 tactics for non-violent resistance, with devising the "playbook" that toppled the Egyptian government.[131] The intriguing connection to a populist NATO-backed civilian rebellion in Serbia where Sharp's techniques had evidently been put to effective use was that at least

---

[129] Diamond, *In the Spirit of Democracy*, 337.
[130] Shadi Hamid, "The Struggle for Middle East Democracy," *Cairo Review of Global Affairs* 1 (2011) 18–29.
[131] Ruaridh Arrow, "Gene Sharp: Author of the Nonviolent Revolution Rulebook," BBC News 21 February 2011; Sheryl Gay Stolberg, "Shy U.S. Intellectual Created Playbook Used in a Revolution," *New York Times*, February 16, 2011.

one or two members of Egypt's contentious April 6th Youth for Change movement had traveled to Belgrade and New York for about a week's worth of training at the Center for Applied Non-Violent Actions and Strategies (CANVAS), where Sharp's tactics are taught.[132] Presumably Americans wanted to see themselves as inspirational for democratic youth. On the other side, too, Cairo's official propaganda blamed the January 25 uprising on contacts between some Egyptian youth and the Western-funded Belgrade think tank.

By this time, CANVAS was a donor-maintained outgrowth of the rebellious but now defunct Optor! Movement. Some Optor! veterans founded the Center as an NGO that successfully raised donor moneys to train young people from many countries in Sharp's principles of non-violent resistance. The evidence that those lessons launched mass demonstrations is tenuous. Only a dozen or so of Sharp's 198 principles initially collected and put into a handbook for Burmese dissidents in Thailand in 1993 were observed in and around Midan al-Tahrir in early 2011, and they were things that had existed in Egyptian, Yemeni, Algerian, and Jordanian protest repertoires for years, if not decades: slogans, caricatures, and symbols; banners, posters, and displayed communications; public prayer and worship; humorous skits and pranks; performances of plays and music; singing; marches; political mourning; assemblies of protest or support; literature and speeches advocating resistance; self-exposure to the elements; pray-ins; alternative communication systems; passive arrest; and defiance of police authority.[133] These street-level forms of expression were far more kinetic than the standard indoor fare of civil society projects as described elsewhere in this chapter, to be sure, and the spirit of civil disobedience was highly apposite. Sharp of course did not however recommend some other acts of insurrection used by Tunisian and Egyptian protesters: self-immolation, torching police stations, setting vehicles on fire, or running protest encampments complete with garbage collection, field clinics, and internet service.

The CANVAS training materials available on the internet did feature such tips as how to stage flash demonstrations to confuse police that were used to good effect by informal horizontal youth networks in Alexandria and other Egyptian cities during 2010, but did not endorse the kind of upheaval that swept the Arab region in 2011. CANVAS' "basic

[132] Tina Rosenberg, "Revolution U: What Egypt Learned from the Students Who Overthrew Milosevic," *Foreign Policy*, February 19, 2011.
[133] Gene Sharp, *From Dictatorship to Democracy: A Conceptual Framework for Liberation*, Fourth U.S. edition (East Boston: The Albert Einstein Institution, 2010).

curriculum" was about planning and organization, not spontaneous subaltern revolt. It seemed a product of the NGOization of a component of a
former rebellion, complete with a brand-name, a non-patented clench-
fisted logo, and managerial lesson-plans as described in this outline:

> There is rarely victory for nonviolent movements without a strategic plan.
> Therefore, an understanding of basic strategic principles (Lesson 7) as well as
> tools and techniques to analyze their past and current situation (Lesson 8 and
> Lesson A1) is important as movements develop their strategic plans. An essential
> part of those plans will be communications. How do movements effectively com-
> municate what they stand for? Developing effective messages and analyzing audi-
> ence segments (Lesson 9) and understanding the tools and types of targeted
> communications (Lesson 10) are essential. Targeted communication is one of the
> most important parts of any movement's strategic plan.[134]

This was a manual for a long-term, calculated, hierarchical campaign.
Under the motto of "unity, discipline, and planning," it assumes a pyramidal structure for coordinated actions according to a "strategic plan."
Also the success story it touts about a pacifist, native, civilian campaign
conveniently leaves out the role of NATO bombardment in toppling
Milosevic while at the same time romanticizing the North Atlantic narrative about democratic intervention.

The progressive Egyptian intelligentsia found this legend of Western-
backed Serbian inspiration for their mass popular mobilization insulting.
There was even a facetious hash tag on Twitter, GeneSharpTaughtMe.
Drawing on observations from Egyptian colleagues, I have argued elsewhere that this training was only marginally relevant to the improvisa-
tional, multifaceted, and unarmed but not entirely non-violent street-level
mobilization in Cairo during the first half of 2011.[135] I never saw or heard
any hint of Euro-American instigation of the Tunisian uprising that started
the whole 'Arab Spring' or the Yemeni protest movement that gained new
momentum after the resignations of Ben Ali and Mubarak, nor of foreign
encouragement of labor strikes, sit-ins, and 'parallel revolutions' roiling
Egypt and the region for several years. At most, Sharp and CANVAS
would count among an array of inspirations that also included Che
Guevara, Nelson Mandela, Palestinian *intifadas*, the American civil rights
movement, Mahatma Gandhi, the Paris Commune, Franz Fanon, *The*

---

[134] CANVAS Core Curriculum, http://www.canvasopedia.org/legacy/content/special/core.
htm.
[135] Carapico, "Egypt's Civic Revolution: Beyond What 'Civil Society Promotion' Had in
Mind," eds. Bahgat Korany and Rabab El-Mahdi, *Arab Spring in Egypt* (Cairo: AUC
Press, 2012) 199–222.

*Battle of Algiers*, and indigenous regional, national, and local cultural symbols, slogans, and performances.

The criminal prosecution of employees of international democracy promotion agencies, mentioned in the Introduction to this book and again at the beginning of this chapter, was only partly about what Egyptians call their revolution. It was about the issues of NGO registration and finance that had consumed so much energy in Egypt for at least two decades. This chapter situated these legal proceedings in the context of a long litigious saga in which the Egyptian government continually sought to harden firewalls around the sovereign civic domain by criminalizing support from abroad as seditious. Indictments against employees of American or German organizations calling themselves 'non-governmental' and 'pro-democracy' seemed to represent an amplification of the pushback or backlash against civil society promotion. As usual, however, it was mainly professional Egyptian or bi-national individuals who faced the prospect of imprisonment.

This chapter closes with a final twist. After the U.S. government posted $5 million in bail to enable Americans under indictment in Egypt to return to the United States, two U.S. citizens took a different stance. One American living in Cairo while working for NDI, who refused to evacuate, and a dual national living in the States, who returned to Egypt for each court hearing, resigned (or were fired from) their positions in mid-2012 to stand trial along with their Egyptian colleagues. A German who evacuated briefly but returned to her home in Cairo also faced the court, while continuing to work in the nearly-empty *Konrad Adenauer Stiftung* office. The Egyptian-American who had been employed by Freedom House had addressed this issue before. "Actions speak louder than words," he wrote in June 2010 about the Obama administration's acquiescence to Mubarak's insistence that all 'aid' be funneled through his crony machine; "Egyptian democrats find themselves without a support system in their fight against government repression in part, due to American ambivalence."[136] Recalling the Ibn Khaldun Center's struggles years earlier, in 2012 he asked the Obama administration to use the leverage of billions of dollars in official aid to insist that Egypt's government "should not decide what the civil society should do or are able to do," and vowed to fight the vindictive political charges alongside other Egyptians.[137]

---

[136] Sherif Mansour, "Why Cairo Believes Obama's Democracy Support Is Nothing More than Empty Words," *Huffington Post*, June 3, 2010.
[137] Sherif Mansour, "Call the General's Bluff," *Foreign Policy*, February 7, 2012.

The story of civil society aid and the pushback against it was full of contradictions manifested in litigious, bitterly contested disputes. Drawing on the testimony of direct participants, I have depicted these as skirmishes between national and global regimes of governmentality, each seeking to channel civic energies into manageable parameters. In the name of anti-imperialism and self-determination, autocratic governments nationalized and regulated all forms of public activism. Conventional inter-governmental development assistance aimed at improving the governance capacity of state institutions often enhanced central administration and control. In the same way, some rule-of-law programs, elections projects, and support for national women's organizations or GONGOs served the interests of national security establishments. The projects that most persistently enraged corrupt officials were those that circumvented their patronage channels and bureaucratic oversight. Metaphorically, non-governmental pathways dena-tionalized some forms of professional activism, including the production of political information, by placing them outside state budgets. Whereas some analysts saw in state capacity-building the potential for political aid to abet the upgrading of authoritarianism, others observed a reverse effect in the pushback – the continual re-regulation, re-registration, subversion, and co-optation of civic activities in response to donor initiatives. Then, the more transnational donor networks pressed, the more dictatorial regimes over-reacted, and the more activists took their projects offshore. This was the second dimension of denationalization. Professional human rights, women's, and NGO networks proliferated, meeting periodically in extra-territorial spaces physically owned and operated by multinational hotel chains. Recognizing a consensual rather than coercive domain, many scholars and participants found there a different sort of governmentality with its own discursive rules and licensing restrictions. When UNDP and other agencies fixed on establishing a "knowledge society" in the Arab world, they were referring to very particular epistemological and professional practices.

The global democracy bureaucracy is a collection of think tanks where highly educated professionals produce specialized knowledge. They are able to devote their full-time energies to research and/or advocacy. Those stationed long-term in North Africa and the Middle East thought about these issues, one way or the other. Not everyone will agree with my analysis, of course. Some will feel that I have been unduly considerate of loathsome dictatorships; others might say I have white-washed the political-aid industry. Anyone with experience would be able to offer additional or counter-examples to those cited here. Nonetheless, few will quarrel with the basic argument that civil society promotion is inherently and intensely political, and many have pointed to its paradoxes.

This chapter traced the interplays, portals, and boundary disputes between national and transnational regimes of governmentality each determined to capture and manage Arab civil society. The ultimate irony is that neither of these purportedly hegemonic apparatuses suppressed the dramatic outpouring of citizen discontent in Tunisia, Egypt, and Yemen.

# Conclusion

## *Political Aid for Justice, Representation, Equality, and Freedom?*

In this book I have advanced the argument that political aid is both inherently political and deeply paradoxical; and that people involved in every sector of democracy promotion are intensely aware of the politics and the paradoxes.

By definition political aid interjects external symbolic, material, and institutional resources into national (and, in the Middle East, pan-Arab) arenas. If all politics involves competition over scarce resources, then political aid naturally stimulates controversy and rivalries. Inevitably resources flow to selected organizations, agents, and causes, but not others. Donors' provision of expertise, technology, publicity, or funds to executive, judicial, legislative, or civic institutions affects the balance of power between and within those bodies. Even if the idea is that international agencies are supporting 'transitions to democracy' or 'women's empowerment,' projects entail complex forms of cooperation and conflict. Practitioners and participants, including many cited here, realize the banalities of interagency and office politics on a commonplace level. This is 'low' politics.

Democracy promotion also reflects the 'high' politics of the international arena where the United States and European powers engage and ally with some Arab regimes and sometimes intervene militarily and/or diplomatically directly to influence outcomes. Certainly military and development assistance, and also political aid, reflect these power politics. However much Western advocates try to place democracy promotion on the altruistic end of the realism-idealism debate, many in the Arab world find connections to the colonial past and imperial present. Moreover as recounted in these chapters client governments variously sought to capitalize on political aid or made a big show of resisting 'foreign interference.' In many instances popular forces, counter-elites, and rights defenders sought to distance themselves from donor agencies and agendas. In all these ways, political aid was politicized.

These circumstances speak to the paradoxes. The social science literature has given us two main theories about the purposes and effects of political aid. One posits the positive diffusion effects of transnational regimes that work to establish norms and practices concerning law, elections, and the protections and participation of women and associational life, and it cites the roles of multilateral initiatives, normative actors, and professional expertise in facilitating political liberalization. The other situates these discourses and institutional arrangement in the overall context of asymmetric North-South or core-periphery exchanges and neo-liberal globalization, finding instead of democratization a way of deepening and intensifying Western hegemony. Examples, testimonials and some counterfactual evidence presented here variously supported both of these antithetical theories, each of which is persuasive in its own right but both of which tend inadequately to distinguish intentions from outcomes. Firsthand accounts also point to a third possibility, that 'target audiences' make creative use of resources within the parameters of constraints.

Across the board empirical evidence and informed opinion support seemingly antithetical hypotheses about how political aid works in practice. Democracy promotion can be both a mode of empowerment and a modality of power. It can be or is both a way of breaching authoritarianism and a tactic for imperial domination. In other words, we cannot discount rival paradigms about the universalization of cosmopolitan norms, on the one hand, and transnational governmentality, on the other. International experts, Arab activists, and scholarly critics specialized in law, elections, women's empowerment, and civil society continually grappled with the emancipatory potential and hegemonic pretenses of international political aid. I found that in each field, articulations between transnational regimes and national circumstances were complex, layered, and fundamentally contradictory: conflicting trajectories of power and empowerment were simultaneously in play.

On one level, transnational democracy promotion is a discourse signifying good intentions and benevolent global leadership, and its output is an incredible volume of reports and commentary that reinforce this narrative. The logic of the rhetoric is that Western or American assistance is necessary but not sufficient for democratic transitions abroad – where, it is assumed, good people look to great powers for expertise, support, and inspiration. Among the possibilities the narrative of democracy promotion seems to foreclose would be progressive change outside the *Pax Americana*. This frame so effectively conveys to Western voters that the people they elect seek freedom and justice in the world that it seems self-evident. When a President Clinton, Bush, or Obama delivers a stirring speech about democratic enlargement, freedom agendas, or a new beginning, American acolytes, pundits, and citizens like to imagine that millions of Arabs are inspired.

This narrative does not travel well, or translate well, as practitioners and close hand observers discovered. The messianic eloquence that seems hegemonic in English has approximately zero street cred in modern standard or local vernacular Arabic; it may be received less as a regime of truth than a pack of lies. People are appalled by violations of the individual, national, and international human rights of Palestinians and Iraqis, provision of the military means for suppression of the Bahraini uprising, extrajudicial drone executions in Yemen, discriminatory visa policies, and ... the list goes on. Whether the larger democracy promotion project in the Middle East is understood as a grand campaign to win hearts and minds or as a strategy for pacification, events, institutions and understandings mediate the results in complex and sometimes counterintuitive ways.

Democracy promotion is not only semantic; it is also an industry, a profession, and a set of institutional practices. This study operationalized democracy advancement as projects, which are discrete, funded activities carried out by professionals. Thus the simple answer to the question 'how does democracy promotion work?' is 'one project at a time, cumulatively over time, through discrete organizational channels.' These tend to self-replicate: democracy brokers beget democracy brokers by reproducing modes of knowledge and institutional conventions. Political aid 'creates demand' for informational services. Associations and bureaucracies for women proliferate, for instance, with similar mission statements, logics and routines. This does not mean, however, that there are not transmutations or that progeny faithfully reproduce parental mores. To the contrary in every country and each sector, people re-purpose the resources of political aid.

Beyond looking at projects as discrete building blocks, this book grouped them around specialized goals and practices in the fields of law, representation, women's rights, and civil society promotion. This approach engaged distinctive literatures, fields of expertise, and forms of activism. In each sector, professionals and scholars grappled with domain disputes and paradoxes of empowerment.

Justice is a field and a language unto itself, highly professionalized, where practitioners are also scholars. Cross-nationally there is common veneration of something called 'the law,' as well as recognition of issue-areas where multi-scalar layers of jurisdiction raise profound issues about what kinds of legislation are peremptory. Law is also constitutive of what we think of as 'the state,' democratic or otherwise. Therefore, any policy that tampers with law is profoundly political. The research presented here illustrated how projects in the broad, somewhat incongruous, justice-and-rule-of-law sector can (depending on circumstances) penetrate, harmonize, fortify, or defy the legal authority of governments. It also showed that political aid sometimes complements universal legal regimes but can also contradict them. More harmonization with global standards seems to occur in high-stakes areas of heavy investment – trade legislation law and counter-terrorism – than regarding other norms on torture or NGO legislation. This is partly because American democracy brokers tend to disregard international law and Europeans pay lip service to human rights but put their money on trade and immigration. In Iraq, moreover, American projects seemed hopelessly out of sync with either international law or the indigenous legal system already influenced by Napoleonic and British models.

Projects work through organized – but not necessarily unidirectional or linear – pathways. The legal sector gave an excellent example of this. Existing judicial systems adapted principles and practices from outside into new legislation, regulation, and institutions. They did so in ways that are more situational and multi-faceted than simply 'diffusion' or 'pushback.' The scholarly literature and project documents directed our attention to the historical and contemporary patterns of inter-Arab legal harmonization and an intermediate layer of law between 'international' and 'municipal' where additional articulations occur. Some political aid projects were inserted inside national jurisdictions. Others interacted with transnational 'Arab' bar associations, human rights networks, and so forth.

International democracy promotion might have lived up to its mission statements in the judicial sector. It is a notably schooled, professionalized, tight field of specialization. Jurists, and even barristers, hold substantive authority relatively autonomous from the executive branch of government; usually they believe in 'the law,' or have an interest in its legitimiza-tion. In Egypt and elsewhere courts are important sites of socio-political struggles, where rights are claimed and defended. Moreover, international legal regimes are relatively robust and well-recognized, an actual force in the world. In addition, there is the demonstrable inter-Arab assimilation, such that principles enshrined in legislation somewhere do spread elsewhere. For the sake of women, the close attention legal experts pay to texts and applications of criminal, family, contract, and labor law is preferable to vague references gender specialists make to 'sharia.' Fortifying legal education and the rule of humanitarian law on a consistent basis would be a good use of political aid. Major donors could work to fortify and expand the jurisdictions of international law.

From the invasion itself to ad hoc decrees to the trial and execution of the dictator Saddam Hussein the American-led occupation of Iraq undermined universal humanitarian law and principles. The memoirs and law review articles of legal experts who initially brought high hopes and professional self-confidence to the consultancies in Iraq under the occupation are full of poignant reflections on ironies, contradictions, missed opportunities, and deviations from well-established legal principles. More than any other, in this field and circumstance professional practitioners became ruefully aware of the politics and paradoxes of political aid.

There were both parallels and differences between the rule of law sector and practices regarding elections, which for many practitioners and observers are the heart of what is meant by 'democracy promotion.' Compared with other activities, projects dealing with elections are uniquely short-term and episodic, and they make the local and international news. A special national event is being performed in which perhaps millions of voters perform rituals that supposedly (but in the cases examined, rarely) determine who will govern. Western powers (sometimes) and incumbent autocrats (always) have a vested interest in 'spinning' the story – whether as a momentous transition or as popular acclaim for the status quo.

In theory, the expertise and monitoring methodologies developed after the end of the Cold War might have served donors' and/or client regimes' interests by crafting more persuasive demonstration elections in the Middle East. The global governance regime could have been a force for stability, a way of manufacturing the appearance of consent for neo-liberal order and pliant dictators, and perhaps even a means of laying the groundwork for orderly regime changes. I was prepared to entertain the hypotheses that expert consultants would design a viable and durable electoral system for Iraq and that political aid would help Ali Abdallah Salih and Husni Mubarak to win credible contests. These accomplishments would have advanced the strategic and ideological hegemony of the United States and 'the West.' In iterative practice, however, it didn't work out that way. Sitting autocrats spurned the rules of the game, and great powers did not enforce those rules. The potential convincingly to manufacture the appearance of consent to client dictatorships or the new order in Iraq was frittered away.

The professional practices of the transnational elections regime offer a methodology for countering 'spin' with relatively objective empirical observations systematically documented in text, notes, and tables. Arabic, English or French book-form reports from professional observer agencies operationalized indicators of relatively competitive, transparent, credible elections. Also, checklists of discrete objective observations – candidates' access to media, registration processes, opening times for polling stations, registration rolls, the presence of soldiers or gunmen, orderly processing, visible transport of boxes, and so forth – were widely distributed, in Arabic (and Kurdish). Arabs joined international delegations to observe each other's votes, and brought insights home. Volunteers took the short course, kept a vigilant eye, tallied checklists, and reported findings that made their way into the pan-Arab media. Cosmopolitan rubrics might, conceivably, have solidified American and/or authoritarian control in individual countries and across the region. Instead, if anything, they had the opposite effect by improving detection and documentation of double standards (as in Palestine) and outright fraud (in Egypt). In this sector the global governance regime did not well serve American hegemony. As in other fields, the failure of the Occupying Authority to apply universal, technocratic standards for plausible elections in Iraq revealed the limits of imperial hubris. 'Electioneering' might have instituted better practices, or created the illusion of popular consent: instead, it did neither. After the two very negative examples of Iraq and Palestine in 2005/06, the transnational monitoring regime, stymied by power politics, lost much of the momentum of the previous decade.

We got beyond Uncle Sam's monologue in the second half of this book. Nonetheless political aid was manifestly political and paradoxical even in sectors less directly affected by 'high' politics. The scholarly literature on gender empowerment and civil society promotion absorbed the disciplines of anthropology, sociology, and cultural studies, and research on globalization. In women's studies many observers and participants encountered tensions between a strong constructivist contingent supportive of the UN-centered UNIFEM/CEDAW regime and a robust critique of the Orientalist prototypes for individual emancipation from family and community. The chapter called Patronizing Women investigated the way texts are transmitted, received, and exercised by Arab women, and it called attention to their incredulity, mistrust, and humor. Feminist colleagues were often bothered by discourses of empowerment laden with cultural determinism, which they (or we) found Orientalist and at the same time irrelevant to popular struggles in Yemen, Palestine, Iraq, Egypt, and elsewhere. This bafflement was rooted in familiarity with the ways Saddam Hussein, Ben 'Ali, and other secular despots offered token representation to women.

Therefore, two kinds of evidence were presented. First, I quoted an abrasive pattern of lectures and quizzes on religio-cultural oppression given to people coping with dire military and economic distress. In witty asides, the occasional heckle, and plenty of thoughtful analysis, women outside the empowerment industry called into question its stock significations of autonomy, voting, gender quotas, *Shari'a*, public comportment, safety, Women's Day, 'sexist stereotypes,' and Western superiority. In these exchanges, outsiders consistently scoffed at the consciousness of Muslims; equally, locals ridiculed foreign hubris and naiveté. The implication was that an emphasis on changing mindsets too guilelessly underestimates the hard constraints of firepower and poverty.

Empowerment was not only a discourse, however; it was also routinized in professional and institutional practices inside and beyond national bureaucracies. Secondly, therefore, the Patronizing Women chapter gave a bit of the history of the interplay between indigenous women's movements, representation at transnational women's conventions, and secular nationalist 'state feminism.' It then related more recent data about where political aid targeted for women went, for what proximate purposes, and what happened next. In practice, of course, material, symbolic, and administrative capital did not help half the population, but only some individuals or agencies designated to 'represent women.' This in turn spawned ordinary political competition over positions, podiums, and power. In this way, women's advocacy was not dissimilar from other projects and/or UN-centered regimes. In the course of specific events, and in the context of post-colonial governance configurations, political capital tended to accumulate in the hands of ruling classes and families. First Ladies, princesses, bureaucrats, a few charismatic public personalities, and U.S. Secretaries of State were further enabled, on national and international stages (and to succumb to the fashion-statement commentary: usually wearing designer dresses and shoes regardless of what was on their heads), to speak 'for' all females. One paradox of idealism institutionalized was that slogans about 'culture change' or 'empowering women' could be deployed either to advance popular rights claims or in the service of incumbent power. This is the risk of treating women as a monolithic group most of whom cannot articulate their own interests.

The chapter on gender offered an interesting case study of constructivism in practice, or how political aid can deepen a multinational, UN-centered regime. As in the fields of law and elections, this regime is not merely diffused or imposed from outside. It flows from regional feminist movements and organizations for women and their co-optation by military dictatorships. It is not just a product of Western democracy promotion: for instance, rogue republics and even Gulf monarchies were just as likely to sign on to CEDAW as recipients of substantial political aid. Political aid would be *a* factor, then, not *the* factor, explaining executive, legislative, or judicial policy-making. Instead, regime theorists might hypothesize that sometimes political aid can help publicize causes, institutionalize practices, and foster specialized epistemic communities.

The evidence supports and qualifies this proposition. That is, central executive authorities (if not courts and legislatures) were more likely to embrace the rhetorical and institutional practices of gender representation than those of either elections monitoring or NGO regimes. The Beijing apparatus appears to be a strong example of multilateral constructivism, outside the U.S. orbit. It is grounded in ideas but realized through institutional practices. This way of looking at things shed light on how conceptually quite different definitions of 'regimes' – regimes of truth, mechanisms of transnational governmentality, national dictatorships – can be mutually constitutive. Therein, however, lay the rub. Saddam Hussein and Zine El Abidine Ben Ali, among others, publicized their commitments to CEDAW or UNIFEM, institutional representation of women, and gender equality – even as they ruthlessly repressed independent civic activism.

In each subfield, contradictions surfaced between the transformative potential of political aid operating in conjunction with international regimes and the ways in which democracy promotion could simply perpetuate Western domination. Activists, professionals, practitioners, and engaged social scientists (overlapping categories, to be sure) told me this, over and over. My overarching political point has been that advocates for social justice and systemic change in Arab countries at the turn of the millennium confronted the contradictory implications of layers of governmentality – and, ultimately, their fragilities. Civil society promotion most dramatically illustrated this conundrum, and the contradictions came to the fore during the explosion of pent-up frustrations the Anglophone press liked to call the 'Arab Spring.'

Of all the categories of democracy promotion, non-governmental political aid was the most disputatious. The chapter on NGOs, GONGOs,
DONGOs, and so forth was mostly about legislation and litigation.
According to participants and engaged scholars, civil society promotion
typified inter-scalar ruptures in the recent era of neo-liberal globalization
when power and politics seemed to be denationalized. Westphalian
notions of national boundaries and diplomatic stations were continually
disputed, defended, and negotiated. Conflicts over civil society registration
and finance highlighted fissures in old-fashioned inter-state channels. For
many observers, domain disputes and turf wars raised anew questions
about sovereignty, self-determination, and the nature of 'the state.' Even
more than in other sectors, the dialectic between nationalized and denationalized activism manifestly played out in theoretical debates and everyday contests over right-of-way, resources, and ideological hegemony. Its
permutations and contradictions were profound. That means we need to
be wary of any explanatory framework that over-determines causality:
neither Western imperialism nor Arab authoritarianism nor other modes
of repression or 'governmentality' are as unmovable as they may seem.

The relatively elite strata of professional civic activists working in Arab
countries often found English-language parlances about 'promoting'
something called 'democratization' rarified and disjointed. 'Promotion'
after all can refer to advertising campaigns. Catchphrases, project clusters,
and institutional formats fixated on some issues to the exclusion of others,
women and men complained. Amidst so much attention to elections and
'culture change,' neither ballot-driven 'regime change' nor 'transitions in
power' were on UN, U.S. or EU agendas. In the aggregate, neo-liberal
entrepreneurial freedoms were more popular with donors than were labor
rights. Women bristled at obsessions with sexual rather than national self-
determination and the privileging of gender over class solidarity. Only in
the Muslim world, some observed, was 'secularism' considered a prereq-
uisite for democratization.

Thus the null set of concerns – themes and phrases that barely registered
in English-language word-counts – included social justice, military rule,
working conditions, existing social contracts, popular safety nets, regular
power transitions, police brutality, and national sovereignty. Yet these
issues – not 'democracy' by name – were the slogans and concepts that
mobilized millions to take to the streets in 2011. All along, in Anglophone
and UN 'donor-speak,' transcriptions of Arab 'deficits' in democracy and
women's rights were chalked up to socio-cultural sediments variously
labeled patriarchal, traditional, tribal, sectarian, or Islamic. Armed forces'

abuses (amply documented by Amnesty International, Human Rights Watch, and dozens of regional watch-dogs) were not given much attention in democracy brokers' reports on problems facing women or NGOs. Indeed, in the rhetoric of transitions to democracy, strangely, the word 'civilian' or word combination 'civilian rule' rarely, if ever, appeared. Religion, 'sharia,' and secularism were mentioned frequently, especially in documents about gender. Militarism and the securitization of governance, by comparison, were not presented as a serious obstacle to realization of justice, representation, female participation, or freedom.

Nor, even in the field of civil society advancement, was the prospect of mass popular uprisings against police brutality part of the democratization template presented to the Arab world in late 2010. Panelists pointed out that 'civil society' referred to effete think tanks rather than popular organizations. The donor construct of civil society *never* included anti-war protests of the sort that spilled into Arab streets during the American-led invasion of Iraq and Israeli bombardments of Gaza, the West Bank, and Lebanon. Consulting reports did not refer to marches, demonstrations or out-of-doors collective mobilization as instances of civic engagement: in the 'transitions to democracy' narrative it is as if they never happened. The discourses and institutional practices of civil society promotion seemed, instead, to foreclose prospects for contentious challenges to despotism. Project conceptualizations put 'democratization' or 'liberalization' in the hands of office-bound professionals fulfilling log-frames laid out in funding proposals featuring three-year 'strategic' plans. Civil society was operationalized in terms of hierarchical organizations and tactical planning, not spontaneously or vertically mobilized multitudes. As Tawakkul Karman told the United Nations General Assembly on November 1, 2011, the 'international community' insisted in describing events in Yemen as a 'crisis,' not a 'revolution.' What Tunisians, Egyptians, and Yemenis called '*thawra*' (revolution) outsiders choose to dub 'the Arab Spring.'

This point registered squarely among Cairo's engaged intelligentsia when 'revolutionary tourists' – not only Middle East scholars enthused by the radical turn of events but transitologists and specialists in 'democratization' with little familiarity with the region who flocked to Egypt to 'see Tahrir Square' first-hand and 'help' Egyptian democrats – reframed events as 'transitions to democracy' in need of expert consultation. The influx of foreigners was a matter of consternation to Egyptian intellectuals who were asked to facilitate their visits. Now, many of the donor-sponsored sessions I attended in the spring of 2011 featured well-informed comparative insights from South Africa, Chile, the Ukraine, and around the globe. Still, the supply of expert transitologists who flew into Cairo after February 11, when Mubarak relinquished power, exceeded demand for their advice on how to manage a transition. Egyptian political party organizers I talked to were not familiar with Gene Sharp and few were interested in IRI's free training modules on how to run an American-style political campaign. Activists in Cairo, Sana'a, and other capitals in upheaval were talking about revolution, not transition. Also, contrary to the Anglophone narrative, popular slogans in Arabic did not vocalize demands for 'democracy' so much as regime change, social justice, popular self-determination, constraints on police brutality, and decent standards of living. So, even naming the uprisings a 'pro-democracy' movement was a kind of appropriation by managers of transitions. The fact that a certain discourse was hegemonic in English did not make it so in Arabic.

This was amply clear to those living 'in the region.' In practice, donor projects endorsing judicial and democratic reform were political and para-doxical on global, regional, national, and grassroots levels. Only oblivious or disingenuous advisors or counterparts working in Egypt, Iraq, Yemen, Algeria, Palestine, or any Arab territory pretended otherwise. Project staff, consultants, and grantees continually confronted competing significations, regulations, and interests – even in quite mundane day-to-day circum-stances. Yet circumstances were not normally mundane before, during, or after the turn of the millennium in the Middle East. Instead, political aid projects were inevitably entangled with international and domestic power alignments, and sometimes radical readjustments. These imbroglios in turn shaped how messages about political transitions, justice, and empow-erment were transmitted, received, operationalized, and re-purposed by various agents and actors. It is one thing to frame a meta-narrative about transitions from authoritarianism in English, or diagram outcomes in a project proposal. It is something else to engineer institutions and practices inside complex societies to match the model, or even to convince commit-ted change agents that international democracy brokers know best.

I have argued that political aid ought to be judged less for how it meets donor objectives than for whether it helps regional human rights activists, elections monitors, feminists, and civil rights workers to meet their prox-imate and medium-term goals. On these grounds, two decades of 'democ-racy promotion' in the Middle East and North Africa have offered at most mixed blessings. Triumphant moments of Palestinian elections or the toppling of Saddam Hussein were annihilated by their punishing denouements. Tyrants manipulated strategically-driven political aid, or prosecuted rights defenders for collaborating with foreign powers. Some activists were seduced by international travel and exposure, yet aware that offshore convention sites were far removed from popular hopes for justice, welfare, representation, empowerment, and sovereignty. Moreover, even as the most professional Arab think tanks and advocacy groups vied for foreign funding the ever-expanding pool of donors and networks also competed for patronage of articulate 'democrats' whose participation could help validate narratives about 'promoting' something called 'democratization.'

In the wake of mass revolts in several Arab countries, many Arab and Arabist scholars are going beyond the question of whether subsequent events conform to a model of gradual transitions from authoritarianism to liberalism. American or European policy analysts want to know whether the stated and/or implicit aims of political aid are being met – is it money well spent; does it enhance a Western self-image and Euro-American interests in security and business opportunities? Engaged scholars in the region are more concerned with whether the political-aid industry advances popular aspirations and cosmopolitan norms for justice, representation, equality, and empowerment. They have expressed qualms, aired controversies, contended with ambiguities, and confronted contradictions. Everyone involved concluded that political aid projects are inherently political, frequently litigated, and often contrary to expressed discursive aims. Participants of various nationalities asked themselves whether political aid advances international legal conventions and shared cosmopolitan values – or simply offers an apparition of managed liberalization under NATO tutelage. This question resonates because both alternative explanations are concomitantly conceivable. It also invites those wondering *whether* political aid works to contemplate not only the stated logics of donors and their delegates but also the reactions of counterparts. Ultimately, rights defenders and citizen watchdogs are better positioned than anyone else to determine whether international democracy promotion promotes justice, representation, and empowerment. Let's ask not whether political aid furthers the interest of donor nations but what democracy promotion does to advance rights and freedoms in 'target' countries. If it works as advertised, political aid furthers human rights, electoral transparency, women's struggles, and freedoms of association and expression. The most authentic authorities on *whether* it works are not the authors of the templates and rubrics but the jurists, monitors, and activists that Western commentators consider secular, moderate, pro-democracy forces. If these groups are unpersuaded of the benefits of political aid, then the larger Western democratization project in the Arab world has been a colossal failure. It is not for me to 'speak for' the wide-ranging opinions of Arab activists. Instead I invite transitologists and democracy brokers and scholarly observers to heed the trepidations and defend the rights of the intellectual vanguard. The ultimate paradox is that political aid projects might support or thwart Arab activism; or, they might be irrelevant to organic struggles for social justice and decent governance in a region long denied either.

# Bibliography of Published Sources

Abdelrahman, Maha. "The Politics of 'UnCivil' Society in Egypt." *Review of African Political Economy* 91 (2002): 21–36.

Abdelrahman, Maha M. *Civil Society Exposed: The Politics of NGOs in Egypt.* Cairo: American University in Cairo Press, 2002.

Abdo, Nahla "Imperialism, the State, and NGOs: Middle Eastern Contexts and Contestations," *Comparative Studies of South Asia, Africa and the Middle East* 30: 2 (2010) 238–249.

Abu-Lughod, Lila, and Rabab El-Mahdi. "Beyond the 'Woman Question' in the Egyptian Revolution," *Feminist Studies* 37:3 (2011): 683–691

Abu-Lughod, Lila. "Dialects of Women's Empowerment: The International Circuitry of the Arab Human Development Report 2005," *International Journal of Middle East Studies* 41 (2009): 83–103.

Abu-Lughod, Lila. "Do Muslim Women Really Need Saving? Anthropological Reflections on Cultural Relativism and Its Others." *American Anthropologist* 104 (2002): 783–90.

Abu-Lughod, Lila. *Dramas of Nationhood: The Politics of Television in Egypt.* Chicago: University of Chicago Press, 2005.

Acharya, Amitav. "How Ideas Spread: Whose Norms Matter? Norm Localization and Institutional Change in Asian Regionalism." *International Organization* 58 (2004): 239–275.

Acuto, Michele. "Wilson Victorious? Understanding Democracy Promotion in the Midst of a 'Backlash.'" *Alternatives* 33 (2008): 461–480.

Adler, Emanuel, and Peter M. Haas. "Conclusion: Epistemic Communities, World Order, and the Creation of a Reflective Research Program." *International Organization* 45 (1992).

Afary, Janet. "The Human Rights of Middle Eastern and Muslim Women: A Project for the 21st Century." *Human Rights Quarterly* 26 (2004): 106–125.

Agati, Mohammad. "Undermining Standards of Good Governance: Egypt's NGO Law and its Impact on the Transparency and Accountability of CSOs." *The International Journal of Not-for-Profit Law* 9:2 (2007).

Ahmed, Huda. "Women in the Shadows of Democracy." *Middle East Report* 239 (2006): 24–26.

Al-Ali, Nadje, and Nicola Pratt. *What Kind of Liberation? Women and the Occupation of Iraq.* Berkeley: University of California Press, 2009.

Al-Ali, Nadje, and Nicola Pratt. "Women in Iraq: Beyond the Rhetoric." *Middle East Report* 239 (2006): 18–23.

Al-Ali, Nadje. "Reconstructing Gender: Iraqi Women between Dictatorship, War, Sanctions and Occupation." *Third World Quarterly* 26 (2005): 739–758.

Al-Ali, Zaid. "What Egypt Should Learn from Iraq." *Open Democracy*, April 21, 2011. Accessed February 6, 2011. http://www.opendemocracy.net/zaid-al-ali/what-egypt-should-learn-from-iraq.

Al-Alloosh, Saad Abdeljabbar. "Overview of Judicial Control of the Constitutionality of Laws in Iraq and Its Prospective Role in Safeguarding Rights and Public Freedoms." Paper commissioned by the World Bank for the Iraqi Judicial Forum, The Judicial System in Iraq: Facts and Prospects, Amman, Jordan, October 2–4, 2004.

Ali, Hadi Aziz. "Civil Courts Procedures in the Service of Litigants, Human Rights Protection and Judicial Performance Improvement." Paper commissioned by the World Bank for the Iraqi Judicial Forum, The Judicial System in Iraq: Facts and Prospects, Amman, Jordan, October 2–4, 2004.

Ali, Kamran Asdar. "Myths, Lies, and Impotence: Structural Adjustment and Male Voice in Egypt." *Comparative Studies of South Asia, Africa and the Middle East* 23 (2003): 321–334.

Al-Istrabadi, Feisal Amin Rasoul. "A Constitution without Constitutionalism: Reflections on Iraq's Failed Constitutional Process." *Texas Law Review* 87 (2009):1627–1655.

Allawi, Ali A. *The Occupation of Iraq: Winning the War, Losing the Peace* (Yale University Press, New Haven: 2007).

Allen, Lori A. "Martyr Bodies in the Media: Human Rights, Aesthetics, and the Politics of Immediation in the Palestinian Intifada." *American Ethnologist* 36 (2009): 161–180.

Allison, Graham, and Robert Beschel. "Can The United States Promote Democracy?" In *Promoting Democracy and Free Markets in Eastern Europe*, ed. Charles Wolf, Jr., 71–104. Santa Monica: Rand, prepared for the Agency for International Development, 1991.

Al-Khudairi, Salma. "NGO Capacity Building Project-Iraq." Australian-Iraqi Forum, May 2005. http://www.aiforum.org.au/docs/NGOCapacityBuildingProject.pdf.

Almadhagi, Ahmed Noman. *Yemen and the United States: A Study of a Small Power and Superpower Relationship, 1962–1994.* London: Tauris, 1996.

Al-Majali, Zaha, and Omar Qaddoura. "Jordan: The Independence and Impartiality of the Judiciary," *Euro-Mediterranean Human Rights Network*, Copenhagen 2008.

Al-Motawakkel. Mohammed A. "International Aspects of the Arab Human Rights Movement." Paper presented to An Interdisciplinary Discussion Held in Cairo in March 1998. Harvard Law School Human Rights Program, Cambridge, MA. 2000.

Al-Sayyid, Mustapha K. "International Aspects of the Arab Human Rights Movement." Paper presented to An Interdisciplinary Discussion Held in Cairo in March 1998, Harvard Law School Human Rights Program, Cambridge, MA. 2000.

Alvarez, Jose E. "Trying Hussein: Between Hubris and Hegemony." *Journal of International Criminal Justice* 319 (2004): 319–329.

Alvarino, Ignacio Alvarez-Ossorio. "The European Strategy for the Middle East." Jean Monnet/Robert Schuman Paper Series 4:19 (2004).

American Bar Association, *Judicial Reform Index for Iraq*, Washington: Iraq Legal Development Project. July 2006. http://www.abanet.org/rol/publications/jri-iraq-2006.pdf.

American Civil Liberties Union. *Blocking Faith, Freezing Charity: Chilling Muslim Charitable Giving in the "War on Terrorism Financing,"* New York: ACLU, June 2009.

Amin, Galal. *The Illusion of Progress in the Arab World: A Critique of Western Misconstructions.* Cairo: American University in Cairo Press, 2006.

Amireh, Amal. "Framing Nawal El Saadawi: Arab Feminism in a Transnational World." *Signs* 26 (2000): 215–249.

Amoko, Apollo. "The 'Missionary Position' and the Postcolonial Polity, Or, Sexual Difference in the Field of Kenyan Colonial Knowledge." *Callaloo* 24 (2001): 310–324.

Appadurai, Arjun. *Modernity at Large: Cultural Dimensions of Globalization.* Minneapolis: University of Minnesota Press, 2006.

Arato, Andrew. "Post-sovereign Constitution-Making and its Pathology in Iraq." *New York Law School Law Review* 51 (2007): 534–555.

Arato, Andrew. "Sistani v. Bush: Constitutional Politics in Iraq." *Constellations* 11 (2004): 174–192.

Aucoin, Louis. "The Role of International Experts in Constitution-Making," *Georgetown Journal of International Affairs* 1 (2004): 89–95.

Avanti, Deborah D. "The Privatization of Security: Lessons from Iraq." *Orbis* 50 (2006): 327–342.

Ayotte, Kevin J., and Mary E. Hussein. "Securing Afghan Women: Neocolonialism, Epistemic Violence, and the Rhetoric of the Veil." *NWSA Journal* 17 (2005): 112–133.

Bali, Asli U. "Justice under Occupation: Rule of Law and the Ethics of Nation-Building in Iraq." *Yale Journal of International Law* 30 (2005): 431–473.

Banks, Cyndi. "'Reconstructing' Justice in Iraq and the Rule of Law." Paper presented to the International Studies Association Conference 2008, San Francisco, March 26–29, 2008.

Banks, Cyndi. "Reconstructing Justice in Iraq: Promoting the Rule of Law in a Post-conflict State." *Hague Journal on the Rule of Law* 2 (2010): 155–170.

Bardawil, Hania. *IFES West Bank and Gaza Resource Centers' Voter Education Project in Advance of the January 20, 1996 Palestinian Legislative Council and Ra'ess Elections, December 1995-January 1996 Final Activity Report.* IFES. Washington, 1996.

Bargouthi, Mustafa "The Slow Death of Palestinian Democracy." *Foreign Policy* July 21, 2010.

Baroudi, Sami E. "Arab Intellectuals and the Bush Administration's Campaign for Democracy: The Case of the Greater Middle East Initiative." *Middle East Journal* 61 (2007): 390–418.

Bassu, Giovanni. "Law Overruled: Strengthening the Rule of Law in Postconflict States." *Global Governance* 14 (2008): 21–38.

Bayat, Assef. "Transforming the Arab World: *The Arab Human Development Report* and the Politics of Change." *Development and Change* 36 (2005): 1225–37.

Bayer, Thomas C. *Morocco Direct Legislative Elections June 25, 1993: Report of the IFES Monitoring and Observation Delegations.* Washington: IFES, 1993.

Bayley, David H. "U.S. Aid for Foreign Justice and Police." *Orbis* 50 (2006): 469–479.

Begos, Kevin. "Faded Dreams of Contracted Democracy." *Middle East Report* 234 (2005): 24–27.

Bellin, Eva "The Robustness of Authoritarianism in the Middle East: Exceptionalism in Comparative Perspective," *Comparative Politics* 36: 2 (2004) 139–157.

Bello, Walden. "The Globalization of Disaster: The Rise of the Relief and Reconstruction Complex." *Journal of International Affairs* 59 (2006): 1–22.

Ben Néfissa, Sarah. "ONG, gouvernance et développement dans le monde arabe." UNESCO Management of Social Transformations, Discussion Paper No. 46, Cairo, April 3, 2001.

Benomar, Jamal. "Constitution-Making after Conflict: Lessons for Iraq." *Journal of Democracy* 15 (2004): 81–95.

Benton, Lauren. *Law and Colonial Cultures: Legal Regimes in World History, 1400–1900.* Cambridge: Cambridge University Press, 2002.

Bergh, Sylvia. "Morocco: A Centrally Steered Semi-Authoritarian State." In *Beyond Orthodox Approaches: Assessing Opportunities for Democracy Support in the Middle East and North Africa.* The Hague: Netherlands Institute for Multiparty Democracy/Hivos, 2010.

Bernard-Maugiron, Nathalie. "Judges as Reform Advocates: A Lost Battle." *Cairo Papers in Social Science* 29 (2006): 60–84.

Bianchi, Robert. *Unruly Corporatism: Associational Life in 20$^{th}$ Century Egypt.* London: Oxford University Press, 1998.

Bibars, Iman. "The Rising Interest in Private Voluntary Organizations and their New Role in Development: A Study of the Impact of the New Role of PVOs on their Performance as Grass Roots Organizations and their Relationship with Large Aid Donors." Paper presented at Princeton University, May 1988.

Bishara, Dina. "Arab States: Rough Sledding for U.S. Party Aid Organizations in the Arab World." *Arab Reform Bulletin* 5: 6 (2007).

Bohman, James. "International Regimes and Democratic Governance: Political Equality and Influence in Global Institutions." *International Affairs* 75 (1999): 499–513.

Bremer III, Paul. *My Year in Iraq: The Struggle to Build a Future of Hope.* New York: Simon and Schuster, 2006.

Brennan, Timothy. "Cosmo-Theory." *The South Atlantic Quarterly* 100 (2001): 659–691.

Brock, Bill. "The Democracy Program: A Strong Foundation." *Commonsense* 6 (1983): 85–121.

Brouwer, Imco. "US Civil-Society Assistance to the Arab World: The Cases of Egypt and Palestine." *European University Institute Working Paper RSC No. 2000/5.* Badia Fiesolana, San Domenico, Italy. 2000.

Brown, Lucy, and David Romano. "Women in Post-Saddam Iraq: One Step Forward or Two Steps Back?" *NWSA Journal* 18 (2006): 51–70.

Brown, Michelle. "Setting the Conditions for Abu Ghraib: The Prison Nation Abroad." *American Quarterly* 57 (2005): 973–997.

Brown, Nathan J. "Law and Imperialism: Egypt in Comparative Perspective." *Law & Society Review* 29 (1995): 103–25.

Brown, Nathan J. *The Rule of Law in the Arab World*. London: Cambridge University Press, 1997.

Brown, Nathan J. "Judicial Review and the Arab World." *Journal of Democracy* 9 (1998): 85–99.

Brumberg, Daniel. "Democratization in the Arab World? The Trap of Liberalized Autocracy." *Journal of Democracy* 13 (2002): 56–68.

Brumberg, Daniel. "Democratization vs. Liberalization in the Arab World: Dilemmas and Challenges for U.S. Foreign Policy." Army War College: Strategic Studies Institute, 2005.

Burke, Edward. *Assessing Democracy Assistance: Yemen*. FRIDE Project Report, Madrid, May 2010.

Burnell, Peter. "From Evaluating Democracy Assistance to Appraising Democracy Promotion." *Political Studies* 56 (2008): 414–434.

Campbell, Leslie. "Iraq's Election Was Free and Fair." *Foreign Policy* (March 30, 2010).

Carapico, Sheila, "Egypt's Civic Revolution: Beyond What 'Civil Society Promotion' Had in Mind," in *Arab Spring in Egypt,* edited by Bahgat Korany and Rabab El-Mahdi, 199–222, Cairo: AUC Press, 2012.

Carapico, Sheila. "Some Yemeni Ideas About Human Rights," in *Alternative Voices on Human Rights in the Arab World*, edited by Anthony Chase and Amr Hamzawy. 137–151, Philadelphia, PA: University of Pennsylvania Press, 2005.

Carapico, Sheila. "NGOs, INGOs, GO-NGOs and DO-NGOs: Making Sense of Non-Governmental Organizations." *Middle East Report* 214, 30:1 (2000) 12–15.

Carapico, Sheila. "Foreign Aid for Promoting Democracy in the Arab World," *Middle East Journal* 56 (2002): 379–395.

Carapico, Sheila. "How Yemen's Ruling Party Secured an Electoral Landslide." *Middle East Report Online*, May 16, 2003.

Carapico, Sheila. "Mission: Democracy." *Middle East Report* 209, 28 (1998): 17–20, 40.

Carapico, Sheila. *Civil Society in Yemen: The Political Economy of Activism in Modern Arabia*. London: Cambridge University Press, 1998.

Cardenas, Sonia, and Andrew Flibbert. "National Human Rights Institutions in the Middle East." *The Middle East Journal* 59 (2005): 411–436.

Carey, Henry F. "The Postcolonial State and the Protection of Human Rights." *Comparative Studies of South Asia, Africa and the Middle East* 22 (2002): 59–75.

Carothers, Thomas, *Democracy Policy under Obama: Revitalization or Retreat*, Carnegie Report, Washington, January 2012.

Carothers, Thomas. "The NED at 10." *Foreign Policy* (1994): 123–129.

Carothers, Thomas. *Aiding Democracy Abroad: The Learning Curve*. Washington: The Carnegie Endowment for International Peace, 1999.

Carothers, Thomas. "The End of the Transition Paradigm." *Journal of Democracy* 13 (2002): 5–21.

Carpenter, Ted Galen. "Jackboot Nation Building: The West Brings 'Democracy' to Bosnia." *The Mediterranean Quarterly* 11 (2000): 1–22.

Cassen, Robert. *Does Aid Work?* Oxford: Clarendon Press, 1987.

Cavatorta, Francesco, and Azzam Elananza. "Show Me the Money! Opposition, Western Funding, and Civil Society in Jordan and Lebanon." In *Contentious Politics in the Middle East: Political Opposition under Authoritarianism*, edited by Holger Albrecht. Miami, FL: University Press of Florida, 2010.

Challand, Benoît. "Comments on Palestinian CSOs: How to Trace Down the Impact of External Aid?": paper presented at the Foundation for the Future Regional Conference on Research on Civil Society Organizations: Status and Prospects, Jordan, January 26–28, 2010.

Challand, Benoît. *Palestinian Civil Society: Foreign Donors and the Power to Promote and Exclude*. London and New York: Routledge, 2010.

Challand, Benoît. "The Evolution of Western Aid for Palestinian Civil Society: Bypassing Local Knowledge and Resources." *Middle Eastern Studies* 44 (2008): 397–417.

Chandler, David. *Bosnia: Faking Democracy after Dayton*. London: Pluto, 1999.

Chandrasekaran, Rajiv. *Imperial Life in the Emerald City*. New York: Knopf, 2006.

Chen, Martha A. "Building Research Capacity in the Nongovernmental Organization Sector." In *Getting Good Government: Capacity Building in the Public Sectors of Developing Countries*, edited by Merilee S. Grindle, 229–253. Harvard Institute for International Development, 1997.

Chen, Martha A. "Engendering World Conferences: The International Women's Movement and the UN." In *NGOs, the UN, and Global Governance*, edited by Thomas G. Weiss and Leon Gordenker. Boulder: Lynne Rienner, 1996.

Chomsky, Noam. *Deterring Democracy*. London: Verso, 1991.

Conetta, Carl. "The Iraqi Election Bait and Switch: Faulty Poll Will Not Bring Peace or U.S. Withdrawal." *Project for Defense Alternatives Briefing Report 17*, 2005: 25.

Conetta, Carl. "Masque of Democracy: Iraqi Election System Still Disfavors Sunni Arabs, Favors Kurds." PDA Briefing Memo 35, The Project on Defense Alternatives, December 10, 2005.

Cortell, Andrew P., and James W. Davis Jr, "Understanding the Domestic Impact of International Norms: A Research Agenda." *International Studies Review* 2 (2000): 65–87.

Craig, David, and Doug Porter. "Framing Participation: Development Projects, Professionals, and Organizations," in *Development and Patronage*, edited by Melakou Tegegn, 50–57. Oxford, UK: Oxfam, 1997.

Craner, Lorne. "Will U.S. Democratization Policy Work?" *Middle East Quarterly* 13 (2006): 3–10.

Crystal, Jill, and Abdallah al-Shayeji. "The Pro-Democratic Agenda in Kuwait: Structures and Context," in *Political Liberalization and Democratization in the Arab World: Arab Experiences*, edited by Bahgat Korany, Paul Noble, and Rex Byrnen, 101–125. Boulder: Lynne Reiner Publishers, 1998.

Dahlerup, Drude, and Anja Taarup Nordlund. "Gender Quotas – a Key to Equality? A Case Study of Iraq and Afghanistan." *European Political Science* (2004): 91–98.

Dalacoura, Katerina. "U.S. Democracy Promotion in the Arab Middle East since 11 September 2001: A Critique." *International Affairs* 81 (2005): 963–979.

Dalpino, Catharine. *Deferring Democracy: Promoting Openness in Authoritarian Regimes*. Washington: Brookings Institution Press, 2000.

Dawisha, Adeed, and Larry Diamond. "Iraq's Year of Voting Dangerously." *Journal of Democracy* 17 (2006): 89–103.

De Bertodano, Sylvia. "Were There More Acceptable Alternatives to the Iraqi High Tribunal?" *Journal of International Criminal Justice* 5 (2007): 294–300.

Dempsey, Gary T. "Fool's Errands: America's Recent Encounters with Nation-Building." *Mediterranean Quarterly* 12 (2001): 57–80.

Denoeux, Guilain P. "The Politics of Morocco's 'Fight Against Corruption.'" *Middle East Policy* 7 (2002): 165–189.

Diamond, Larry. *Squandered Victory: The American Occupation and the Bungled Effort to Bring Democracy to Iraq*. New York: Henry Holt & Co, 2005.

Diamond, Larry, "Building Democracy after Conflict: Lessons from Iraq." *Journal of Democracy* 16 (2005): 9–23.

Dillman, Bradford. "Round Up the Unusual Suspects: American Policy toward Algeria and its Islamists." *Middle East Policy* 8 (2002):126–143.

Docena, Herbert. "Silent Battalions of 'Democracy.'" *Middle East Report* 232 (2004): 14–21.

Doebbler, Curtis F. J. "An Intentionally Unfair Trial." *Journal of International Criminal Justice* 5 (2007): 264–271.

Donnelly, Jack. "International Human Rights: A Regime Analysis." *International Organization* 40 (1986): 599–642.

Dougherty, Melissa L. "A Comparative Analysis of International Tribunals: The Formation of an Iraqi Judiciary to Try Sadaam Hussein." Bepress Legal Series: Working Paper 588, 2005.

Dunne, Michele, and Amr Hamzawy. "Does Egypt Need International Election Observers?" The Carnegie Endowment Middle East Project, October 15, 2010.

Edwards, Jim. "Rebuilding Iraq's Judicial System from the Ground Up." *New Jersey Law Journal* 3 (2003).

Elbayar, Kareem. "NGO Laws in Selected Arab States." *International Journal of Not-for-Profit Law* 7 (2005): 3–27.

El-Baz, Shahida. "Globalisation and the Challenge of Democracy in Arab North Africa." *Africa Development* 30 (2005): 1–33.

El-Ghobashy, Mona. "Egypt's Paradoxical Elections." *Middle East Report* 238 (2006): 20–29.

El-Kassem, Nadeen. "The Pitfalls of a 'Democracy Promotion' Project for Women of Iraq." *International Journal of Lifelong Education* 27 (2008):129–151.

Elyachar, Julia. "Empowerment Money: The World Bank, Non-Governmental Organizations, and the Value of Culture in Egypt." *Public Culture* 14 (2002): 493–513.

Elyachar, Julia. "Mappings of Power: The State, NGOs, and International Organizations in the Informal Economy of Cairo." *Comparative Studies in Society and History*, 45:3 (2003): 571–605.

Encarnación, Omar G. "Beyond Civil Society: Promoting Democracy after September 11." *Orbis* 47: 4 (2003): 705–720.

Encarnación, Omar G. "Tocqueville's Missionaries: Civil Society Advocacy and the Promotion of Democracy." *World Policy Journal* 17 (2000): 9–18.

Erickson, Christian. "Counter-terror Panoptics: Surveillance Programs and Human Rights NGO Opposition in Comparative Context." Paper presented at the annual meeting of the International Studies Association, 48th Annual Convention, Chicago, February 28, 2007.

Escobar, Arturo. *Encountering Development: The Making and Unmaking of the Third World*. Princeton: Princeton University Press, 1995.

Esmier, Samera. "The Violence of Non-Violence: Law and War in Iraq." *Journal of Law and Society* 34 (2007): 99–115.

*Euro-Mediterranean Partnership Regional Cooperation: An Overview of Programs and Projects 2007/08*. Brussels: European Commission, 2008.

European Parliament's Committee on Foreign Affairs and Committee on Development. *EU Election Observation: Achievements, Challenges*. Brussels: European Commission, 2008.

European Union Election Observation Mission. *Lebanon Final Report on the June 7, 2009 Parliamentary Elections*. Brussels: European Commission, 2009.

Evans, Tony. "International Human Rights Law as Power/Knowledge." *Human Rights Quarterly* 27 (2005): 1046–1068.

Exum, Andrew, and Zack Snyder. "Democracy Demotion in Egypt: Is the United States a Willing Accomplice?" *Policy Watch* 1212, March 23, 2007.

Fanon, Franz. *A Dying Colonialism*. New York: Grove Press, 1965.

Feldman, Noah. *What We Owe Iraq: War and the Ethics of Nation Building*. Princeton: Princeton University Press, 2004.

Ferguson, James, and Akhil Gupta. "Spatializing States: Toward an Ethnography of Neoliberal Governmentality." *American Ethnologist* 29 (2002): 981–1002.

Ferguson, Michele L. "'W' Stands for Women: Feminism and Security Rhetoric in the Post-9/11 Bush Administration." *Politics and Gender* 1 (2005): 9–38.

Finnemore, Martha, and Kathryn Sikkink. "Taking Stock: The Constructivist Research Program in International Relations and Comparative Politics." *Annual Review of Political Science* 4 (2001): 391–416.

Fischer, Jeff. "Council of Representatives Election Composite Report, Iraq, December 15, 2005, Final Report." Washington: IFES Center for Transitional and Post-Conflict Justice, February 20, 2006.

Fischer, Jeff, and Clement Henry. *Pre-Election Technical Assessment, Tunisia, December 15–December 22, 1993*. Washington: IFES, 1993.

Fisher, William F. "Doing Good? The Politics and Antipolitics of NGO Practices." *Annual Review of Anthropology* 26 (1997): 439–464.

Fonte, John. "Democracy's Trojan Horse." *The National Interest* 76 (2004): 117–127.

Forsythe, David P., and Barbara Ann Rieffer. "U.S. Foreign Policy and Enlarging the Democratic Community." *Human Rights Quarterly* 22 (2000): 998–1010.

Frank, Michael J. "Trying Times: The Prosecution of Terrorists in the Central Criminal Court of Iraq." *Florida Journal of International Law* 18 (2006): 1–133.

Gallagher, Margaret. "Lipstick Imperialism and the New World Order: Women and Media at the Close of the Twentieth Century." Paper prepared for Division for the Advancement of Women Department for Policy Coordination and Sustainable Development United Nations, December 1995.

Gause, F. Gregory. "Can Democracy Stop Terrorism?" *Foreign Affairs* 84 (2005): 62–76.

Gendzier, Irene L. "Play it Again Sam: The Practice and Apology of Development." In *Universities and Empire: Money and Politics in the Social Sciences during the Cold War*, edited by Christopher Simpson, 57–95. New York: The New Press, 1998.

Giammusso, Maurizio. "Civil Society Initiatives and Prospects of Economic Development: The Euro-Mediterranean Decentralized Co-operation Networks." *Mediterranean Politics* 4 (1999): 25–52.

Gillespie, Richard. "A Political Agenda for Region-building? The EMP and Democracy Promotion in North Africa." University of California at Berkeley: Institute of European Studies, Paper 040530, 2004.

Goudie, Andrew. "International Development: Beyond the White Paper is a Good Government Agenda Practical? An Approach to Governance." Department for International Development, Overseas Development Institute, London, March 25, 1998.

Gruner, Angela. "Loss of Guiding Values and Support: September 11 and the Isolation of Human Rights Organizations in Egypt." *Mediterranean Politics* 8 (2003): 133–152.

Guest, Iain. "Defending Human Rights in the Occupied Palestinian Territory – Challenges and Opportunities." *Friedrich Ebert Foundation* 57 (Jerusalem: February 2007).

Guilhot, Nicolas. "Limiting Sovereignty or Producing Governmentality? Two Human Rights Regimes in U.S. Political Discourse." *Constellations* 15 (2008): 502–516.

Guilhot, Nicolas. *The Democracy Makers: Human Rights and International Order*. New York: Columbia University Press, 2005.

Hagan, John, Gabrielle Ferrale, and Guillermina Jasso, "How Law Rules: Torture, Terror, and the Normative Judgments of Iraqi Judges." *Law and Society Review* 42 (2008): 605–643.

Haider Ala Hamoudi. "Toward a Rule of Law Society in Iraq: Introducing Clinical Legal Education into Iraqi Law Schools." *Berkeley Journal of International Law* 23 (2005): 112–136.

Hajjar, Lisa. "Cause Lawyering in Transnational Perspective: National Conflict and Human Rights in Israel/Palestine." *Law and Society Review* 31 (1997): 473–504.

Halabi, Zeina. "Arab Civil Society: Assessing Interpretations and Determining Challenges." Paper commissioned by Henrich Böll Foundation, Middle East Office and Arab NGO Network for Development, September 2004.

Hammami, Rema. "NGOs: The Professionalization of Politics." *Race and Class* 37 (1995): 51–63.

Hanafi, Sari. "Donors, International NGOs, and Palestine NGOs: Funding Issues and Globalized Elite Formation." In *NGOs and Governance in the Arab World*, edited by Sarah Ben Nefissa and Nabil Abd al-Fattah, 337–360, Cairo: American University Cairo Press, 2005.

Hanafi, Sari, and Linda Tabar. "The Intifada and the Aid Industry: The Impact of the New Liberal Agenda on the Palestinian NGOs." *Comparative Studies of South Asia, Africa and the Middle East* 23 (2003): 205–214.

Hani, Al-Hourani. "Civil Society in Jordan: A Literature Review." Paper presented at Foundation for the Future Regional Conference on Research on Civil Society Organizations: Status and Prospects, Dead Sea Convention Centre, Jordan, January 26–28, 2010.

Hasso, Frances S. "Empowering Governmentalities Rather than Women: *The Arab Human Development Report 2005* and Western Development Logics." *International Journal of Middle East Studies* 41 (2009): 63–82.

Hatem, Mervat F. "Economic and Political Liberation in Egypt and the Demise of State Feminism." *International Journal of Middle East Studies* 24 (1992): 231–251.

Hatem, Mervat F. "In the Eye of the Storm: Islamic Societies and Muslim Women in Globalization Discourses." *Comparative Studies of South Asia, Africa and the Middle East* 26 (2006): 22–35.

Hawthorne, Amy. "Middle Eastern Democracy: Is Civil Society the Answer?" Carnegie Papers: Middle East Series, Democracy and Rule of Law Project #44, Washington, 2004.

Hawthorne, Amy. "Do We Want Democracy in the Middle East?" *Foreign Service Journal* (February 2001) 43–49.

Herman, Edward S. "The Election in Iraq: The U.S. Propaganda System is Still Working in High Gear." *ZNet Iraq*, February 13, 2006.

Herman, Edward S., and Frank Brodhead. *Demonstration Elections: U.S.-Staged Elections in the Dominican Republic, Vietnam, and El Salvador.* South End Press, Cambridge, MA, 1984.

Hersch, Seymour M. "Did Washington Try to Manipulate Iraq's Election?" *The New Yorker*, July 25, 2005.

Heydemann, Steve. *Upgrading Arab Authoritarianism.* The Brookings Institution, Analysis Paper, No. 13. Washington: The Saban Center for Middle East Policy, 2007.

Heyzer, Noeleen, and Ilana Landsberg-Lewis. "UNIFEM and Women's Climb to Equality." In *Muslim Women and the Politics of Participation: Implementing the Beijing Platform*, edited by Mahnaz Afkhami and Erika Friedl, 153–161. Syracuse: Syracuse University Press, 1997.

Hicks, Neil. "Transnational Human Rights Networks and Human Rights in Egypt." In *Human Rights in the Arab World: Independent Voices*, edited by Anthony Chase and Amr Hamzawy, 64–88. Philadelphia, PA: University of Pennsylvania Press, 2006.

Hilal, Jamal. "Civil Society in Palestine." Paper presented to the Foundation for the Future Regional Conference on Research on Civil Society Organizations: Status and Prospects, Dead Sea Convention Centre, Jordan, January 26–28, 2010.

Hippler, Jochen. "Democratisation of the Third World after the End of the Cold War," in *The Democratisation of Disempowerment: The Problem of Democracy in the Third World*, edited by Jochen Hippler, (London: Pluto Press, 1999): 1–32.

Hirschman, Albert O. *Development Projects Observed.* Washington: Brookings Institution, 1967.

Hobsbawm, Eric J. "Spreading Democracy." *Foreign Policy* Sept/Oct (2004): 40–41.

Hochstetler, Kathryn, Ann Marie Clark, and Elisabeth J. Friedman. "Sovereignty in the Balance: Claims and Bargains at the UN Conferences on the Environment, Human Rights, and Women." *International Studies Quarterly* 44 (2004): 591–614.

Holden, Patrick. "Hybrids on the Rim? The European Union's Mediterranean Aid Policy." *Democratization* 12 (2005): 461–480.

Howell, Jude, and Jenny Pearce. "Civil Society: Technical Instrument or Social Force for Change?" In *New Roles and Relevance: Development NGOs and the Challenge of Change*, edited by David Lewis and Tina Wallace, 76–87. Bloomfield, CT: Kumarian Press, 2000.

Huber, Bettina. "Governance, Civil Society, and Security in the Euro-Mediterranean Partnership: Lessons for a More Effective Partnership." EuroMeSCo Paper 39 (Lisbon 2004).

Huber, Daniela. "Is the EU Losing Credibility in Palestine?" FRIDE Policy Brief No. 50, Madrid, June 2010.

Hudson, Michael C. "To Play the Hegemon: Fifty Years of U.S. Policy toward the Middle East." *The Middle East Journal* 50 (1996): 329–343.

Human Rights Watch. "Jordan: Parliament Should Reject U.S. Impunity Deal." December 8, 2005.

Human Rights Watch. "Iraq: Flawed Tribunal not Entitled to U.N. Legitimacy." January 15, 2004.

Human Rights Watch. "Iraqi Elections: Human Rights Concerns: Questions and Answers from Human Rights Watch," January 21, 2005.

Human Rights Watch. *No Exemptions from International Justice for the Gravest Crimes*. London: Human Rights Watch, December 7, 2005.

Human Rights Watch. "Egypt: Margins of Repression: State Limits on Non-governmental Organization Activism." New York: Human Rights Watch, 2005.

Human Rights Watch. "Human Rights and Algeria's Presidential Elections: A Human Rights Watch Background Paper," April 1999.

Ibrahim, Akram Nash'at. "Modernizing the Iraqi Penal Code to Serve and Protect Human Rights." Paper commissioned by the World Bank for the Iraqi Judicial Forum, The Judicial System in Iraq: Facts and Prospects, Amman, Jordan, October 2–4, 2004.

Ibrahim, Saad Eddine. "Arab Social-Science Research in the 1990s and Beyond: Issues, Trends, and Priorities." In *Research for Development in the Middle East and North Africa*, edited by Eglal Rached and Dina Craissati, 111–140. Ottawa and Cairo: IDRC AND CRDI, 2000.

IFES, IRI, and NDI. *"Palestinian Elections: A Pre-Election Assessment Mission Report."* Washington, August 2002.

Ikenberry, John G., and Charles A. Kupchan. "Socialization and Hegemonic Power." *International Organization* 44 (1990): 283–315.

International Crisis Group. *The Broader Middle East and North Africa Initiative: Imperiled at Birth.* Brussels/Amman: ICG Middle East and North Africa Briefs, June 7, 2004.

International Crisis Group, *Iraq: Can Local Governance Save Central Government?* ICG Middle East Report No.33, 27 October 2004.

International Human Rights Network. *"Human Rights NGO Capacity Building-Iraq: Next Steps Report."* IHRN, Oldcastle, Ireland, February 2005.

Ismael, Jacqueline S., and Shereen T. Ismael. "Gender and State in Iraq." In *Gender and Citizenship in the Middle East*, edited by Suad Joseph, 185–211. Syracuse: Syracuse University Press, 2000.

Ismael, Tareq Y., and Jacqueline S. Ismael. "Whither Iraq? Beyond Saddam, Sanctions and Occupation." *Third World Quarterly* 26 (2005): 609–629.

Jad, Islah. "The NGO-ization of Arab Women's Movements." *IDS Bulletin* 35 (2004): 24–42.

Jad, Islah "NGOs: Between Buzzwords and Social Movements," *Development in Practice*, 17: 4–5 (2007): 622–629.

Jamal, Amany A. *Barriers to Democracy: The Other Side of Social Capital in Palestine and the Arab World*. Princeton: Princeton University Press, 2007.

Jamal, Manal. *After the Peace Process: Foreign Donor Assistance and the Political Economy of Marginalization in Palestine and El Salvador*. PhD diss., McGill University, 2006.

Jamal, Manal. "Foreign Donor Assistance and Democracy Promotion in Palestine." Paper presented to the 6th Mediterranean Social and Political Research Meeting, Montecatini Termi, 16–20 March, 2005.

Jenkins, Rob. "Collateral Benefit: Iraq and Increased Legitimacy for International Trusteeship." *Dissent* 53 (2006): 72–75.

Jerusalem Media and Communication Center. *Foreign Aid and Development in Palestine*. Jerusalem, 1999.

Johansson-Nogues, Elisabeth. "Civil Society in Euro-Mediterranean Relations: What Success of EU's Normative Promotion?" *EUI Working Papers*, RSCAS, 2006/40, Brussels, 2006.

Johnson, Erik C. "Policy Making beyond the Politics of Conflict: Civil Society Think Tanks in the Middle East and North Africa." In *Think Tanks and Civil Societies: Catalysts for Ideas and Action*, edited by James G. McGann and R. Kent Weaver, 337–365. New Brunswick and London: Transaction Publishers, 2000.

Kamat, Sangeeta. "NGOs and the New Democracy: The False Saviors of International Development." *Harvard International Review* 25 (2003): 65–69.

Kampmark, Binoy. "The Trial of Saddam Hussein: Limits and Prospects." *Contemporary Review* 288 (2006): 192–200.

Kandil, Amani. "A Critical Review of the Literature about the Arab Civil Society." Paper presented at Foundation for the Future Regional Conference on Research on Civil Society Organizations: Status and Prospects, Dead Sea Convention Centre, Jordan, January 26–28, 2010.

Kandiyoti, Deniz. "Between the Hammer and the Anvil: Post-conflict Reconstruction, Islam and Women's Rights." *Third World Quarterly* 28 (2007), 503–517.

Karam, Azza. "Strengthening the Role of Women Parliamentarians in the Arab Region: Challenges and Options." Paper presented at Queens University, Belfast, October 1999.

Karkutli, Nadim, and Dirk Buetzier, *Final Report: Evaluation of the MEDA Democracy Programme 1996–98*. Brussels, April 1999.

Katz, Marisa. "Rhetoric v. Reality: Democratease." *The New Republic*, June 2005.

Katz, Stanley Nider. "Democratic Constitutionalism after Military Occupation: Reflections on the United States' Experience in Japan, Germany, Afghanistan, and Iraq." *Common Knowledge* 12 (2006):181–196.

Kausch, Kristina. "Defenders in Retreat: Freedom of Association and Civil Society in Egypt." FRIDE Report, Madrid, 2009.

Kelemen, Daniel R., and Eric C. Sibbitt. "The Globalization of American Law." *International Organization* 58 (2004): 103–136.

Keohane, Robert. *After Hegemony: Cooperation and Disorder in World Political Economy*. Princeton: Princeton University Press, 1984.

Khadr, Asma. "International Aspects of the Arab Human Rights Movement." Paper presented to An Interdisciplinary Discussion Held in Cairo in March 1998." Harvard Law School Human Rights Program, 2000.

Khakee, Anna. *Assessing Democracy Assistance: Morocco*. FRIDE Project Report, Madrid, 2010.

Khaladi, Rashid. *Resurrecting Empire: Western Footprints and America's Perilous Path in the Middle East*. New York: Beacon Press, 2004.

Khallaf, Mahi. "Civil Society in Egypt: A Literature Review." Paper presented to the Foundation for the Future Regional Conference on Research on Civil Society Organizations: Status and Prospects, Dead Sea Convention Centre, Jordan, January 26–28, 2010.

Khrouz, Driss Ali Hajji, and Muhamed Boussetta. "The Development Research Environment in Morocco: Situation and Prospects." In *Research for Development in the Middle East and North Africa*, edited by Eglal Rached and Dina Craissati, 161–186. Ottawa: International Development Research Center, 2000.

Klein, Keith, and Adila R. Laidi. *Pre-Election Assessment West Bank and Gaza*. Washington: IFES, 1994.

Koh, Harold. "How is International Human Rights Law Enforced?" *Indiana Law Journal* 74 (1998): 1396–1417.

Kolhatkar, Sonali, and James Ingalls. *Bleeding Afghanistan: Washington, Warlords, and the Propaganda of Silence*. New York: Seven Stories Press, 2006.

Korayem, Karima. "The Research Environment in Egypt." In *Research for Development in the Middle East and North Africa*, edited by Eglal Rached and Dina Craissati. Ottawa: International Development Research Center, 2000.

Kramer, Ronald, Raymond Michalowski, and Dawn Rothe. "The Supreme International Crime: How the U.S. War in Iraq Threatens the Rule of Law." *Social Justice* 32:2 (2005): 52–81.

Kurrild-Klitgaard, Peter. "Blood, Baath, and Beyond: the Constitutional Dilemma of Iraq." *Public Choice* 119 (2004): 13–30.

Landolt, Laura K. "(Mis)constructing the Third World? Constructivist Analysis of Norm Diffusion." *Third World Quarterly* 25 (2004): 579–591.

Langeswiesche, William. "Welcome to the Green Zone: The American Bubble in Baghdad." *The Atlantic Monthly* (2004): 61–88.

Langohr, Vickie. "An Exit from Arab Autocracy." *Journal of Democracy* 13 (2002): 116–122.

Langohr, Vickie. "Too Much Civil Society, Too Little Politics: Egypt and Liberalizing Arab Regimes." *Comparative Politics* 36 (2004): 181–204.

Lasensky, Scott. "Underwriting Peace in the Middle East: U.S. Foreign Policy and the Limits of Economic Inducements." *Middle East Review of International Affairs* 6 (2002).

Lemoine, Ray, and Jeff Neumann, *Babylon by Bus.* New York, Penguin Books, 2006.

Leve, Lauren G. "'Failed Development' and Rural Revolution in Nepal: Rethinking Subaltern Consciousness and Women's Empowerment." *Anthropological Quarterly* 80 (2007): 127–172.

Lewis-Anthony, Siân, "The Initiatives in the Field of Judicial Reform in the Euro-Mediterranean Region," Euro-Mediterranean Human Rights Network Copenhagen, July 20, 2009.

Lockman, Zachary. *Contending Visions of the Middle East: The History and Politics of Orientalism.* Cambridge: Cambridge University Press, 2004.

Loza, Sara et al. *Final Report Assessment of PVO Activity under the Local Development II Project.* Submitted by the Social Planning, Analysis, and Administration Consultants to USAID/Cairo, April 30, 1991.

Luke, Timothy W. "Unbundling the State: Iraq and the 'Recontainerization' of Rule, Production, and Identity." *Environment and Planning A* 39 (2007): 1564–1581.

Lust-Okar, Ellen, and Amaney Ahmad Jamal. "Rulers and Rules: Reassessing the Influence of Regime Type on Electoral Law Formation." *Comparative Political Studies* 35 (2002): 337–367.

Magen, Amichai. "The Rule of Law and Its Promotion Abroad: Three Problems of Scope." *Stanford Journal of International Law* 51 (2009): 51–115.

Magen, Amichai. *Evaluating External Influence on Democratic Development: Transition.* Center on Democracy, Development, and The Rule of Law, Stanford University, CDDRL Working Papers Number 111, Palo Alto, California, March 2009.

Mahmoud, Medhat. "Judicial System in Iraq: A Review of the Legislation Regulating Judicial Affairs in Iraq." Paper commissioned by the World Bank for the Iraqi Judicial Forum, The Judicial System in Iraq: Facts and Prospects, Amman, Jordan, October 2–4, 2004.

Malo, Hoshyar Salam. "The Future of Civil Society in Iraq: A Comparison of Draft Civil Society Laws Submitted to the Iraqi Council of Representatives." *International Journal of Not-for-profit Law* 10 (2008).

Manji, Firoze, and Carl O'Coill. "The Missionary Position: NGOs and Development in Africa." *International Affairs* 78 (2002): 567–583.

Marks, Laura U. "What Is That *and* between Arab Women and Video? The Case of Beirut." *Camera Obscura* 18 (2003): 40–69.

Marshall, Jennifer A., Melissa G. Pardue, and Grace V. Smith. "Beyond the Words at Beijing+10: How U.N. Policy Falls Short of Women's Best Interests." *The Heritage Foundation Backgrounder*, February 28, 2005.

Martin-Diaz, Alicia. *The Middle East Peace Process and the European Union.* Commission of the European Communities, Brussels: European Parliament Directorate General for Research Working Paper: Political Series POLI-115EN, 1999.

Mayer, Ann Elizabeth. "Reform of Personal Status Laws in North Africa: A Problem of Islamic or Mediterranean Laws?" *The Middle East Journal* 49 (1995): 432–46.

McGann, James G. "Pushback against NGOs in Egypt." *International Journal of Not-for-Profit Law* 10 (2008).

Meital, Yoram. "The Struggle over Political Order in Egypt: The 2005 Elections." *The Middle East Journal* 60 (2006): 257–279.

Melia, Thomas O., "The Democracy Bureaucracy: The Infrastructure of American Democracy Promotion," Discussion paper for the Princeton Project on National Security Working Group on Global Institutions and Foreign Policy Infrastructure, Washington, September, 2005.

Messick, Brinkley. "Prosecution in Yemen: The Introduction of the Niyaba." *International Journal of Middle East Studies* 15 (1983): 507–518.

Messick, Brinkley. *The Calligraphic State*. London: University of California Press, 1993.

Mettraux, Guenael. "The 2005 Revision of the Statute of the Iraqi Special Tribunal." *Journal of International Criminal Justice* 5 (2007): 287–293.

Mitchell, Timothy. *Rule of Experts: Egypt, Techno-Politics, Modernity*. Berkeley: University of California Press, 2002.

Mitchell, Timothy. *Colonizing Egypt*. Cairo: American University in Cairo Press, 1988.

Mokhtari, Shadi. "After Abu Ghraib: Exploring Human Rights in America and the Middle East." Cambridge: Cambridge University Press, 2009.

Molyneux, Maxine. "The Law, the State, and Socialist Policies with Regard to Women: The Case of the People's Democratic Republic of Yemen 1967–1990." In *Women, Islam, and the State*, edited by Deniz Kandiyoti. London: Temple University Press, 1991.

Morrow, Jonathan. "Iraq's Constitutional Process II: An Opportunity Lost." USIP Special Report No. 155, Washington, 2005.

Moustafa, Tamir. "Got Rights? Public Interest Litigation and the Egyptian Human Rights Movement." In *Human Rights in the Arab World: Independent Voices*, edited by Anthony Chase and Amr Hamzawy, 153–173. Philadelphia: University of Pennsylvania Press, 2006.

Mowitt, John. "In the Wake of Eurocentrism: An Introduction." *Cultural Critique* 47 (2001): 3–15.

Munson Jr., Henry. "International Election Monitoring: A Critique Based on One Monitor's Experience in Morocco." *Middle East Report* 209 (1998): 37–39.

Muravchik, Joshua. *Exporting Democracy: Fulfilling America's Destiny*. Washington: The American Enterprise Institute, 1991.

Murphy, Richard W., and F. Gregory Gause. "Democracy and U.S. Policy in the Muslim Middle East." *Middle East Policy* 1 (1997): 58–67.

Mutua, Makua. "Human Rights International NGOs: A Critical Evaluation." In *NGOs and Human Rights: Promise and Performance*, edited by Claude E. Welch, Jr., 151–163. Philadelphia: University of Pennsylvania Press, 2001.

Naim, Abd al-Allahi Ahmad. "Human Rights in the Arab World: A Regional Perspective." *Human Rights Quarterly* 23 (2001): 701–732.

Nakhleh, Khalil. "A Critical Look at Foreign Funding to Palestine: Where Is It Heading." In *Funding Palestinian Development*, edited by Nader Izzat Said, 25–31. Ramallah: Birzeit University Planning for Development Series No.2, 1998.

Nashat, Saeid N., "A Look into the Women's Movement in Iraq." *Farzaneh* 6:11, 2003, 54–65.

National Democratic Institute, *Promoting Participation in Yemen's 1993 Elections.* Washington: NDI, 1994.

National Democratic Institute. *Final Report on the 2009 Lebanese Parliamentary Elections.* Washington: NDI, March 1, 2009.

National Democratic Institute. *Final Report on the Moroccan Legislative Elections.* Washington: NDI, September 7, 2007.

National Democratic Institute for International Affairs and the Carter Center. *The January 20, 1996, Palestinian Elections.* Washington: National Democratic Institute, 1997.

National Endowment for Democracy. *The Backlash against Democracy Assistance.* Report prepared for Senator Richard J. Lugar, Chairman, Committee on Foreign Relations, United States Senate, NDI. Washington, June 8, 2006.

National Endowment for Democracy. *Defending Civil Society: A Report of the World Movement for Democracy.* Washington: National Endowment for Democracy, February 2008.

Nazer, Hisham M. *Power of a Third Kind: The Western Attempt to Colonize the Global Village.* London: Praeger, 1999.

Norris, Pippa. "Increasing Women's Representation in Iraq: What Strategies Would Work Best?" Report prepared at the Kennedy School of Government for the NED, February 16, 2004, Cambridge, MA.

Olsen, Gorm Rye. "The European Union: An Ad Hoc Policy with a Low Priority." In *Exporting Democracy: Rhetoric vs. Reality,* edited by Peter J. Schraeder, 131–145. Boulder, CO: Lynne Rienner, 2002.

Ong, Aihwa. *Neo-Liberalism as Exception: Mutations in Citizenship and Sovereignty.* London: Duke University Press, 2006.

Oomen, Barbara. "Donor-Driven Justice and Its Discontents: The Case of Rwanda." *Development and Change* 36 (2005): 887–910.

Ottoway, Marina, and Martha Brill Olcott. *The Challenge of Semi-Authoritarianism.* Washington: Carnegie Endowment for International Peace Democracy and Rule of Law Project, no. 7, 1999.

Ottoway, Marina. "Promoting Democracy in the Middle East: The Problem of U.S. Credibility." Carnegie Endowment for International Peace Working Papers, Democracy and Rule of Law Project, no. 35: Washington, 2003.

Pace, Roderick, Stelios Stavridis, and Dimtris Xenakis, "Parliaments and Civil Society Cooperation in the Euro-Mediterranean Partnership." *Mediterranean Quarterly* 15:1 (2004): 75–92.

Payne, Rodger A. "Persuasion, Frames, and Norm Construction." *European Journal of International Relations* 7 (2001): 37–61.

Pegram, Thomas. "Diffusion across Political Systems: The Global Spread of National Human Rights Institutions." *Human Rights Quarterly* 32 (2010): 729–760.

Petchesky, Rosalind P. "Rights of the Body and Perversions of War: Sexual Rights and Wrongs Ten Years past Beijing." *International Social Science Journal* 57 (2005): 301–318.

Petras, James. "NGOs: In the Service of Imperialism." *Journal of Contemporary Asia* 29 (1999): 429–440.

Petras, James. "Imperialism and NGOs in Latin America," *Monthly Review* 49:7 (1997) 10–27.

Pevehouse, Jon C. "Democracy from the Outside-In? International Organizations and Democratization." *International Organization* 56 (2002): 515–549.

Pinto-Duschinsky, Michael. "Foreign Political Aid: The German Political Foundations and Their U.S. Counterparts." *International Affairs* 67 (1991): 33–66.

Pinto-Duschinsky, Michael. "The Rise of 'Political Aid.'" In *Consolidating the Third Wave Democracies,* edited by Larry Diamond, Marc F. Plattner, Yun-han Chu, and Hung-mao Tien, 295–324. Baltimore and London: Johns Hopkins University Press, 1997.

Pollack, Kenneth, "*A Switch in Time: A New American Strategy for Iraq.*" Washington: The Brookings Institution. February 15, 2005.

Pratt, Nicola. "Gendering Political Reconstruction in Iraq." University of East Anglia Papers in European and International Studies, Working Paper 3, Norwich, UK, March 2005.

Pratt, Nicola. "Bringing Politics Back In: Examining the Link Between Globalization and Democratization." *Review of International Political Economy* 11 (2004).

Pratt, Nicola. "Human Rights NGOs and the 'Foreign Funding Debate' in Egypt." In *Human Rights in the Arab World: Independent Voices,* edited by Anthony Chase and Amr Hamzawy, 114–126. Philadelphia: University of Pennsylvania Press, 2006.

Presbey, Gail M. "Challenges of Founding a New Government in Iraq." *Constellations* 12 (2005): 521–541.

Pressley, Don, and Lawrence Groo. "Streamlining U.S. Democracy Assistance." *Georgetown Journal of International Affairs* 6 (2005) 113–121.

Prince, Keir. "Palestinian Authority Reform: Role of the International Community." *Arab Reform Bulletin* 5, November, 2007.

Pripstein Posusney, Marsha. "Behind the Ballot Box: Electoral Engineering in the Arab World." *Middle East Report* 209 (1998): 12–15.

Pripstein Posusney, Marsha. "Multi-Party Elections in the Arab World: Institutional Engineering and Oppositional Strategies." *Studies in Comparative International Development* 36 (2002) 34–62.

Puckett, Blake K. "'We're Very Apolitical': Examining the Role of the International Legal Assistance Expert." *Indiana Journal of Global Legal Studies* 16 (2009): 293–310.

Puddington, Arch. "The Pushback against Democracy." *Journal of Democracy* 18 (2007): 125–137.

Quandt, William W. Between Ballots and Bullets: Algeria's Transition from Authoritarianism. Washington: Brookings Institution, 1998.

Quigley, Kevin F. F. "For Democracy's Sake: How Funders Fail – and Succeed." *World Policy Journal* 13 (1996): 109–119.

Riddell, Roger C. *Foreign Aid Reconsidered.* Baltimore: Johns Hopkins University Press, 1987.

Roberts, Hugh. "Algeria's Contested Elections." *Middle East Report* 209 (1998): 21–24.

Robinson, William I. "Globalization, the World System, and 'Democracy Promotion' in U.S. Foreign Policy." *Theory and Society* 25 (1996): 615–665.

Robinson, William I. "What to Expect from U.S. 'Democracy Promotion' in Iraq," *New Political Science* 26: 3 (2004)441–447.

Roca, Pierre-Jean. "Insiders and Outsiders: NGOs in International Relations." In *NGOs and Governance in the Arab World*, edited by Sarah Ben Nefissa and Nabil Abd al-Fattah 39–54. Cairo: AUC Press, 2005.

Rondinelli, Dennis A. *Development Projects as Policy Experiments: An Adaptive Approach to Development Administration.* London: Methuen & Co., 1983.

Roy, Olivier. "The Predicament of 'Civil Society' in Central Asia and the Greater Middle East." *International Affairs* 81 (2005): 1001–1012.

Roy, Sarah. "U.S. Economic Aid to the West Bank and Gaza Strip: The Politics of Peace." *Middle East Policy* 4 (1996): 50–77.

Ruben, Elizabeth. "Fern Holland's War." *The New York Times Magazine*, September 19, 2004.

Ruggie, John Gerard. "What Makes the World Hang Together? Neo-Utilitarianism and the Social Constructivist Challenge." *International Organization* 52 (1998): 855–588.

*Rule of Law Development in the West Bank and Gaza Strip: Survey and State of the Development Effort.* Gaza: UNESCO, May 1999.

Al-Sa'adawi, Nawal. "The Seventh International AWSA Conference Rationale and the Way Forward." *Meridians: Feminism, Race, Transnationalism* 6:2 (2006) 22–32.

Sabbagh, Amal. "Overview of Women's Political Representation in the Arab Region: Opportunities and Challenges." In *The Arab Quota Report: Selected Case Studies*, Quota Report Series from Workshop in Cairo, December 5–6, 2004. Stockholm: International Institute for Democracy and Electoral Assistance, 2007.

Sadiki, Larbi, "To Export or Not to Export Democracy to the Arab World: The Islamist Perspective." *Arab Studies Journal* 6 (1998): 60–75.

Sadowski, Yahya M. *Political Vegetables? Businessman and Bureaucrat in the Development of Egyptian Agriculture.* Washington: Brookings Institution, 1991.

Saeed, Hayder. "Civil Society in Iraq." Paper presented to the Foundation for the Future Regional Conference on Research on Civil Society Organizations: Status and Prospects, Dead Sea Convention Centre, Jordan, January 26–28, 2010.

Said, Edward. "Palestinian Elections Now." *Counterpunch*, June 17, 2002.

Sakr, Naomi "Women's Rights and the Arab Media." Report for the Centre for Media Freedom/Middle East and North Africa, London, 2000.

Salam, Nawaf. "Civil Society in the Arab World: The Historical and Political Dimensions." *Islamic Legal Studies Program.* Harvard University: Occasional Publications 3, October 2002.

Sassen, Saskia. *A Sociology of Globalization.* New York: W. W. Norton, 2007.

Saunders, Rebecca. "Uncanny Presence: The Foreigner at the Gate of Globalization." *Comparative Studies of South Asia, Africa, and the Middle East* 21 (2001): 88–98.

Scharf, Michael. P. "The Iraqi High Tribunal: A Viable Experiment in International Justice?" *Journal of International Criminal Justice* 5 (2007): 258–263.

Schedler, Andreas. "The Menu of Manipulation." *Journal of Democracy* 13 (2002): 36–50.

Schenker, David. *Palestinian Democracy and Governance: An Appraisal of the Legislative Council.* Washington: Washington Institute for Near East Policy, 2000.

Schlesinger, James. "The Quest for a Post-Cold War Foreign Policy," *Foreign Affairs* 72 (1993): 17–28.

Schlumberger, Oliver. "Arab Political Economy and the European Union's Mediterranean Policy: What Prospects for Development?" *New Political Economy* 5 (2000): 247–268.

Scott, James C. *Domination and the Arts of Resistance: Hidden Transcripts.* New Haven, Yale University Press, 1990.

Scott, James C. *Seeing Like a State: How Certain Schemes to Improve the Human Condition Have Failed.* New Haven: Yale University Press, 1998.

Scott, James M. "Transnationalizing Democracy Promotion: The Role of Western Political Foundations and Think Tanks." *Democratization* 6 (1999): 146–170.

Shadi, Mokhtari. *After Abu Ghraib: Exploring Human Rights in America and the Middle East.* Cambridge: Cambridge University Press, 2009.

Shalakany, Amr. "I Heard It All Before: Egyptian Tales of Law and Development." *Third World Quarterly* 27 (2006): 833–853.

Sharp, Jeremy M. "Egypt: 2005 Presidential and Parliamentary Elections." CRS Report for Congress, September 21, 2005.

Sheehi, Stephen. "Arabic Literary-Scientific Journals: Precedence for Globalization and the Creation of Modernity." *Comparative Studies of South Asia, Africa, and the Middle East* 25 (2005).

Shehadeh, Raja. "Human Rights and the Israeli Occupation." *CR: The New Centennial Review* 8 (2008): 33–55.

Shohat, Ella. "Area Studies, Gender Studies, and the Cartographies of Knowledge." *Social Text* 72: 20:3 (2002): 67–78.

Shukrallah, Hani. "International Aspects of the Arab Human Rights Movement." Paper presented to An Interdisciplinary Discussion Held in Cairo in March 1998. Harvard Law School Human Rights Program, Cambridge, MA, 2000.

Sikkink, Kathryn. "Human Rights, Principled Issue-Networks, and Sovereignty in Latin America." *International Organization* 47 (1993): 411–441.

Simpson, Matthew T. "Iraqi High Court Authority: A State-Practice Review of the Source of High Court Authority and an Assessment of 2005 Iraq Constitution." Islamic Law and Law of the Muslim World Paper No. 07–01, 2007.

Sissons, Miranda, and Ari S. Bassin., "Was the Dujail Trial Fair?" *Journal of International Criminal Justice* 5 (2007): 272–286.

Smith, Andrew R., and Fadoua Loudiy. "Testing the Red Lines: On the Liberalization of Speech in Morocco." *Human Rights Quarterly* 27 (2005): 1069–1119.

Smith, James C. *The Idea Brokers: Think Tanks and the Rise of the New Policy Elite.* New York: The Free Press, 1991.

Snyder, Jack. *From Voting to Violence: Democratization and Nationalist Conflict.* New York: W. W. Norton, 2002.

Stacher, Joshua A. "Rhetorical Acrobatics and Reputations: Egypt's National Council for Human Rights." *Middle East Report* 235 (2005): 2–7.

Stiles, Kendall W. "Civil Society Empowerment and Multilateral Donors: International Institutions and New International Norms." *Global Governance* 4 (1998): 199–216.

Stone, Diane. "Think-Tanks, Global-Lesson-Drawing, and Networking Social Policy Ideas." *Global Social Policy* 1 (2001): 338–360.

Stover, Eric, Hanny Megally, and Hania Mufti. "Bremer's 'Gordian Knot': Transitional Justice and the U.S. Occupation of Iraq." *Human Rights Quarterly* 27 (2005): 830–857.

Suad, Joseph. "Elite Strategies for State-Building: Women, Family, Religion, and State in Iraq and Lebanon." In *Women, Islam, and the State*, edited by Deniz Kandiyoti, 176–200. Philadelphia: Temple University Press, 1991.

Sullivan, Denis J. "NGOs in Palestine: Agents of Development and Foundation of Civil Society." *Journal of Palestine Studies* 25 (1996): 93–100.

Synnott, Hilary. "State-Building in Southern Iraq." *Survival* 47 (2005): 33–56.

Tadros, Mariz. "Between the Elusive and the Illusionary: Donors' Empowerment Agendas in the Middle East in Perspective." *Comparative Studies of South Asia, Africa, and the Middle East* 30.2 (2010): 224–237.

Tallawy, Mervat. "International Organizations, National Machinery, Islam, and Foreign Policy." In *Muslim Women and the Politics of Participation: Implementing the Beijing Platform*, edited by Mahnaz Afkhami and Erika Friedl, 128–140. Syracuse: Syracuse University Press, 1997.

Tamas, Peter A. "Spoken Moments of a Pernicious Discourse? Querying Foucauldian Critics' Representations of Development Professionals." *Third World Quarterly* 28 (2007): 901–916.

Taraki, Lisa. "Society and Gender in Palestine: A Critique of International Policy Documents." Working Paper 2, Birzeit University: Women's Studies Programme, Ramallah, 1995.

Telhami, Shibley. "Exporting Democracy to the Middle East." *Dissent* (2007): 57–58.

Tetreault, Mary Ann. "The Sexual Politics of Abu Ghraib: Hegemony, Spectacle, and the Global War on Terror." *NWSA Journal* 18 (2006): 33–50.

Tetreault, Mary Ann. *Stories of Democracy: Politics and Society in Contemporary Kuwait.* New York: Columbia University Press, 2000.

Thompson, Elizabeth F. *Justice Interrupted: Historical Perspectives on Promoting Democracy in the Middle East.* Washington: USIP Special Report 225, June 2009.

Tocci, Nathalie. "Has the EU Promoted Democracy in Palestine? And Does It Still?" *CFSP Forum* 4 (2006): 7–10.

Tripp, Charles. *A History of Iraq.* Cambridge: Cambridge University Press, 2007.

True, Jacqui, and Michael Mintrom. "Transnational Networks and Policy Diffusion: The Case of Gender Mainstreaming." *International Studies Quarterly* 45 (2001): 27–57.

UNDP. *Arab Human Development Report 2009: Challenges to Human Security in Arab Countries.* United Nations Development Program, Regional Bureau for Arab States, New York, 2009.

Vallersundi, Ana Palacio. "The Barcelona Process: A Euro-Mediterranean North-South Partnership." *Georgetown Journal of International Affairs* 1 (2004): 145–151.

Van de Pas, Annie. "Egypt: Engaging in a Pyramid Power System." In *Beyond Orthodox Approaches: Assessing Opportunities for Democracy Support in the Middle East and North Africa*. The Hague: Netherlands Institute for Multiparty Democracy/Hivos, 2010.

Van Nieuwkerk, Karin. "From Repentance to Pious Performance," *ISIM Review* 20 (2007): 54–55.

Vogt, Ulrich. "The Existing Relations between Arab and European NGOs," in "The Role of NGOs in the Development of Civil Society: Europe and the Arab Countries," proceedings of a Bruno Kreisky Forum-Arab Thought Forum seminar in Amman, Jordan, on December 6–7, 1997, Amman and Vienna, 1997 (PDF)

Waltz, Susan. "Universal Human Rights: The Contribution of Muslim States." *Human Rights Quarterly* 26 (2004): 799–844.

Warrick, Catherine. *Law in the Service of Legitimacy: Gender and Politics in Jordan*. Surrey, UK: Ashgate Press, 2009.

Wedeen, Lisa "Conceptualizing Culture: Possibilities for Political Science," *The American Political Science Review* 96:4 (2002): 713–728.

Wedeen, Lisa. "Seeing Like a Citizen, Acting Like a State: Exemplary Events in Unified Yemen." *Comparative Studies in Society and History* 45 (2003): 680–713.

Wedeen, Lisa. *Peripheral Visions: Publics, Power and Performance in Yemen*. London: University of Chicago Press, 2008.

Wehrey, Frederic et al. *The Iraq Effect: The Middle East after the Iraq War*. Santa Monica: Rand, Project Air Force, 2010.

Weilemann, Peter R. "Experiences of a Multidimensional Think-Tank: The Konrad-Adenauer-Stiftung." In *Think Tanks and Civil Societies: Catalysts for Ideas and Action*, edited by James G. McGann and R. Kent Weaver, 169–186. New Brunswick and London: Transaction Publishers, 2000.

Weylen, Georgina. "Analyzing Women in the Politics of the Third World." In *Women and Politics in the Third World*, edited by Haleh Afshar, 7–24. London: Routledge, 1996.

Whitaker, Beth Elise. "Exporting the Patriot Act? Democracy and the 'War on Terror' in the Third World" *Third World Quarterly* 28 (2007): 1017–1032.

Whitehead, Laurence. "Losing 'the Force'? The 'Dark Side' of Democratization after Iraq." *Democratization* 16 (2009): 215–242.

Wiarda, Howard J. *Civil Society: The American Model and Third World Development*. Boulder: Westview, 2003.

Wiktorowicz, Quintan. "Civil Society as Social Control: State Power in Jordan." *Comparative Politics* 33 (2000): 43–61.

Wilcke, Christoph. "Castles Built of Sand: U.S. Governance and Exit Strategies in Iraq." *Middle East Report* 232 (2004): 4–13.

Wilcox, Jr., Philip C. "U.S. Policy and Palestine: Reform and Peace are Interdependent." *Arab Reform Bulletin* 4:9 (2006).

Wittes, Tamara Koffman, *Freedom's Unsteady March: America's Role in Building Arab Democratization*. Washington: Brookings Institution Press, 2008.

Wittes, Tamara Koffman, and Andrew Masloski. "Democracy Promotion Under Obama: Lessons from the Middle East Partnership Initiative." *Policy Paper 13*. Washington: The Saban Center for Middle East, the Brookings Institution, 2009.

Wittes, Tamara Koffman. *The New U.S. Proposal for a Greater Middle East Initiative: An Evaluation.* Washington: The Saban Center at the Brookings Institution, May 10, 2004.

Wolff, Sarah. "Constraints on the Promotion of the Rule of Law in Egypt: Insights from the 2005 Judges' Revolt." *Democratization* 16 (2009): 100–118.

Women for Women International. *Windows of Opportunity: The Pursuit of Gender Equality in Post-War Iraq,* Women for Women International Briefing Paper, Washington, January, 2005

The World Bank. "Morocco: Country Assistance Evaluation," May 14, 2001 Report No. 22212, Washington, 2001.

Würth, Anna, and Claudia Engelmann. "Governmental Human Rights Structures and National Human Rights Institutions in the Middle East and North Africa." In *Islam and Human Rights*, edited by Hatem Ellisiesie, 239–256. Frankfurt: Peter Lang Verlag, 2008.

Youngs, Richard. *Democracy Promotion: The Case of European Union Strategy.* Working Document No. 167. Brussels: Center for European Policy Studies, 2001.

Youngs, Richard. *How to Revitalize Democracy Assistance: Recipients' Views.* FRIDE Working Paper 100. Madrid, 2010.

Youngs, Tim. *The Palestinian Parliamentary Elections and the Rise of Hamas.* Research Paper 06/17, London: House of Commons Library, 2006.

Zanger, Sabine C. "Good Governance and European Aid: The Impact of Conditionality." *European Union Politics* 1 (2000): 293–317.

# Index

## Other Books in the Series